SHAKESPEARE:
WORLD VIEWS

SHAKESPEARE: WORLD VIEWS

Edited by
Heather Kerr,
Robin Eaden,
and Madge Mitton

DELAWARE

Newark: University of Delaware Press
London: Associated University Presses

Associated University Presses
440 Forsgate Drive
Cranbury, NJ 08512

Associated University Presses
16 Barter Street
London WC1A 2AH, England

Associated University Presses
P.O. Box 338, Port Credit
Mississauga, Ontario
Canada L5G 4L8

The paper used in this publication meets the requirements of the American National Standard for Permanence of Paper for Printed Library Materials Z39.48-1984.

Library of Congress Cataloging-in-Publication Data

Shakespeare—world views / edited by Heather Kerr, Robin Eaden, and Madge Mitton.
    p.   cm.
  Essays presented at the Second Conference of the Australian and New Zealand Shakespeare Association, held at the University of Adelaide in February 1992.
  Includes bibliographical references.
  ISBN 0-87413-565-6 (alk. paper)
  1. Shakespeare, William, 1564–1616—Criticism and interpretation—Congresses.   I. Kerr, Heather, 1957–   . II. Eaden, Robin, 1943–
. III. Mitton, Madge, 1941–   . IV. Australian and New Zealand Shakespeare Association Meeting (2nd : 1992 : University of Adelaide)
PR2976.S3388 1996
822.3'3—dc20   95-22020
                                                                                          CIP

PRINTED IN THE UNITED STATES OF AMERICA

Contents

CONTENTS

Preface

THE fifteen essays in this collection represent the variety of approaches to Shakespeare encountered at the Second Conference of the Australian and New Zealand Shakespeare Association, held at the University of Adelaide in February 1992. A companion volume of proceedings, *Shakespeare and the World Elsewhere*, comprises a further nineteen papers also focused on the conference theme "Shakespeare Outside England."[1] As the present collection makes clear, the theme was open to liberal interpretation and the reader will find ample evidence of what Michael Billington calls Shakespeare's "chameleon quality." Indeed, Billington's essay "Was Shakespeare English?" is symptomatic of a tendency to produce Shakespeare as a marker of cultural pluralism, what has been characterized as a "respect for cultural difference, a principled tolerance of the multiple traditions, social practices, ethics, self-identifications that come under the global sign of 'culture.'"[2] The conference evidenced a general willingness to entertain strikingly heterogeneous Shakespeares, a pluralist tolerance that could accommodate, according to Jyotsna Singh (p. 40) "a postmodernist move to decenter all totalizing assumptions" and still find room for universalizing gestures like Billington's claim that Shakespeare is "the creator of infinitely transposable poetic and dramatic myths." Shakespeare seemed to function as an accommodating umbrella of affinity for scholars from widely disparate locations.

In this volume the competing local Shakespeares made available to us also speak of the continuing importance of those Shakespeares as a "site upon which the battle of the humanities is being waged" (Singh, 31). This apparently paradoxical understanding of Shakespeare as at once fragmented and monolithic, as local and global, as a site for affinity and contest, suggests that Shakespeare remains an unsettled, even unsettling cultural location. This volume gives an overview of some of the ways in which texts and performances, scholars, actors, and directors, in a variety of national and institutional locations, continue to unsettle Shakespeare as a stable indicator of cultural values.[3]

The conference theme, "Shakespeare Outside England," enabled consideration of cultural and historical differences such as the variously inflected performance traditions in Asia, Australasia, and Europe,[4] the "reinvention" of Shakespeare in revolutionary France and in Germany, and politicizing appropriations by Brecht and by the Czech resistance, as well as by the discourses of postcolonialism and postmodernism.

The collection has been gathered around two broad and overlapping categories. These might be called the politics of reading and performance. We open with Michael Billington's wide-ranging exploration of theatrical appropriations, which are understood to reproduce Shakespeare not as a specifically English ideal but as a kind of transnational machinery for realizing cultural values. Some of the implications for any too easy celebration of Shakespeare's infinite variety are taken up in Paul Washington's examination of "This Last *Tempest*: Shakespeare, Postmodernity, and *Prospero's Books*" with which we close. If Shakespearean performances everywhere seem to speak to Billington of Shakespeare's availability to modernity, Washington instead sees the new historicist attention to local and particular uses of Shakespeare enacting "a crisis of postmodernity" in which New Historicism and postmodernity work against each other.

This study of the "uses and inscriptions" of *The Tempest*, that paradigmatically postcolonial text, may be read alongside Jyotsna Singh's engagement with "The Postcolonial/Postmodern Shakespeare": "any genealogical analysis of Shakespeare's popularity and influence within a colonial and postcolonial context," she suggests, "is marked by anomalies and contradictions that blur boundaries between the elite colonial bard and the indigenous Shakespeares." Trevor Code, too, examines *The Tempest* and *Antony and Cleopatra* from what he thinks of as antipodean and marginal positions, both "inside" and "outside" the plays.

These interpretive strategies work to unsettle confident claims for Shakespearean universality. Similarly, readings from the changing Europe of Habicht and Prochazka might combine with Morley's study of Brechtian appropriation or Martin's survey of Swedish performance history, Golder's study of a French revolutionary *Othello*, and Carruthers's work on Suzuki's *Macbeth*, or Billington's survey of recent Japanese productions to open up questions of what are at stake for Western practices undertaken within a number of potentially competing cultural locations.

Moving away from particular geopolitics, Ann Blake represents "Shakespeare's Comic Locations" as willfully unsettled and unsettling geographies. In contrast, Mercedes Maroto Camino analyses the tragedy of Lucrece as a site of conflict where patriarchal power embraces land and women in a single act of domination, a process of "mapping" that makes the sexual conquest of Lucrece an unequivocally political issue: patriarchal and feminist cartographies are clearly at odds.[5]

The space of performance is central to what the late Philip Parsons's essay calls the "Elizabethan Experiment," productions with the Sydney Theatre Company, exploring the actor-audience relationship for which Shakespeare wrote. Penny Gay works to critique the aims and outcomes of these experiments in her companion essay, focused on productions of Dr. Faustus, 1 Henry IV, Hamlet, Othello, and King Lear. These explorations of a project designed to reconstruct Elizabethan performance conditions in Sydney in the late twentieth century are set alongside David Carnegie's study of the dramaturgy of Elizabethan stage hangings. Taking the opportunity afforded by the creation in New Zealand of full-sized stage hangings for the Shakespeare Globe Centre reconstruction in London of the first Globe, Carnegie employed four actors to help test theories about the particularities for the actor and playwright of stage business involving the theater hangings. With the focus strictly on performance values, the project to replicate the Globe in London and the motivations informing the Wellington Shakespeare Society's commissioning of the hangings remain unexamined, even if tantalizingly available to those concerned with the study of contemporary investments in Shakespeare as guarantor of cultural value.

Indeed, the very emergence of an Australian and New Zealand Shakespeare Association in 1990 is a phenomenon not without interest to cultural critics who may find that its formation and activities engage with disconcerting directness in what Singh calls the "anomalies and contradictions" of the settler-cultural production of Shakespeare. This volume marks one intervention, one way to "talk back" to other sites for the reinvention of Shakespeare, entering into conversations, enjoining debates, sometimes even doing metaphorical battle with the uses to which Shakespeare is being put around the world.

Quotations from Shakespeare are from the Riverside edition unless otherwise specified.

Heather Kerr
Robin Eaden
Madge Mitton

Notes

1. Robin Eaden, Heather Kerr, and Madge Mitton, eds., *Shakespeare and the World Elsewhere* (Adelaide: Australian and New Zealand Shakespeare Association, 1993).

2. David Bennett, ed. *Cultural Studies: Pluralism and Theory* (Melbourne: Melbourne University Press, 1993), ix.

3. Marion Campbell and Philip Mead, eds., *Shakespeare's Books: Contemporary Cultural Politics and the Persistence of Empire* (Melbourne: Melbourne University Press, 1993), explores these issues in the postcolonial context particularly.

4. Michael Mullin offers an overview of "Shakespeare in America," in Eaden et al., *Shakespeare and the World Elsewhere*, 80–88.

5. See Ros Diprose and Robyn Ferrell, eds., *Cartographies: Poststructuralism and the Mapping of Bodies and Spaces* (St. Leonards: Allen and Unwin, 1991).

Acknowledgments

Our thanks are due to the University of Adelaide Foundation, the Flinders University of South Australia, the Adelaide Festival Centre Trust, the British Council, the International Shakespeare Association, and individual sponsors of the Second Conference of the Australian and New Zealand Shakespeare Association held at the University of Adelaide, February 1992.

The editors wish to thank the International Shakespeare Association and Werner Habicht for permission to print a shortened version of the Occasional Paper number 5, *Shakespeare and the German Imagination* (1994). We also thank the Johns Hopkins University Press for permission to publish a revised version of Jyotsna Singh's "Different Shakespeares: The Bard in Colonial/Postcolonial India," *Theatre Journal* 41 (December 1989): 445–58.

For permission to reproduce photographs of theatrical performances the editors wish to thank Beata Berstrom, Hans Hasselgren, Bengt Wanselius, Lesley Leslie-Spinks, Stina Ekblad, and Rei Zunde. We are grateful to the Syndics of the Fitzwilliam Museum, Cambridge, for permission to reproduce Titian's *Tarquin and Lucretia*. Jan Van de Straet's *America* is reproduced by kind permission of the Burndy Library of the Institute for the History of Science and Technology.

Thanks are also due to the staff of Special Collections, Barr Smith Library, the University of Adelaide, particularly Cheryl Hoskin and Susan Woodburn, and to the English Department at the University of Adelaide for their support. For assistance with production of the volume our thanks to Jamie Macintyre. Finally, the editors wish to acknowledge the unfailing support of the conference conveners, Alan Brissenden and Tim Mares, and the enduring patience of the contributors during the process of gathering and editing the essays collected here.

Was Shakespeare English?

MICHAEL BILLINGTON

Was Shakespeare English? The question may seem faintly absurd. If he wasn't, then millions of tourists have been duped in their annual excursion to the birthplace in Stratford-on-Avon. I ask the question because of changing attitudes to Shakespeare, particularly in performance. For centuries Shakespeare has been appropriated as a symbol of England: the supremacy of its language, the durability of its monarchy, the variety of its character. He has become as much a part of our national identity as Churchill, Empire and the Last Night of the Proms. But as England—and the United Kingdom generally—shrinks in global significance, so Shakespeare himself takes on a different perspective. Seeing him produced in a variety of cultures and languages, I have been struck by his infinite adaptability. He changes colors like the chameleon, seeming Germanic in Germany, Mediterranean in Italy, politically subversive in eastern Europe, and mythic and folkloric in Japan, where it is not uncommon to take his stories and adapt them into Kabuki or Kyogen form. Maybe this is simply a reflection of my own globe-trotting. But I suspect something more significant is going on: that Shakespeare is increasingly being uprooted from his historical and geographical context and treated as a multidimensional myth to be infinitely plundered.

That Shakespeare was once claimed as a national icon is easily proved. Back in 1769 David Garrick supervised and staged a somewhat accident-prone, rain-sodden Shakespeare Jubilee in Stratford-on-Avon. Among the verses penned by Garrick was one running as follows:

> Our Shakespeare compar'd is to no man,
> Nor Frenchman, not Grecian, nor Roman,
> Their swans are all geese to the Avon's sweet swan,
> And the man of all men was a Warwickshire man
> Warwickshire man,

>Avon's swan,
>And the man of all men was a Warwickshire man.[1]

Speaking as a native of Warwickshire myself, I suppose my breast should swell with pride at such sentiments; but I fear Garrick's blithe dismissal of the rest of Western civilization now seems absurd.

But the notion of Shakespeare as the quintessence of Englishness persisted for a long time. Rereading *Mansfield Park* recently, I was struck by a passage in which Henry Crawford, who claims not to have read Shakespeare since he was fifteen, argues:

>"But Shakespeare one gets acquainted with without knowing how. It is part of an Englishman's constitution. His thoughts and beauties are so spread abroad that one touches them every where, one is intimate with him by instinct. No man of any brain can open at a good part of any one of his plays without falling into the flow of his meaning immediately." (chap. 34)

This is Shakespeare by osmosis: part of the gentlemanly tradition of English life. But from Victorian times to the present day Shakespeare has also been given a more specific political identity: as a symbol of Anglo-Saxon unity, linguistic dominance, the masculine virtues. It is a process brilliantly described by Terence Hawkes in his essay "Swisser Swatter," in which he describes how Shakespeare was enshrined as the centerpiece of an Edwardian series, English Men of Letters, and how he remains a powerful ideological weapon always available in times of crisis: as late as 1982 G. Wilson Knight, in a volume entitled *Authors Take Sides on the Falklands*, was citing Cranmer's royal prophecy at the end of *Henry VIII* as a forecast of the Anglocentric world order at which we should aim.[2]

By a nice irony the very qualities for which Shakespeare was once praised—his alleged patriotic chauvinism—are those that damn him in the eyes of the politically correct. He is now often scorned as that most contemptible of creatures: a white European middle-class male who failed to live up to the ideals of Marxism, feminism or vegetarianism. I recently came across a poem by D. J. Enright—another Warwickshire man—which wittily satirizes the notion that Shakespeare is a permanent political embarrassment:

>He was anti-Scottish: it took an English army
>To settle the hash of that kilted butcher

Macbeth. He made jokes about the Welsh, the
French, the Danes, the Italians and the Spanish.
He accused a West Indian (or possibly Algerian)
Of trying to rape a white girl unsuccessfully.
If it wasn't a base Judean he displayed
As criminally careless with pearls, then
It was an equally base Indian. Thank God
He hadn't heard of the Australians![3]

So what is the truth? Is Shakespeare an archetypal embodiment of a certain kind of Englishness: patriarchal, xenophobic,
essentially conservative? Or is he, as Enright ironically implies,
a shifty, ambiguous character who pictured the human condition
"as one of unending and uneasy struggle"? Obviously you can
prove anything you wish by selective quotation. But my contention, based on thirty-five years of constant Shakespearean
playgoing, is that Shakespeare is an essentially pluralist, multidimensional figure who is reinvented afresh by each new generation and by every different culture. As Hawkes says, there is no
unchanging, permanent Shakespearean play to which we can
finally turn. To me, Shakespeare is much more like a vast global
mirror in which we see our own reflections.

Although we are discussing Shakespeare outside England, I'd
like to look for a moment at the way he is currently performed
in his native land. Two things are immediately obvious about
modern England. One is that it is a multiracial society in which
people with white, black, brown, and yellow skins live together
in uneasy harmony. The other key fact is the unstoppable process
of growing integration with Europe, with more and more political
power being ceded to Strasbourg and Brussels: in my experience
a rising generation sees itself as fundamentally European rather
than English or even British. What is intriguing is the way both
these phenomena are represented in modern Shakespeare
production.

The move toward multiracial Shakespeare has been gathering
momentum for some time. Over a decade ago the National Theatre staged a *Measure for Measure* set, none too convincingly, in
the Caribbean. The Royal Shakespeare Company has long made
a policy of employing black actors, avoiding the suspicion of
tokenism by casting Hugh Quarshie as Hotspur and Josette Si-
mon as Isabella. Black theater companies have also started to
mount their own productions, eroding the assumption that
Shakespeare is the exclusive property of the white middle class.

The test, I suspect, will come when Stratford offers its first black actor as Hamlet or Lear. But it's a measure of how far we have progressed that Cheek by Jowl's *As You Like It* boasts a black Rosalind and Jaques: a fact on which hardly a single critic commented. The reason, of course, is that Rosalind is played by a man and Jaques is treated as gay; which raises the intriguing idea that we are so preoccupied by sex that we happily accept color-blind casting.

But I would also argue that English Shakespeare is currently being Europeanized. By that I mean, it is deeply affected by the staging techniques of western Europe and the politics of eastern Europe. You see this most visibly in recent productions of the history plays, which have always been taken as a touchstone of Englishness, the most profound expression of Shakespeare's concern with the governance of his native isle. Ron Daniels recently directed an RSC *Richard II* packed with visual references to eastern Europe pre-1989. Richard himself started as a befurred tyrant and ended as a shaven-headed figure sitting on a steel bed-frame in prison-camp clothes: Shakespeare's England simply became a metaphor for a dark, enfolding autocracy moving from medieval crossbows to modern rifles. Adrian Noble's recent production of *Henry IV Parts One and Two* is more respectful to period but fascinatingly radical in its use of Euroexpressionism: the Eastcheap tavern is a multileveled scarlet stew full of distorted, de Chirico–like perspectives, Justice Shallow's orchard is evoked through a ladder and a flutter of white muslin, and in Part Two the sleepless, guilt-ridden king wanders into the Eastcheap tavern, instantly linking the high life with the low. Noble and his designer, Bob Crowley, are clearly out to rescue the plays from the medieval neorealism of Stratford tradition: indeed one critic inquired "Why does a play about England look so determinedly foreign?" Completing the pattern, Richard Eyre has directed a National Theatre *Richard III* as a modern fascist nightmare: it starts in a 1930s England of khaki greatcoats and morning suits and gradually acquires the iconography of Hitlerism with McKellen's Richard seen in black uniform high on a podium, his good arm ready to rise in ritual salute. Greeted with literal-minded reservations in England, the production has been wildly acclaimed throughout western and eastern Europe.

All these productions—from Cheek by Jowl's *As You Like It* to the National's *Richard III*—suggest several things. One is that Walter Raleigh's notion of Shakespeare, in the English Men of Letters series, as the embodiment of maleness—a Phallus in

Wonderland—looks questionable today: indeed Declan Donnellan's startling production of Shakespeare's pastoral comedy discovers in the play an echo of our own fascination with cross-dressing, gender-bending, and sexual confusion. The updating and relocation of the history plays also suggest that we are far more interested in Shakespeare as an analyst of power and dissector of totalitarianism than as a chronicler of kings: one of the points that emerged from Eyre's *Richard III* was Shakespeare's prophetic understanding of the way the twentieth century's great dictators—including Hitler, Stalin, and Mussolini—have achieved supremacy through pseudoconstitutional means. But I suppose what all these productions prove is that "Englishness" is itself a very loaded term. England itself is now a very pluralist country that includes Muslim sects, the second- and third-generation products of Caribbean and Asian immigrants, Commonwealth residents, European refugees. We are a very mixed nation indeed culturally. We eat in tapas bars, watch American movies, drink German and Danish lager, and all the time are moving closer to Europe. Given all this, it is hardly surprising that what you might call "thatched-cottage Shakespeare" is gradually being replaced by productions that are multiracial, sexually exploratory, and visually nonrealistic. Even in England, Shakespeare seems increasingly wide-ranging and internationalist.

In productions hailing from outside England, I am constantly struck by the way Shakespeare effortlessly adapts to the prevailing preoccupations. Strip the plays of their original language and you are left with a series of all-embracing mythological narratives: a reminder of the way Shakespeare's plays work not just through their poetry but through a complex tissue of visual signs and symbols. The most obvious example is *Hamlet*. I was brought up, in the Bradley tradition, to see it as a character study of a flawed hero and as a moral debate about the ethics of revenge. In the Soviet Union and eastern Europe the play has famously become a potent, politically subversive weapon aimed at corrupt and decadent tyrannies: one in which Elsinore, rather than Hamlet, is the hero.

One of the most famous examples in recent times was Yuri Lyubimov's version of *Hamlet* staged for Moscow's Taganka Theater. No one who saw it will ever forget the dominant image of a vast mobile curtain, woven out of rope, that either swiveled round from a central point, advanced menacingly forward or traversed the stage driving the characters before it. It became an eavesdropper's paradise, a castle wall, a protective cover, an instrument of aggression (as when Claudius swung it round at one point thereby sweeping poor Ophelia into a waiting grave). But its real power was to remind one that Elsinore is a police state and that walls have holes as well as ears. Significantly when Lyubimov recreated that production in England, with local actors, it lost much of its potency: the reason was not so much that Lyubimov was indifferent to the poetry as that the production, outside the context of Brezhnev's Russia, lost its instant political relevance. Not only Shakespeare plays, but productions also, change their meaning depending on where they are staged.

But proof that *Hamlet* is not just a specific text but a revolving metaphor was provided by Alexandra Tocilescu's remarkable production from Bucharest's Bulandra Theater. This was created in 1985 when the evil Ceausescu was still in power. But instead of taking the obvious line and showing Elsinore as a barbaric despotism, the production seemed to be set in a dusty museum on the point of collapse. Claudius and Gertrude may have been greeted everywhere by sycophantic applause and ritual anthems. But the court was a shabby relic full of wire-netted cases stuffed with skulls, armor, musical instruments, unread tomes. There was even an onstage piano player knocking out wistful nocturnes and waltzes in a mood of exhausted melancholy. I have rarely seen a production that caught so well the desolation and bankruptcy of tyranny. Ideas that seem a cliché in the West—such as portraying Fortinbras as a ruthless pragmatist who here had Horatio stabbed to death—also became chillingly appropriate for Romania. Seeing the production in 1990, I was reminded that Romania had recently witnessed not a political revolution but a brutally effective coup. In the West *Hamlet* still tends to be read as a study of an individual dilemma. In eastern Europe, it becomes something else: an echoing poem about the emptiness and vulgarity of absolutism.

Since the tragedies and the histories inevitably deal with the dynamics of power, the rise and fall of princes, the tension between the individual and the state, the conflict between order and chaos, they can be adapted to virtually any society; though, on that score, it is worth pointing out that *King Lear* gradually seems to be replacing *Hamlet* as the key play for the late twentieth century. It is as if we find in it a precise echo of the inexplicable nature of the universe, of a world that contains the extremes of charity and cruelty, of goodness and evil blended in unholy confusion. Eighteenth-century England could only cope with the play by rewriting it: by giving it rationality and sense. But the greatness of *Lear* resides in the very fact that it does not make sense: that it is, literally, a sense-less play and the greatest absurdist tragicomedy ever written, which is why it has become common to cultures throughout the world.

But the true test of my theory that Shakespeare is a dramatist of no fixed abode and endlessly shifting identity has to be the comedies. Here, after all, are works apparently rooted in an observable England: an England of violet and primrose, hedges and yew trees, bumptious weavers and malaprop constables. Writing in London, Shakespeare seems to have retained an astonishing sense-memory of his Warwickshire youth. He also filled his comedies with deeply English wordplay and topical jokes: nowhere more so, you might say, than in *Twelfth Night* with its references to Mistress Mall's picture, the lady of the Strachy who married the yeoman of the wardrobe, and Brownists and politicians. Here, you might say, is a comedy so English as to be untransposable.

In fact, there is a long history of foreign productions. The French have a particular affinity with the play, Jacques Copeau doing a famous production at the Vieux-Colombier in 1914 that, by all accounts, achieved a miraculous quicksilver fluency. Terry Hands, who directed the play at the Comédie Française in 1976, also told me a number of interesting stories about that production. The French, being much more interested in the vagaries of passion than the English, focused intensely on the romantic aspects of the play and keenly wanted to know what happened between Orsino and Viola. Hands also claimed that one of his French actors solved a famous textual mystery. You remember that Feste inquires of Malvolio "For what says Quinapulus?"—a bewildering reference to an unknown figure. But the French actor playing Feste instinctively said—"*qui n'a pas lu.*" In other words, "For what says he who has not read?" Excited by this discovery, Hands wrote to the editor of the New Arden edition only to be met with the rebuff "Shakespeare very rarely, if ever, uses French in his plays and I think this is unhelpful." So much for the interchange between the theater and academia.

But last year I saw a Hamburg production of *Twelfth Night—Was Ihr Wollt*—at the Thalia Theater directed by Jürgen Flimm that convinced me that the play gains a new resonance in German. What the German director brought to the play was a fascination with ideas you all too rarely find in England: in this case *Twelfth Night* became an exploration of the Platonic idea of love as a link between the sensible and the eternal world. The result, on stage, was to push the play's sexual confusion as far as it could go. Thus the bosomy and voluptuous Olivia found in Cesario an image of earthly perfection, which led her to unbutton her bodice and hitch up her skirts in a direct attempt at overt seduction. The self-loving and narcissistic Orsino also bore a close resemblance to Cesario whom he clasped to his bosom and cradled lovingly in his lap. And Sebastian and Antonio embraced not only each other but the Platonic idea that truth and beauty may be achieved by mutual affection between persons of the same sex. In short, the play became an infinitely beguiling study in the varieties of Platonic love.

I began to understand why the Germans refer possessively to "unser Shakespeare": this production explored depths of romantic passion I have rarely seen investigated in England. I must also confess that the play's comedy is much harder to translate. Flimm's production was often very funny, but in a physically strenuous way as if he were trying to compensate for the difficulty of capturing Shakespeare's pun-filled prose in German. Thus we saw Sir Toby played—a touch improbably—as a lithe, balletic drunk who at the prospect of Malvolio's yellow stockings hurled himself thrice to the ground with unusual ferocity. And Maria, at the same point, wet her knickers with excitement. But, for all that, the play's themes of sexual confusion, mistaken identity, and madness emerged in all their mythical power. I shall long remember Viola stripping off her doublet in self-hatred on "Disguise, I see thou art a wickedness" and the tormented, vengeful cries of Malvolio reverberating offstage during Feste's final song. The emotional core of the play easily transcended its specific local references.

But this inevitably raises the question of Shakespeare in translation. When we see or read a Shakespeare play in another language, are we in a sense getting Shakespeare at all? Peter Brook once said that you inevitably lose 70 percent of Shakespeare in translation. Jean-Louis Barrault in a 1948 lecture went rather further. "Shakespeare's entry on the French stage," he claimed,

> begins with a crime. In order to cross the Channel he has to be shorn of his poetic garb. The poetic atmosphere of his art which rises towards suprareality and ideal forms is cruelly dispelled by the cold light of our severely rationalized language. Shakespeare, whose thought belongs more to poetry than to pure reason, has his wings severely clipped by the logic which destroys rhythm and music.[4]

It seems to me, however, there is both loss and gain in translating Shakespeare. Self-evidently what you lose is the precision of his puns—a German told me it was almost impossible to capture the double meaning of Feste's "I do live by the church"— the extraordinary alternation between high and low vocabulary, the dense, compacted clang and clatter of his verse. I was looking at a Spanish translation of *Hamlet* recently and was intrigued to see what the translator—a fluent and idiomatic English speaker—had made of the First Player's reference to "bisson rheum." Unsurprisingly, I discovered that it took five words of Spanish to convey the meaning of two in English.

Yet, having seen Shakespeare recently played in French, German, Italian, Romanian, Russian, Georgian, and Japanese, most of which I don't speak, I am convinced something strange and mysterious happens. Released from a preoccupation with line-by-line meaning, I find that hidden areas of the play spring to life. What an English audience takes for granted is often ignored: aspects of a play we would overlook shine out clearly when transmitted through the prism of another language, culture, and history. I can only prove this by example. Last summer for instance, the Comedy Theater of Bucharest brought to London their production of *A Midsummer Night's Dream*. The production was in the final stage of rehearsal when the miners were brought to Bucharest, wielding staves, to quell demonstrations. Distaste for abused power was evident in the way Oberon seemed to be constantly accompanied by four Securitate men in hats and dirty raincoats. But I was more struck by something else. How often in English, Canadian, American, and, I dare say, Australian productions has one seen the Pyramus and Thisbe interlude treated as an extended vaudevillian romp. But, to these Romanian actors, the idea of putting on a play before an official audience had other overtones. It symbolized, in fact, the power of theater as an active resistance movement. Bottom, for instance, delivered his death-speech with immense tragic weight and, when he finally expired, a ripple of shock ran through the giggling spectators. Even more remarkable was the way Bottom instructed the actors to reject the money insultingly thrown at their feet by Philostrate. In Romania, one was reminded, the souls of the actors were not to be purchased even by state subsidy. Thus can foreign Shakespeare open one's eyes to possible new meanings.

I also had the salutary experience recently of seeing *The Merchant of Venice* played by the Vienna Burgtheater in a production by Peter Zadek: a bicultural figure who was born in Berlin, brought up in England from 1933 to 1958, and is now one of the major German-language directors. Obviously *The Merchant* is a play that today causes almost insuperable problems. In England, various ways round them have been found. A famous Jonathan Miller production, with Laurence Olivier, silkily evaded them by translating the action to a turn-of-the-century Venice reminiscent of the novels of Italo Svevo; but since Olivier's Shylock seemed such a prosperous, frock-coated, integrated part of the business community, one wondered why he raged at his status as an outsider. More honestly, a recent Bill Alexander production for the RSC took the text much more literally: Antony Sher's Shylock was a fierce, proud, gloriously unassimilated Levantine Jew upon whose gaberdine Antonio genuinely spat and at whom mobs jeered and threw stones when he ventured outside the ghetto. Interestingly—in the light of my thesis that Shakespeare transcends Englishness—Sher said that he brought his memories of the white treatment of South African Blacks to his interpretation.

But what intrigued me about Zadek's Viennese production was that it made money rather than race or religion the dominant theme. *The Merchant*, after all, is a play about money lent, borrowed, lost, gained, and used as an instrument of power. Accordingly, Zadek set his production in a contemporary Wall Street. Solario and Solanio became small-time brokers reading the financial papers. Bassanio, fashionably pig-tailed, turned up in Belmont with his business associates who offered shrewd market advice about which casket to plump for. And Shylock was played by Gert Voss less as a heroic victim than a cool capitalist who, in the trial scene, far from being devastated by his losses, wrote out promissory notes and made a dignified exit, presumably to ring up his Swiss bank-manager.

This is obviously not the whole of *The Merchant of Venice*. If you deny Shylock an overt sense of persecution or alienation, you make him a bloodthirsty version of Michael Douglas's Gekko in *Wall Street* rather than a historically tormented figure seeking legitimate revenge. But Zadek's approach brought out another aspect of the play: that Venice is, in Sigurd Burckhardt's words, "a closed world, inherently conservative, because it knows that it stands or falls with the sacredness of contracts."[5] It is a point Antonio fully grasps, since he points out that if the course of law be denied, it

> Will much impeach the justice of the state,
> Since that the trade and profit of the city
> Consisteth of all nations.
>
> (3.3.29–31)

And it is a point echoed by Shylock in the trial scene when he observes "If you deny me . . . / There is no force in the decrees of Venice" (4.1.101–2). But it took a Viennese production, liberated from the orthodoxies of Anglo-Saxon Shakespeare, to realize fully the commercial obsession of Shakespeare's comedy.

I am not trying to suggest that Shakespeare is better in translation. I am simply suggesting that the plays acquire a different resonance and richness—a new patina of meaning—when seen through foreign eyes. One problem, possibly peculiar to England, is that the most popular plays in the canon are revived with such routine frequency that it becomes difficult to shed the accretions of the past and to see the plays through a genuinely fresh perspective. Indeed, one of my complaints as a critic is the gradual narrowing of the Shakespeare repertory, influenced partly by the academic syllabus. The great comedies and tragedies come wheeling round season after season but you can go, even in England, quite a long time without seeing *King John*, *Henry VIII*, *Two Gentlemen of Verona*, *All's Well*, or others among the unfashionable plays. Simply because *The Dream* or *Macbeth* are done so often, one tends to lose the blinding shock of revelation.

It takes, I believe, a foreign production to offer us a radical new vision, or to remind us that Shakespeare is like a cosmic mirror in which each culture finds its own reflection. *Macbeth* is a good case in point. I recently saw a very provocative German production by Katharina Thalbach that, freed from the constraints of Tartan realism, treated the play as a grotesque Ubu-like horror story, filled with gallows humor, about despotic insecurity. One moment will also stay with me for a long time: the prolonged, awestruck silence among the thanes as the moral significance of Duncan's murder and the implication of the Macbeths in his killing slowly sank in.

But it is to Japan, where Shakespeare is studied and performed with scholarly intensity, that one can look for the ultimate proof of the mythic power of his drama. One of the great discoveries of the Edinburgh Festival in recent years has been the Japanese director, Yukio Ninagawa, who is a cross-cultural magician saturated in the art and music of the West but also definably a prod-

uct of the East. His production of *Macbeth*, set in the samurai
world of sixteenth-century Japan, had a particular quality one
always looks for in Shakespearean production and rarely finds:
the sense of a legendary story being retold. He achieved this
through the simple device of placing two aged crones at either
side of the stage who parted a walled curtain and then watched
events mysteriously unfold. They became a silent chorus unashamedly weeping as Macbeth sank into barbarism.

But the extraordinary quality of Ninagawa's *Macbeth* was its
lyricism. Instead of a play about murder and retribution, it became a study in the transience of earthly power. The dominant
images were of a blood-red sun, which turned to the color of ash
as Macbeth reached the pit of earthly despair; of an embossed
throne set within the context of a Buddhist altar; and of endlessly
falling cherry blossoms, which to the Japanese symbolizes mortality as well as beauty. The action was also underscored by the
plangent strains of the Fauré *Requiem*, the Samuel Barber *Adagio
for Strings*, and a Purcell chaconne. It became not simply the
tragedy of an individual but a poetic meditation on the way all
human striving is subject to the passage of time; and, as the two
old women closed the curtain on Malcolm before the end of his
final speech, we realized that even his beneficent reign would be
no more than a beam in the eye of eternity. If I had only three
hours left to spend in a theater before I died, I think I would
choose to spend it watching the Ninagawa *Macbeth*.

Japan offers the clearest proof of my contention that we limit
Shakespeare if we define him purely by his Englishness. On the
one hand, the Japanese theater offers faithful literal translation
of the plays. On the other hand, it also absorbs them into its own
tradition. In Britain, we recently saw a Japan Festival—mounted,
needless to say, with their money—that offered versions of *Hamlet*, *Lear*, and *The Merry Wives*. The *Hamlet*, for instance, was
staged as a Kabuki show and was based on an 1868 adaptation
of the play. The style was the exact antithesis of Western theater.
There were no concessions to realism. The story was told with
the aid of two groups of musicians behind transparent screens,
with a chanting narrator accompanied on the banjolike shami-
sen. The same eighteen-year-old actor tripled as Hamlet, Ophelia,
and Fortinbras. And when the corpse of the dead Hamlet had
to be whisked off stage, the actor simply disappeared behind a
billowing black cloth. Contrary to the Romanian production I
mentioned earlier, Fortinbras was played not as a tyrannous thug
but as a purifying, virile presence. The experience could not

have been more remote or strange. This was Shakespeare Japanese-style. And yet, such is the power of the original fable, it transmitted itself through the lattice barriers of language and theatrical convention. I have now seen French, German, Italian, Romanian, Russian, and Japanese *Hamlets* and each time the play has taken on new colors and shades of meaning while retaining its transfixing hold.

What all this proves is open to speculation and debate. You could say it simply shows that a middle-aged English critic is extremely susceptible to foreign influence: that, having seen the plays so often in my own tongue and studied them since youth, I am overpowered by seeing them in translation; that foreign Shakespeare, like a new foreign restaurant, stimulates the palate.

But I hope my experience has wider significance than this. Obviously, I believe the plays have to be constantly renewed and rediscovered in English. I think we—in England—are at a significant turning point in the production of Shakespeare. There is a feeling that verse speaking has grown slack for a number of reasons: the decline in reading verse aloud at home or school, the pervasive influence of television, the shift away from a verbal culture. Directors like Adrian Noble and Peter Hall constantly argue for a return to the first principles of Shakespearean verse speaking. At the same time, there is a call for Shakespearean production to incorporate the physical and mimetic skills of other cultures. Recently at Stratford's Other Place there was a week-long studio experiment in which a group of Asian actors worked alongside RSC regulars on the text of *Antony and Cleopatra.* I am reliably informed that it led to a remarkable synthesis of different cultural traditions and opened all kinds of doors.

By provocatively enquiring "Was Shakespeare English?" I am trying to do two things. One is to suggest that, without forfeiting the rigorous, Leavisite approach to text that has characterized much Shakespearean production over the past three decades, we have to revise our notion of Englishness. We have to acknowledge that it now includes people of African, Caribbean, Indian, Pakistani, Chinese, or Japanese parentage and that they have particular skills and disciplines that will enliven and change the approach to Shakespeare. It would be absurd to have a teeming, multiracial society on the streets and a white colonialist attitude inside the theater.

But my larger point is that Shakespeare is too vast, too uncontainable to be regarded as the property of any one country or cultural tradition. There is obviously a peculiar frisson to hearing and seeing Shakespeare on his home-ground in Stratford-on-Avon. England or Britain generally also has a head-start of several centuries in the regular production of his plays—though we should remind ourselves how recent is the tradition of presenting faithful, uncut, unadapted texts: from the mid-seventeenth to the mid-nineteenth century Shakespeare was presented in all kinds of barbarous, rewritten versions. But I have no wish to see Shakespeare become part of the English heritage industry, nor do I think we should be colonially condescending toward non-English Shakespeare. As I have tried to indicate, the loss in the specificity of language is countered by the gain in new insights. In the end, Shakespeare is too elusive, shifting, variable, and pluralistic to be the property of any single language or country.

Let me end with a story. John Kani, the black South African actor, told me that when *Othello* was presented by the Market Theatre in Johannesburg a few years ago, it met with a bewildering variety of responses. To the white, liberal audience that makes up part of the Market Theatre's constituency it was greeted as the familiar somber tragedy about the heroic gullibility of its hero. To the black audiences from the townships, who crowd into the Market Theatre at the weekends after payday, it became a topical, pungent, and appallingly relevant social drama about the eternal fraudulent deceptiveness of the white liar. This was Shakespeare played in English; but meaning wholly different things to different people and proving yet again the incontrovertible truth that the plays are unvarnished, truth-telling mirrors in which we find the strangest reflections.

Notes

1. David Garrick, in J. C. Trewin, *The Night Has Been Unruly* (London: Robert Hale, 1957), 19–20.

2. Terence Hawkes, "Swisser Swatter: Making a Man of English Letters," in *That Shakespeherian Rag: Essays on a Critical Process* (London: Methuen, 1986), 51–72; G. Wilson Knight, in *Authors Take Sides on the Falklands*, ed. C. Woolf and J. Moorcroft Wilson (London: Woolf, 1982), 66–67.

3. D. J. Enright, "All's Well That Ends, or Shakespeare Unmasked" (1973), in *The Methuen Book of Theatre Verse*, ed. J. Field (London: Methuen Drama, 1991), 95–97.

4. Jean-Louis Barrault, "Shakespeare and the French," lecture delivered at the Edinburgh Festival (1948); in *Shakespeare in Europe*, ed. Oswald LeWinter (Harmondsworth: Penguin, 1970), 347.

5. Sigurd Burckhardt, "*The Merchant of Venice*: The Gentle Bond," *ELH* 29 (1962) p. 243; rpt. in *Shakespeare's Comedies*, ed. Laurence Lerner (Harmondsworth: Penguin, 1967), 159.

The Postcolonial/Postmodern Shakespeare

JYOTSNA SINGH

I

I<small>N</small> a lecture entitled "The Hero as Poet: Dante; Shakespeare," delivered on 12 May 1840, Thomas Carlyle raises an odd rhetorical question: "Consider now if they asked us, will you give up your Indian Empire or your Shakespeare, you English: never have had any Indian Empire or never have had any Shakespeare?" Presenting this as a "grave question" Carlyle offers a telling response:

> Offical persons would answer doubtless in official language; but we, for our part too, should not we be forced to answer: Indian Empire or no Indian Empire; we cannot do without Shakespeare! Indian Empire will go, at any rate, someday; but this Shakespeare does not go, he lasts forever with us.[1]

While, ostensibly, Carlyle's question sets up an either/or polarity between a political entity, the Indian Empire, and a cultural icon, "Shakespeare," it also yokes together the entities it seeks to separate, suggesting a connection between imperial might and cultural self-aggrandizement. Carlyle acknowledges the temporary, even arbitrary, political power of the rulers, but nonetheless promotes their cultural authority by universalizing the bard's popularity. In thus linking Shakespeare to the Indian Empire, Carlyle ironically, and unwittingly, reveals that empire building is a cultural as much as a military or political activity and that Shakespeare continues to function as an instrument of imperial hegemony. In Gramscian terms, this would mean a continuing encroachment of political life into the different arenas of civil society.[2]

British national identity in the Victorian period, as we all know, was shaped by the country's status as a colonial power. Queen Victoria's Diamond Jubilee, for instance, was celebrated

in 1897 through glorified images of the British Empire and
Shakespearean England.[3] While these "innocent" celebrations of
the empire were taking place in the metropolis, English literary
education was being made serviceable to British political interests in the colonies. Most notably, Thomas Babbington Macaulay's 1835 English Education Act for the Indian colonies
promoted English literature over Sanskrit and Arabic texts by
representing Western literary knowledge as objective, universal,
and rational. Its aim was to co-opt a native elite class as a "con-
duit of Western thought and ideas."[4]

Given this fact, it is not surprising that critics and teachers in
the postcolonial world—in Africa, in the Caribbean, and in India—continue to struggle with the impact of Shakespeare's authority, sometimes obscuring the origins of his popularity in
official colonial policy, and at other times resisting his authority
through native revisions. For instance, in India the imperial legacy of a universal, transhistorical Shakespeare has been undeni-
ably institutionalized by Indian universities; the Indian theater,
however, since the early 1900s, has witnessed an opposing movement of vernacular appropriations of Shakespeare, mediated by
heterogeneous forces of race, language, and native culture. And
in Africa and the Caribbean, similar contradictory impulses have
been apparent: Shakespeare has constituted an important part
of colonial intellectual formation in Africa, and in Kenya, for
instance, there is a curious tradition of the recitation and citation
of Shakespeare among legal professionals.[5] However, there has
also been an opposing movement against the Eurocentric canon
and, as Nixon and Cartelli demonstrate, a number of dissenting
intellectuals—George Lamming, Aimé Césaire, and Ngugi Wa
Thiong'o—appropriated Shakespeare's The Tempest as a way of
(in George Lamming's words) "getting out from under this ancient mausoleum of [Western historic achievement]."[6] Using
Shakespeare's text as a means of emphasizing the calls for de-
colonization, they recast Prospero, the supposedly "enlightened
European," as a totalitarian with an absolute will to power and
Caliban, the slave, as a revolutionary resistance fighter and a
maker of history.[7]

Thus, any genealogical analysis of Shakespeare's popularity
and influence within a colonial and postcolonial context, we
will find, is marked by anomalies and contradictions that blur
boundaries between the elite colonial bard and the indigenous
Shakespeares. Here, I don't imply an effacement of institutional
boundaries within which texts are produced and circulated—

boundaries between the theater and the university, for instance—but, rather, I suggest a complex and contradictory relation between Shakespeare's works and the ideology of Western/British cultural hegemony in colonies such as India, regardless of the particular setting. Echoes of this cultural struggle and strife can also be found in the Anglo-American academy today, and perhaps in Australia and New Zealand too, where Shakespeare studies have become an important site upon which the battle of the humanities is being waged, as his authority is evoked in numerous debates about "value," "canonicity," and "standards." Regardless of where one stands in this debate, one can clearly note the challenge of politically oriented criticism to Shakespeare's privileged position within pervasive class-bound, and frequently racist, notions of culture—a position that for centuries remained largely undetected and unchallenged.

It is within the context of these debates, then, that this essay is written. As we approach Shakespeare's works in the twentieth century, and in an increasingly interconnected, postmodern global culture, we have become keenly aware that not only do they illuminate the culture of Elizabethan and Jacobean England, but through their subsequent reception and reproduction they have continued to shape a variety of cultural paradigms and institutions—both in the West and in the "third world." Taking this historical perspective, it becomes apparent that the meaning and "value" of Shakespeare's works emerge from a complex interplay of negotiations and struggles, and nowhere do these struggles seem more crucial to issues of national, racial, and ethnic identity than they do in the former colonies of the West.

II

The history of British cultural hegemony in India offers a telling testimony to the nature of this clash of cultures. Considering how the colonial rulers introduced Shakespeare to Indian cultural life in the early nineteenth century, it would be appropriate to use the term "Shakespeare as Empire" to describe their strategy. To begin with, I will examine the role of the English theaters as instruments of empire in nineteenth-century Calcutta, the intellectual and political center of colonial presence in India at the time. Starting in 1775, when the Calcutta theater, or the new Playhouse, opened under the patronage of the Governor-General, Warren Hastings, and continuing for a period of about a hundred years, English theaters entertained a largely British audience of

political figures, officers, merchants, scholars, and clerks of the
East India Company. In their early years at least, these were exclusive theaters, stressing their distance from the natives so that
even the ushers and doorkeepers at the Calcutta theater were
English. While aristocratic Indians were gradually associated
with these theatres—both as viewers and contributors—the primary aim of staging plays by Sheridan, Congreve, Massinger, and,
most notably, Shakespeare was to keep alive the myth of English
cultural superiority, a myth that was crucial to British political
interests in India, and in which Shakespeare, undoubtedly, was
a privileged signifier.[8]

By most accounts, Shakespeare's plays were performed frequently in English theaters in nineteenth-century Calcutta. For
instance, *Hamlet* and *Richard III* were among works performed
at the Calcutta theater (which was managed by a Mr. Bernard
Massing or Massinck, specially sent from England by David Garrick, the noted Shakespearean actor, to introduce the theater of
the mother country to the colonies). The Chowringhee theater,
which opened in 1813, was the venue for the following plays:
'Henry IV in 1814, *Richard III* in 1815, and *The Merry Wives of
Windsor* in 1818. The Sans Souci, which opened in 1839, was
another popular venue for Shakespearean plays. Mrs. Esther
Leach, a prominent actress at the time, arranged for artists to be
brought from London, among whom was a James Vining. Having
acted at Drury Lane and Covent Garden, Vining gave important
performances at the Sans Souci, including his appearance as
Shylock in *The Merchant of Venice* in 1843.[9] A performance at
the Sans Souci that remains memorable is that of Baishnav
Charan Adhya as Othello with Mrs. Anderson (the daughter of
Mrs. Leach) as Desdemona; according to one observer: "A Bengali youth in an English theatre catering to a [largely] English
audience in . . . the nineteenth century, is certainly a memorable
event in the history of Calcutta's theatres."[10]

When the Indian actor donned the "white mask" of a Shakespearean actor in the English production of *Othello*, he clearly
enacted his difference from the white world, both of fictional
Venice and colonial Calcutta. In doing so, he complicated and
displaced the stark "Manichaean" dichotomy of "black and
white," which, Franz Fanon believes, governed the relations between European colonizers and their non-European subjects; instead of being appropriated by the colonial text, Adhya revealed
the ambivalence of its cultural authority through a native strategy

of resistance, best described, by Homi Bhabha, as "camouflage, mimicry, white skin/black masks."[11]

A sense of how some members of the largely English audience responded to this event can be derived from a letter in a contemporary edition of the *Calcutta Star* that unflatteringly calls the actor a "real unpainted nigger."[12] While exposing the "hidden" dark face of the Indian actor, the writer seems anxious about the possible cultural and racial contamination of the English stage and society in Calcutta. An exclusion of all natives from colonial social life, which the worried letter to the *Calcutta Star* seems to suggest, was obviously not a viable policy; instead, as I mentioned earlier, the English decided to mediate the gap between themselves and the "millions they governed" by "interpreters," whom Macaulay aptly defined as a "class of persons Indian in blood and colour, but English in tastes, in opinion, in morals and intellect."[13]

It was this class of aristocratic Anglicized Indians who gradually gained access to the Calcutta theaters—a privilege that loosely coincided with the official policy of promoting English language and literature in India. In a recent landmark study, Gauri Vishwanathan argues that the colonial administrators found an ally in English literature for maintaining control over the natives under the guise of a liberal education. This was done by representing Western literary knowledge as universal, transhistorical, and rational—and specifically, as a source for moral values that emphasized social duty and order.[14] The moral education of natives proposed by Charles Grant, in his 1792 tract *Observations on the State of Society among Asiatic Subjects of Great Britian*, now became the basis of literary studies in India. A moral approach to literature, Grant had argued, "views politics through the safe medium of morals, and subjects them to the laws of universal rectitude."[15] So when nineteenth-century rulers emphasized English literature as a source for universal morality, they prevented the natives from inculcating liberal thought that could endanger British presence in India. Clearly, they had found a masterful strategy for domination and control. Thus, in introducing English literature to the Indians—or in allowing them access to the Calcutta theaters—the colonial rulers were not being egalitarian, but rather were engaged in a "hegemonic activity" by which, in Gramsci's terms, the consent of the governed is secured through intellectual and moral manipulation rather than through military force. Charles Trevelyan's official confidence in this policy, elaborated in his book *On the Educa-*

tion of the People of India (1838), pointedly reveals how the rulers idealized the empire, while occluding its harsh exploitative effects: "The Indians daily converse with the best and wisest Englishmen through the medium of their works and form higher ideas of our nation than if their intercourse was of a more personal kind."[16]

III

Shakespeare was an important source of the "higher ideas" that policy makers such as Trevelyan and Macaulay had in mind when they located "sound Bible Protestant principles" in his works. In declaring these canonical literary works as sources of revered moral values, the colonizers were assured that a "love" for Shakespeare, among others, would develop among the elite classes. The empire's political and cultural investment in the Shakespearean book in nineteenth-century Calcutta is vividly described by the Indian critic, S. K. Bhattacharya:

> While the English playhouses by their production of English, especially Shakespeare's plays created an appetite for theatrical performances, the foundation of Hindu College in 1816, and the teaching of Shakespeare . . . created in the minds of the students—the intelligentsia of modern Bengal—and taught them, not only how to appreciate Shakespeare criticism, but also to recite and act scenes from his plays. This fashion spread to every academic institution. In 1837 Bengali students staged scenes from The Merchant of Venice in the Governor's house, in 1852 and 1853, the students of the Metropolitan academy and David Hare academy staged Shakespeare's plays while the old and new students of the Oriental academy staged Othello in 1853, The Merchant of Venice in 1854, and Henry IV in 1855. Shakespeare's dramas became an indispensable part of English education and a popular item in all cultural productions. The Bengali theatre which made its mark in the later decades was the natural outcome of this new-found passion.[17]

It is remarkable that this critic, writing as recently as 1964, identifies the native "appreciation" for Shakespeare as a spontaneous response, a "fashion" or a "new-found passion" that had a "natural" outcome in the emergence of the Bengali theater. While acknowledging that the English "created" a "literary taste" among elite Bengalis, the critic nonetheless views English literature as a transcendentally benevolent and nonpolitical influence. In keeping with Thomas Carlyle's prophecy, it seems the myth of the "universal bard" continues to persist in the postcolonial era, and in order to understand the insidious effects of this myth, let us turn to a telling essay, entitled "In States Unborn—Shakespeare Overseas," by the English critic D. J. Enright.

Enright regrets the "disrepute" into which English literature abroad has fallen and half heartedly acknowledges that "English literature is irrevocably compromised [in the former colonies] because it was thrust upon subject races as a political, an imperialistic measure." Then, in a reversal, he blames newly independent states for undermining English literature, because "it speaks out for largeness, tolerance, a degree of individual freedom," which these free countries "are unable to afford." While he believes that the English have an exclusive claim on ideals such as freedom and tolerance, he somewhat paradoxically views Shakespeare's characters as "the genuine progeny of common humanity, such as the world will always supply." Thus Shakespeare is crucial to Enright's plea for the continuing enlightenment of former subjects:

> Shakespeare was the great recording genius of our Renaissance. Now Asia and Africa are experiencing their Renaissance. These regions received their industrial revolution . . . from us. Their arts lagged an era behind . . . Their art was inviolate, shackled to the past. But they came to want it to yield its long-preserved virginity, to be free. They knew they could not go on forever producing *haiku* or *kabuki*, or variations of the *Ramayana*. . . What holds for them, for it deals with a world which is modern (rather than medieval) and bursting with energy (rather than sophistication) is pre-eminently the plays of Shakespeare.

While Shakespeare, Enright argues, is undoubtedly an enlightening influence on the natives, "Eastern interpretations" of the plays can only contribute "minor modifications rather than radical revision." Thus in Enright's vision of a postcolonial history we are not to expect "an Indian Shakespeare, a Malayan Shakespeare, a Japanese Shakespeare, and so forth, but rather a contemporary Shakespeare more or less common to all countries."[18]

In promoting a Shakespeare "common to all," the English critic not only erases cultural or racial differences among former subjects of the British Empire, but also denies them human agency and originality. Enright's strategy typifies hegemonic Western discourses in which, as James Clifford suggests, the supposedly backward non-European peoples "no longer invent local futures"; instead, they remain constituted as passive and reverential subjects in the ideology of Western superiority.[19] Clifford's diagnosis is reflected in the frequent praise heaped on Shakespeare by Indian critics—a praise that generally occludes the socioeconomic factors that continue to legitimate and promote English literary studies in India. According to Ania Loomba, "all of Delhi University's approximately 140,000 students must study English literature for at least one year, among whom around 20,000 may read Shakespeare."[20] Who are these students? In what ways are they constituted as subjects in the ideology of the universal English text? Writing in 1972, critic and teacher S. Nagarajan reveals how teaching English literature perpetuates the class system: "The reactions to [Shakespeare] vary . . . from Westernized students coming from affluent families and English schools to the students who come from unanglicized families and regional language schools. Perhaps it is the second category we should concentrate upon—at least they are in the majority."[21]

Such a schism between classes is still evident in Indian society. Yet critical and pedagogical discourses on Shakespeare often constitute and naturalize all students or readers, including the unanglicized majority, as admirers of the timeless Shakespeare. The reasons for the importance of English literature for language teaching are not incidental. According to Steve Whittey, "during Independence, the bourgeoisie found the continued use of a European language advantageous for social and political control. They could maintain their own privileged position through their monopoly over the colonial language."[22] A proof of such attitudes can be found in the recent remarks of Alyque Padamsee, India's top stage director; when asked about the relevance of English theater (in the context of his recent production of *Othello*), his reply ironically revealed the connection between the Indian class structure and the English language: "India is the largest English-speaking country in the world."[23] Furthermore, as R. Sunder Rajan argues, the indigenous power structures in Indian universities are buttressed by the "hegemonic authority" of the Western, neocolonial commercial and political interests, manifested by the Anglo-American universities, the university and commercial presses, and quasi-governmental agencies such as the USIS and the British Council.[24]

Given these basic class inequities in India, it is not surprising that discourses on English literature are generally formalistic and reverential. And if English literary figures are to be revered, who better than Shakespeare? What such discourses occlude is the presence of a vast majority of Indians who do not study

English as a first language, and whose sense of awe for the Shakespearean text is intrinsic to their linguistic struggle and has no relevance to the value of the text. Thus a recurring praise of the "universal Shakespeare" denies both colonial history and postcolonial class differences. Typifying such an approach is the essay by G. Mulyil published in the Literary Criterion in 1963. Viewing the study of English literature as "an intimate east-west encounter," the critic envies the "earlier generation who were given a more thorough grounding in the language and literature of the rulers," especially in Shakespeare, "the Englishman's most treasured possession," who appeals to all races with his "rich humanity." Acknowledging "the problem of translation," the critic nonetheless reinforces class elitism when he regrets that "where in the past a few people knew a great deal about Shakespeare, today a large number know a little about him."[25] In all these accounts the specter of the underprivileged cannot be exorcized, even though their presence is considered bothersome to the project of English education.

Other Indian critics, writing in the 1960s, 1970s, and even the 1980s reveal similar contradictions in their position on Shakespeare's influence. A recent critical anthology, Shakespeare in India, also reinforces Shakespeare's "universal" status. While the editors announce a "love of Shakespeare in [their] country,"[26] the emphasis of the book is on textual criticism. In this way the essayists do not make any break with the Anglo-American critical tradition, nor do they attempt to situate their work within their cultural and social milieu. Presented as the work of "India's foremost Shakespeare critics," Shakespeare in India ultimately legitimates the neocolonial hegemony of the English book. Produced and marketed in the West by the prestigious Oxford University Press, it is given an "acceptable" status in the West, even as it represents the Indian critical practice as essentially imitative and derivative.

Overall, it seems that while mainstream critical perspectives have not accounted for the more popular influences of Shakespeare, different regional theaters in India have produced alternative Shakespeares, often for the unanglicized majority. Most theater historians agree that contemporary Indian theater originated in Bengal in the mid-nineteenth century. Although Indian folk theater had existed in rural areas for centuries, there was no direct evolution from classical Sanskrit theater to new, contemporary forms. Therefore, when English-educated Bengalis, especially in Calcutta, were exposed to Shakespeare and other classic dramatists, they sought to emulate productions in the English theaters. And not surprisingly, the first Bengali theater in Calcutta opened with a production of *Julius Caesar*. A number of other Shakespearean productions followed, but by the mid-nineteenth century there was a dawning sense of a need for original Bengali plays. Shakespeare's works disappeared from the Bengali stage around the 1920s, and Bengali plays became more responsive to social and political realities.

When Shakespearean plays reappeared on the Bengali stage around 1948 they reflected contemporary social realities, and the name most notably associated with this revival is that of Utpal Dutt. A prominent actor and director, Dutt is a revolutionary intellectual who reacted violently to his Western colonial education ("the fact that he could recite Virgil and Shakespeare dismayed him,")[27] and yet his theatrical training came from touring with Geoffrey Kendall's Shakespearean company in 1947. After independence, Dutt's Little Theatre Group produced a new play by Shakespeare every month, but with increasing social awareness they realized that they could not presume to be radical so long as they continued to perform plays exclusively for a minority audience, the Westernized intellectuals of Calcutta.[28]

Returning to the Little Theatre Group in 1950, Dutt now produced plays only in Bengali for a largely middle-class audience. Among notable productions was a Bengali translation of *Macbeth*, which toured remote villages in Bengal. By immersing *Macbeth* in the ritual world of the Jatra, the vigorous folk theater of Bengal, and thus by transforming Shakespeare's language into a bold, declamatory form of incantation typical of the Jatra, Dutt celebrated an alternative dramatic practice, outside existing systems of cultural authority. Jatra actors usually perform with highly charged religious fervor, using rhythmic gestures and incantatory speech; familiar with these indigenous conventions, the villagers responded to *Macbeth* as compelling myth. While views vary on the aesthetic success of Utpal Dutt's production, one cannot doubt that it challenged the elitist culture's exclusive claims over Shakespeare's works by transplanting them onto the non elite native's cultural terrain. Dutt has often stated that "the classics were not the prerogative of an elite. They would cease to exist unless they were brought to the people."[29] This notion does not imply a timeless, universal Shakespeare loved by one and all; rather, it takes into account class, education, and race, among others, as material factors in any mode of cultural production.

Other regional revivals of Shakespeare on the Indian stage have also, from time to time, drawn on the idiom of popular culture, though they have not been as politically motivated as Dutt's. For instance, the "craze for Shakespearean drama" on the Bombay stage from the mid-nineteenth century to 1913 was "not due to any special regard for Shakespeare's poetry or genius," but rather to the plays' providing "a good story with a few romantic and thrilling situations."[30] Performed in a number of Indian regional languages, including Urdu, Marathi, and Gujerati, these plays appealed to the Bombay audiences by providing "plenty of spectacles, swift moving action, noise, scenes of bloodshed, music, song and dialogue in stylized language."[31] In these obviously eclectic, irreverent adaptations, the Shakespearean text is no longer sacrosanct; instead it is invaded by heteroglossia, or multiplicity of styles and forms in the Bakhtinian sense, that disrupt the cultural authority of the official English Shakespeare.

Although such regional revivals have not transformed the institutional investment in the "universal bard," they nonetheless reveal the audacious claims frequently made by the unanglicized majority of Indians on the canonical colonial Shakespeare—whose works are liguistically inaccessible to them and yet crucial as "cultural capital" for their education. Even in an English-language production of *Othello* recently performed in Bombay and Delhi, the protagonist was depicted as an Islamic Moor and the racial conflicts in the play struck a topical chord in a society torn by cultural and religious strife.[32] Yet overall, as we have seen, and as Ania Loomba and others have suggested, Shakespeare continues to serve as an accommodating ideal in Indian academy and society, erasing colonial history and expelling the tensions of class struggle and language divisions in the postcolonial era. As a result, English literary studies inevitably suppress the popular, the vernacular, and the marginalized aspects of the culture. It is these aspects of culture and society that must be foregrounded if one is to expose the continuing complicity between imperial and Western systems and indigenous systems of power—or between Macaulay's ghost and the descendants of his anglicized "interpreters." The question, then, that remains to be asked is where in the Western postmodern academy can the voices of the unanglicized majority, the underprivileged masses in Africa, in the Caribbean, and in South Asia—those who will never understand the canonical Shakespeare—be expressed and accounted for? And to what purpose and what effect?

IV

Contextualizing Shakespeare within colonial/postcolonial history for the Western academy clearly constitutes a postmodernist move to pluralize and decenter all totalizing assumptions of the center, the metropolis, the mother country; in this sense, it is what Linda Hutcheon and Ann Kaplan have identified as the positive or Utopian impulse in postmodernism.[33] In emphasizing discontinuity and difference from the established traditions of Renaissance studies, recent scholarship—under the labels of new historicism, feminism, Marxism, and postcolonial theory—has "objected to the tradition of Burkhardt that viewed the Renaissance as the heroic, originary moment of modern [implicitly Western] individualism . . . [in which it discovered] the origins of permanent qualities, if not of human, then at least of humanist nature."[34] In doing so, these critics have repudiated the liberal-humanist tradition, which buttressed Shakespeare's claims to a timeless universality, while naturalizing various social hierarchies—of gender, rank, and race, among others.

Postmodernity has been aptly defined by one critic as the moment at which the West "has lost its cultural and ideological coherence . . . the traditional bonds of bourgeois culture are dissolved . . . state power is faced with a legitimation crisis, and the great narratives of [Western] modernity have stuttered to a stop."[35] Within this crisis of representation, Western critics have begun to realize that it is difficult to locate unmediated presence anywhere, in history, in culture, or in the psyche. And voices emanating from the margins—from the postcolonial or, some would say, neocolonial territories—have intensified this sense of crisis by repudiating all universalist claims concerning the nature of human experience. Thus, in perspective, Shakespeare's works are neither universal nor benign embodiments of the "civilizing values" of the West, but instead, are inextricably linked to the West's political and cultural hegemony.

Few would deny that these attempts to "rewrite" the Renaissance in relation to postcolonial discourses are well-intentioned efforts to decenter the old map of knowledge. Hence, everywhere in the Western academy "postcolonial Shakespeares" are intervening in the Burkhardtian celebrations of the "Renaissance Man"—the coherent, unified, mostly male subject who was also traditionally the imagined reader of canonical works. The provocative title of the conference at which this paper was presented, "Shakespeare Outside England," testifies to such a move to reconsider the bard from outside the dominant traditions. On the other hand, however, one cannot help being aware of how studies of non-European Shakespeares can also be hooked to the economy of "globalism" in which foreign cultures are simply reproduced in the West as new commodities. For instance, an article in the *Chronicle of Higher Education*, June 1989, proclaims that business schools seek "to internationalize curricula to meet the demands of global economy," training graduates in the cultures and business practices of other countries. If the postcolonial perspective is caught up in such elisions between cultural practices and business interests, then it clearly faces the danger of becoming what Ann Kaplan defines as a "commercial or co-opted" form of postmodernist discourse,[36] simply translating the marginality of otherness into a discourse available for a commodity culture's consumptions. Thus, it can simply become another "language game" played around "the effect of fragmented subjectivity which has begun to replace alienation as the existential condition of intellectuals in the dominant, Western consumer society."[37]

While believing in the possibility—and in the necessity—of decentering the traditional, hegemonic map of knowledge, I am also forced to wonder whether postcolonial discourse can in any way position itself outside multinational, neocolonial capitalism? Therefore, I am uncomfortably aware that even while I attempt to speak for the unanglicized majority of Indians and other postcolonial subjects, I am in effect co-opting them for my own purposes, for in a sense I am here, at this moment, by virtue of the history of empire. And finally, I can take no solace from my own ambiguous and divided subject position: on one hand, in an Indian context, I am one of Macaulay's subjects educated to be "English in tastes, opinions, morals, and in intellect"; and yet in the Western academy I am simply a "native informant" interpreting a non-European culture in the language of the colonizers.

Notes

1. Thomas Carlyle, "Lecture on the Hero as Poet: Dante; Shakespeare," in *Four Lectures* (London, 1840).

2. See Edward Said's discussion of Gramsci in *Orientalism* (New York: Vintage Books, 1979), 11.

3. Marion F. O'Connor, "Theatre of the Empire: 'Shakespeare's England' at Earl's Court, 1912," in *Shakespeare Reproduced: The Text in History and Ideol-*

ogy, ed. Jean E. Howard and Marion F. O'Connor (London: Methuen, 1987), 68–69, 76–77.

4. Gauri Vishwanathan, "The Beginnings of English Literary Study in India," *Oxford Literary Review* 9 (1987): 10. This is a pioneering study that shows how the export of literature played a role in ensuring the ideological hegemony of the British Empire.

5. David W. Cohen and E. Atieno, "The Surveillance of Men: Notes towards an Essay on Gender in Kenya," unpublished essay.

6. Rob Nixon, "Caribbean and African Appropriations of *The Tempest*," *Critical Inquiry* 13 (1987): 558. See also Thomas Cartelli, "Prospero in Africa," in *Shakespeare Reproduced: The Text in History and Ideology*, ed. Jean E. Howard and Marion F. O'Connor (London: Methuen, 1987), 99–115.

7. Nixon, "Caribbean and African Appropriations," 570–73.

8. For a fuller account of the development of English theaters in colonial Calcutta, see P. Guha-Thakurta, *The Bengali Drama: Its Origin and Development* (London: Kegan, Paul, 1988), 40–48; Sushil K. Mukherjee, *The Story of the Calcutta Theatres: 1753–1980* (Calcutta: K. P. Bagchi, 1982), 1–7; and Rustom Bharucha, *Rehearsals of Revolution: The Political Theatre of Bengal* (Honolulu: University of Hawaii Press, 1983), 7–9.

9. Mukherjee, *Calcutta Theatres*, 3–4; Guha-Thakurta, *Bengali Drama*, 42–43.

10. Mukherjee, *Calcutta Theatres*, 7.

11. Frantz Fanon, *Black Skin, White Masks*, trans. Charles Lam Markmann (New York: Grove Press, 1967), 44–45; Homi Bhabha, "Signs Taken for Wonders: Questions of Ambivalence and Authority under a Tree Outside Delhi," *Critical Inquiry* 12 (autumn 1985): 144–65.

12. Kironmoy Raha, *Bengali Theatre* (New Delhi: National Book Trust, 1978), 10.

13. Macaulay's 1835 Minute, cited by Ania Loomba, *Gender, Race, Renaissance Drama* (Manchester: Manchester University Press, 1989), 31.

14. Vishwanathan, "English Literary Study in India," 10.

15. Cited by Vishwanathan (ibid., 12).

16. Charles Trevelyan, *On the Education of the People of India* (London, 1838), 176.

17. S. K. Bhattacharya, "Shakespeare and Bengali Theatre," *Indian Literature* 7 (1964): 29.

18. D. J. Enright, "In States Unborn—Shakespeare Overseas," *Times Literary Supplement*, 23 April 1964: 27–28.

19. James Clifford, *The Predicament of Culture: Twentieth-Century Ethnography, Literature, and Art* (Cambridge: Harvard University Press, 1988), 5.

20. Loomba, *Gender, Race, Renaissance Drama*, 28.

21. S. Nagarajan, "The Teaching of Shakespeare in India," *Indian Writing in English*, Proceedings of a seminar on Indian English held at the Central Institute of English (Hyderabad, 1972), 47.

22. Quoted by Loomba (*Gender, Race, and Renaissance Drama*, 31), from Steve Whittey, "English Language as a Tool for British Neocolonialism," *East Africa Journal* 8 (1971): 4–6.

23. For a fuller account of Padamsee's views on Shakespeare in India, see "Between Othello and His Maker," interview with Alyque Padamsee, *Statesman* (New Delhi), 28 March 1991.

24. Rajeshwari Sunder Rajan, "'After Orientalism': Colonialism and English Literary Studies in India," *Social Scientist* 158 (1986): 29–31.

25. G. Mulyil, in the *Literary Criterion* (Hyderabad), special Christmas issue, December 1963: 79–81.

26. S. Nagarajan and S. Vishwanathan, eds., *Shakespeare in India* (Oxford: Oxford University Press, 1987), vi.

27. Nandini Bhattacharya and Pardipta Bhattacharya, "A Weapon of Change," interview with Utpal Dutt, *Sunday* (Calcutta), 3 November 1985: 3.

28. See Bharucha, *Rehearsals of Revolution*, 55–56.

29. For a detailed account of Dutt's views, see Bhattacharya, interview with Utpal Dutt.

30. C. R. Shah, "Shakespearean Plays in Indian Languages, I," *Aryan Path*, November 1955: 485.

31. Ibid., 485.

32. A review of *Othello* in *Times of India* (New Delhi), 27 March 1991, describes the views of the director, Alyque Padamsee, as follows: "In the strong racial conflict in the play he sees, for example, a parallel of our own communal problems. 'My Moor is an islamic moor' he tells us."

33. Linda Hutcheon, *The Poetics of Postmodernism: History, Theory, Fiction* (London: Routledge, 1988); Ann Kaplan, introduction to *Postmodernism and Its Discontents: Theories, Practices*, ed. Ann Kaplan (London: Verso, 1988).

34. Don E. Wayne, "New Historicism," *Encyclopaedia of Literature and Criticism*, ed. Martin Coyle, et al. (London: Routledge, 1990), 796.

35. Hal Foster, *Recodings: Art, Spectacle, Cultural Politics* (Seattle: Bay Press, 1985), 157.

36. Kaplan, introduction to *Postmodernism and Its Discontents*.

37. Wayne, *New Historicism*, 802.

Shakespeare and Czech Resistance

Martin Prochazka

CZECH Shakespeareanism can be understood as an "affirmative culture"—"the assertion of a universally obligatory, eternally better and more valuable world that must be unconditionally affirmed: a world essentially different from the factual world of the daily struggle of existence, yet realizable by every individual . . . from within."[1] However, apart from identifying Shakespeare and his plays with this ideal value system, the acts of affirmation have always included or implied gestures of resistance against foreign rule, cultural domination, or political hegemony. The use of Shakespeare by various Czech resistance movements (from the late eighteenth-century "National Revival" to "Charter 77") can hardly be discussed without taking note of this tension between universal humanist ideals and contemporary political issues.[2]

Another distinction may be drawn between the gestures of resistance (political events and theatrical productions) and theater institutions created by the resistance movements or connected with them. Throughout modern Czech history, theater has been a political, as well as cultural institution. In the nineteenth century, for instance, the absence of political and legal foundations for a Czech nation had made the popular leaders cherish great hopes in the National Theater as a substitute for the long-delayed constitution, which was expected to legitimize Czech national identity. In the 1930s, avant-garde artists envisaged the project of the Theater of Labor as a means of cultural, and finally political, reorganization of the state. These theatrical (as well as political) institutions were based on different value hierarchies from those implied in the gestures of resistance. In contrast to *emancipatory* acts and efforts, they were embodiments of *mancipatio*, the acceptance of values and authority as a gift from some higher political, metaphysical, or ideological power (the monarch, the nation, the working class). As Marcel Mauss has shown, the gift establishes an asymetric, hierarchical relationship, the receiver's

44

obligation to the giver.[3] This obligation to political powers and traditional authorities also shaped the affirmative character of the use of Shakespeare by Czech resistance movements.

In discussing individual Shakespeare productions I have decided to concentrate on their institutional framework, in which the gestures of emancipation and resistance interpenetrate and collide with acts of *mancipatio* and subjection. Apart from resistance movements, my attention is focused on several crucial historical moments of resistance in modern Czech history that not only produced distinct political representations of Shakespeare's art but also gave specific meanings to four representative theatrical institutions. The peasants' rebellion of 1775, followed by the abolition of serfdom and the establishment of the centralized absolutist regime of Joseph II, influenced the repertory of the Patriotic Theater which staged the first Czech translations and adaptations of Shakespeare. The foundation of the National Theater can be seen as one of the outcomes of the vain attempt of 1848 to achieve autonomy within the Austrian Empire. On its stage took place the Shakespeare festival of 1916, which was closely connected with the movement for national independence. Shortly before Czechoslovakia fell victim to Hitler in 1938, E. F. Burian's efforts to incorporate the aesthetic program of the avant-garde theater into the anti-Fascist broad left movement found expression in his adaptation of *Hamlet* and the project of the Theater of Labor. And the most informal theatrical institution, the Living Room Theater of Czech "dissidents," resulted from resistance to the general demoralization and destruction of cultural life after the invasion by the Warsaw Pact armies in 1968. All these institutions created social spaces, in which the "affirmative culture" of Czech Shakespeareanism attained specific aesthetic forms and social dimensions.

I   Troublesome Loyalty: *Macbeth* at the Patriotic Theater

The late eighteenth-century productions of Shakespeare in Czech translation were staged at the Patriotic Theater. Its wooden structure was erected in the main Prague marketplace (now Wenceslas Square) in 1786. Because of its location and its unpretentious, makeshift appearance, it soon acquired a popular nickname, "The Booth" (Bouda).

The project of the Patriotic Theater was an outcome of sweeping changes in the Austrian Empire in the last quarter of the eighteenth century. A few years before, the abolition of serfdom had given the peasants freedom of movement and caused a constant flow of country people to the cities. As a result, the Czech language began to assert itself against the bilingual German-Czech, which had so far prevailed among the lower classes in the cities. Parallel to this spontaneous social and linguistic emancipation ran the efforts of scholars and some nationalist aristocrats to "revive" Czech language and literature, marginalized by the Hapsburgs for a hundred and fifty years.

In the meantime, the Austrian government started an extensive program of consolidation. The Emperor, Joseph II, wanted to transform the monarchy into a centralized state governed by a bureaucratic elite. For this purpose he could use the popular support that had been his since the abolition of serfdom, and even Czech revivalist efforts.

The social and cultural *emancipation* of the people had to be restated as a change of feudal allegiance. The emperor himself had assumed the roles of the defender of peasants' rights, the friend of Czech patriots, and the patron of linguistic and cultural revival. He even went to see a Czech play at "The Booth." Under his auspices, the emancipatory efforts were transformed into ceremonial bestowals of privileges. Thus the feudal authority was reestablished by *mancipatio*, the traditional ceremony of accepting the gift. Freedom and the public use of the Czech language were constructed as gifts, establishing new relationships between the emperor and his "favorite" Czechs, but in reality between the absolutist state and a potentially mutinous ethnic group. The patterns of these relationships were obvious: father and son, ruler and subject, God and the people.

We do not know much about the performances of the Czech translations of Shakespeare during this period. But it is quite certain that *Macbeth* was the first Shakespeare play staged, even before the opening of the Patriotic Theater. The translator, Karel Ignác Thám, used a German adaptation by F. J. Fischer and a Czech chapbook version (1782), which transposed the heavily cut and adapted text into undemanding prose.[4]

The production of *Macbeth, or The Witches' Prophecy* (Makbet, aneb Proroctví čarodějnic, 1786) might have followed the company's practice of inserting short Czech plays into ballet shows in order to meet the demands of Czech as well as German-speaking lower-class audiences. In a way typical of popular entertainment in this period, Thám emphasized the theatrical aspects of the witches scenes and represented Lady Macbeth as the only agent of Macbeth's corruption, a vile schemer and cozener.

Unlike the Restoration *Macbeth* adapted by William Davenant (who also changed the language to make it appeal to public taste and added operatic and ballet interludes),[5] Thám's version did not put much stress on the characters of Macduff and Lady Macduff. Nor did it strive to create a symmetrical pattern contrasting the powers of good and evil in human nature. On the other hand, it considerably weakened the evil aspects of the main heroes' characters and deeds by centering the action around the witch intrigue and distancing the murder of the king as much as possible: the part of Duncan was omitted.

These changes reflected the preferences of popular taste, but they might also result from anxiety at presenting the murder of a monarch on the stage of a theater that itself was a "gift" from the emperor. There is also a good reason to believe that Thám had to avoid showing the defilement of the sacred ties that formed the traditional basis of feudal power and authority. Macbeth's deed was not presented as a breach of the double bond of family ties and subject-state relationship, or as the violation of basic moral obligations between giver and receiver, guest and host ("First, as I am his kinsman and his subject, / Strong both against the deed. . ." 1.7.13–14). Instead, it was shown to be the result of witchcraft, the hero's weakness, and female depravity.

This was also the reason Thám's *Macbeth*, in contrast to his almost contemporary translation of Schiller's *Robbers*, was not banned by the vigilant censorship. Yet the issues of rebellion against aristocratic landholders and of the rebels' submission to the power of a just monarch were clearly articulated in other plays staged at that time at "The Booth" and watched probably by some participants in the peasants' revolt of 1775. These may now provide the missing political context of the *Macbeth* production.[6] It is quite likely that Thám's adaptation had been deliberately distanced from contemporary representations of rebellion against the feudal order, in which the act of emancipation was finally sanctioned by renewed *mancipatio* (in the form of the filial duty, love, and gratitude of the people to the monarch) and the restoration of political stability was represented as the reestablishment of the identity of the state-subject and father-son relationships.[7] Because of the absence of *mancipatio* articulated in terms of a filial bond (Malcolm's and Fleance's fathers as well as Macduff's and Siward's sons are killed), *Macbeth* was hard to fit into the representational order of the "neoconservative" state ideology.

Nevertheless it had been integrated, though in the form of a literary text, not a performance. The 1786 edition contained a preface on the importance of the *reading* of plays for the moral cultivation of human nature. Unlike numerous Enlightenment arguments emphasizing universal aspects of this process, the essay concentrated on prospects for the education of low-class Czech theatergoers. The general value of literacy was specified in terms of *mancipatio* (literacy as a "gift" to the common people establishing a hierarchical relationship between them and the state elite) and upward social mobility. The result of this *mancipatio* was envisioned as a linguistic emancipation of the people—the elevation of the Czech language, used so far only by the commoners, to a higher social status.

This emancipation was in turn redefined in theatrical terms by Prokop Šedivý who was Thám's co-worker and the translator of *King Lear* (1791). Using Schiller's Mannheim lecture of 1784 ("Was kann eine gute stehende Schaubuhne eigentlich wirken?"), Šedivý stressed the meaning of theater for the education of the people, suppressed Schiller's reflections on the importance of individual genius in this process, and amplified the argument in favor of the communal and universal nature of the theater as a national institution and as a seedbed for the people's cultural growth.[8] As we shall see, this idea became a key issue in the process of Shakespeare's appropriation by Czech culture. It defined an institutional framework in which Shakespeare could be constructed as a "representative man" as well as a universal value standard.[9]

II "The Nation to Itself": The Shakespeare Festival of 1916

Shortly after the revolutionary wave of 1848 and 1849 which gave the Czechs the promise of constitutional monarchy and political equality with the Germans, a manifesto appeared articulating the need for a permanent National Theater. Written by František Palacký, a leading nationalist historian and politician, on behalf of the newly established committee of leaders of the movement, it stressed the political and cultural importance of such a theater in the new circumstances of the multinational state and, more broadly, in the competition between civilized European nations. Though Palacký used the old Enlightenment argument justifying theater as "the school of life and manners," he did not define it as a corrective and supporter of state power. Rather, he attempted to derive the legitimacy of national theater from the legal nature of the modern state, with respect to the earnestly desired transformation of the Austrian Empire into a constitutional monarchy. By granting equal rights to nations as political subjects, the constitution was believed to create the space necessary for the assertion of their diverse cultural identities. Contemporary notions of this space found expression in the architecture of the National Theater.

The basic function of this theater-as-institution was to restate the unattainable political goals of emancipation in general ethical and aesthetic terms. The major aim of the Czech resistance had to be represented in the form of an invented tradition establishing—in spite of the political uncertainties of the present[10]— a strong link between the past and the future of national life. The theater should serve as material evidence of national history's becoming the locus of collective memory and proof of the value of the nation's cultural tradition.

This desire is amply articulated in the emblematic decoration of the theater building (opened in 1881 and, after the fire, again in 1883). In the foundations of the neo-Renaissance pile, cornerstones from different parts of the country are placed to represent the identity of the building with the territory occupied by the nation. The dress- and upper-circle foyers are decorated with paintings, frescoes and sculptures commemorating the grandeur of the ancient, legendary past and allegorizing different aspects of the land and the character of the people. The auditorium is conceived as a sacred space, a temple of the muses whose curtain shows the Genius of the nation descending to the people to endow them with artistic and intellectual creativity. Above all this the beholder's eye can rest on the inscription "The Nation to Itself," locating the acts of giving and acceptance, the ministerial and magisterial functions, in this architectural space where the past is made present in the form of material artifacts and conjured into a mythical "sacred gift," bestowing creative potentiality on the national community to safeguard its future growth. It is not surprising that this structure, designed to transform the past into a palpable, visual image of a "strong" tradition, can at the same time represent the simultaneity of national existence.

The "strong" tradition represented in the architecture of the National Theater also shaped the major event of Czech cultural life during World War I, the Shakespeare festival of 1916.[11] Intended as a representative show of Czech performing arts, a demonstration of the versatility of the current dramatic repertory and of the company's superiority to the Prague German Theater (which, owing to financial and management problems, had failed to produce a festival of Wagner operas), the festival was proof of an ambitious effort to balance nationalist concerns and international influences in the sphere of acting, directing, and stage design. Jaroslav Kvapil, who was the *spiritus agens* of the whole venture, had developed a distinct personal, but also fairly cosmopolitan, style (refined by the influences of Stanislavski, Max Reinhardt, E. G. Craig, and Adolph Appia), which contrasted with the rigid institutional architecture of the theater. But the major purpose of the festival, the assertion of Czech national identity and sovereignty, was inseparable from the theater and the representational order of its building.

Preparing the festival, Kvapil had considerable problems with Austrian censors, who were quite aware of its political meaning and institutional framework. They had good reason to ban at least one performance—both parts of *Henry IV* in one evening—because of the quite justified suspicion that people would connect the monumentally staged coronation ceremony with rumors that one of the sons of George V of England would soon become king of the free Czech state. But the censors might also have followed overtly political aims: Kvapil was a member of "Mafie" (The Mafia), a clandestine Czech organization fighting for national independence. (In spite of the ban, the production was in fact staged after the festival because of the regime's increasing carelessness about political problems at home.)

All these details may imply a fairly complex paradigm of resistance enclosed in the traditional institution of the National Theater and aimed against the Austrian Empire and its war machine.[12] The festival was an attempt to restate the former ethical and aesthetic representations of national community vis-à-vis the alienated state power. In this context, the gesture of resistance can be understood as an attempt to shift the emphasis from the institutional foundations (both of the National Theater and of the Austrian Empire) to creative work as a demonstration of communal unity. This demonstration was made possible by using Shakespeare as a universal cultural value, "cultural capital."[13] The appropriation of this capital in the form of a defiant gesture against Austrian authorities and local German culture was meant to stress the international nature of the event—the ability to communicate with creative people across battlefields, state limits and cultural and ideological barriers. Shakespeare was therefore represented not as a fixed value (in terms of the greatness of his genius), but as a dynamic potential of historicity ("a history in all men's lives").

This was also the implication of the opening lecture delivered by the renowned critic F. X. Šalda. Šalda saw Shakespeare's drama as the moment of liberation from the determinism of Fate in ancient tragedy, and the establishment of "concrete humanity," consisting in the fullness and complexity of dramatic characters. According to the reviewers, the Shakespeare festival staged this "concrete humanity" in the form of the dynamic relationship between character and role (understood in psychological and historical, rather than theatrical terms).[14] The universal representative quality of the plays was compared with the social structure of the audience representing the whole nation.[15] Thus the nineteenth-century slogan "The Nation to Itself" had been reformulated in universalist terms, but the general pattern of *mancipatio* remained the same. Shakespeare's "concrete humanity" was a gift bestowed ceremonially on the "nation" assembled in the auditorium. But instead of conjuring the glorious past as the great origin of the uncertain yet hopeful present, Shakespeare's drama was invoked as a prototype of the historical activity of individuals and nations oriented toward the future. In a general way, this change can be described as the transmutation of originality into what Bristol calls "cultural goodness" (*Shakespeare's America*, 51), which may function as "cultural capital" in spite of its being articulated in terms of artistic creativity.

In the case of the National Theater the specific problem of this transmutation was that it had to make amends for the constant failures of Czech political representatives to agree on the strategic and rhetorical means of national emancipation.[16] This explains why Shakespeare's œuvre, in spite of attempts to transform it into "cultural capital," still functioned in accordance with the institutional design of the National Theater, merely as a "sacred gift."

Let us take the staging of *Henry IV*, which was found most subversive by the censors. Even after substantial cuts (*1 Henry IV* was condensed into two acts) and concentration on the main themes, the play remained too long (five hours), and confused the spectators by double dramatic gradation, absence of symmetry between serious and comic plots, and the lack of parallels developing the contrast between Hotspur and Falstaff. In this way, the major political issue (the conflict between traditional kingship shattered by civil war and burdened with crime and the emerging character of "pragmatic politician, for whom the indi-

vidual competence is the chief value")[17] was detached from the
dramatic action. The new center of the play was the character of
Falstaff. Yet his representation on the stage could not provide
the structural unity of the play: instead, it became the vehicle
for "the fragmentation of the sublime historical action into a
number of comic genre scenes,"[18] and for the virtual denial of
the political message of the production ("a negative expression
of the desire for a hero who would redeem the time and overcome
its conflicts").[19] The gap opening in dramatic texture had then
to be filled in a traditional way. Falstaff was acted in an easy and
undemanding manner like the popular entertainer in nineteenth-
century comedies and farces.[20] The result was that the audience
was amused by the "lighthearted jokes" and did not even notice
the intricate political and moral implications of the Falstaff-Hal
relationship.[21] Further, the rather tedious development of dramatic action had eventually to be redeemed by the splendor of
the coronation ceremony. This scene was perceived as a fundamental restatement of the political agenda of the play. It presented the desire for political autonomy in a ritualized form as
a *mancipatio* renewing feudal continuity in the most familiar
terms of the father-son relationship. It also included "the praise
of royal insignia" which—in the politically privileged space of
theater-as-institution—could imply the recreation of the nation-
state by the enactment of theatrical ritual.

Though the Shakespeare festival aimed to transform the œuvre
into "cultural capital" and thus to open new ways of negotiating
the relationship between tradition and resistance, it failed to ful-
fill this expectation. This was due to the restrictions enforced by
the institutional character of the National Theater, which did not
allow any departure from the old concept of tradition based on
the acceptance of national values as "sacred gifts" and on the
ritual confirmation of the relationship with Supreme Authority.
Apart from the crisis of theater representation, it also reflected
some problems inherent in Czech nationalist political programs.

It may not be surprising that this use of Shakespeare as a com-
pensation for the shortcomings of nationalist politics provoked
a critical response. A minor dramatist condemned the festival
for presenting Shakespeare as "eternal" and observed that
his plays "have nothing to say" to the contemporary public.[22]
Though this attack was based on an idea that the audience had
become aware of a discrepancy between the myth of Shakespeare's "genius" and the datedness, alienness, and coarseness of
his plays, it actually showed how ineffectual was the traditional

institution of the National Theater as a center of political resistance. Read in a different way, the review seems to signal the rejection of Shakespeare as the currency of the "placeless market" of cultural exchange and the location of this exchange in the hegemonic system of the market economy, in which "Shakespeare, Rubens, Rabelais," unless transformed into "cultural capital," can only represent elemental, uncontrollable and disruptive forces of the earth, "volcanoes which seldom throw out gold."[23]

III Collective Ownership: *Hamlet* and the Theater of Labor

In 1938, several months before Czechoslovakia was torn apart by the Treaty of Munich and left at the mercy of Nazi Germany, the theater director, dramatist, actor, poet, and musician Emil Frantisek Burian and the architect Miroslav Kouril published the project of the "Theater of Labor." The design showed a long, low, rectangular functionalist building resembling a factory shed. In Burian's vision, this bleak industrial structure would enclose a new cultural center for the country which would supplant the National Theater. Being the "expression of the strength of the working people," this institution would accomplish the transformation of cultural life on the way toward an "aesthetic state" of society.[24]

The project was not so utopian as it may appear. Some of its features resulted from Burian's rich experience in theater management, staging, playwriting, and organizing diverse cultural activities (art exhibitions, poetry readings, and concerts). In 1933 he founded in Prague an avant-garde theater that almost immediately became one of the most important stages in central Europe, launching from five to twelve new productions of plays, operas, dramatizations, and recitation performances a year. In the first season the theatre was called *D 34*; the number was increased by one each year until 1940 (*D 41*), when the playhouse was closed by the Nazis.

As a director, Burian had developed a distinctive method of staging generally called "poetic theater." Though he remained faithful to some principles of the political theater of Piscator and Brecht, he deliberately resisted the lure of German expressionism. Rather, he strove to transfer the playful creativity of early Czech avant-garde poetry (Vítězslav Nezval's and Jaroslav Seifert's *poetismus*—"poeticism") to the stage. It was this activity, and not the direct employment of "estrangement" techniques and strategies, that he envisaged as transforming theater into a weapon against the alienating power of the capitalist economy and the violence of totalitarian regimes.

Burian's stagecraft was based on the strong concept of the director's subjectivity. The director had to be a creative reader of the text, able to extricate it from the bonds of normative tradition, locate its subjectivity, and transpose its linguistic form into complex theatrical gestures. In this way, Burian's work can be described as a creative repetition of the writing of later romantics (especially the Czech poet Karel Hynek Mácha, but also A. S. Pushkin, E. T. A. Hoffmann, Heinrich Heine, and Georg Buchner), who, instead of believing that it was possible to internalize and subjectivize the strong "humanist" tradition, turned their attention to slippage of meaning and the impossibility of stating their own subjectivity. What was repeated was the emancipatory gesture of romantic irony that—in Mácha's case—amounted to violence done to the language, conceived by the nationalists as a "strong tradition," and indeed as the sacred gift of God. To exercise this violence was to create an independent sound and image structure, to form an individual, fully subjectivized "poetic language." Such a language could then become the basis for independent aesthetic experience ("creative reading") and could be transposed into a different, kinetic language of the theater. All these reflections were quite consonant with the theories of poetic language and "semantic gesture" developed by Jan Mukařovský, the leading personality of the Prague Linguistic Circle.[25]

In addition to this theoretical background, Burian developed fully his concept of stagecraft as a synaesthetic art, expressing itself by means of stage metaphors and thus articulating the space. In contrast to the National Theater space, which became an emblem of *mancipatio*, Burian's art emphasized the *emancipatory* function of spatial articulation. Burian believed that this was the major function of *political* theater: to expropriate the text, to extricate it from a certain tradition, amounted to appropriating it in a new spatiotemporal form that would draw the audience close to the actors and thus establish a new community.

This community, a prototype of the "aesthetic state," was to be as much poetical as functional. Though having a collective management and manner of work, the actors, artists, and artisans had to subject themselves to directorial authority based on superior imagination, creativity and interpretative insight. And so did the audience, confronted with the estranging and sometimes deeply alienating techniques of representation. For instance, Burian developed a special style of orchestration of voices (which was called "voiceband") based on musical articulation deliberately opposed to the meaning and rhythm of language. He followed the late romantics, dadaists, and expressionists in their attempts to make parallels between the actor and the puppet. He dazzled but also dazed the audience by the coordination of choreography, lighting, set movements, and film projection, which assailed their senses and forced them to enter the newly created space.

This practice was a significant attempt to change the concept of tradition within the theater-as-institution.[26] Whereas all the earlier forms of this establishment were founded on the pattern of *mancipatio*, of the acceptance of state power or national culture as a sacred gift, Burian's idea of theatrical space was introduced in the name of collective ownership.

With this ideological program Burian sought a way to make his institution competitive in the framework of capitalist economy. Apart from developing methods of collective management, he theorized a new scheme of *mancipatio* derived from the idea of the theater as a prototype of creativity in human labor. In this perspective, the communal ownership of space was also based on the sacred gift model. But, instead of the monarch or the nation, the *abstract* donor was "the culture of the working people." The director and the actors were receivers and at the same time mediators and *concrete* donors bestowing the gift on the audience. Thus, the argument of tradition as a creative power and as a necessary consciousness of continuity was restated in terms of the ensemble of arts as the agent and focus of *mancipatio*. Yet this act of receiving was no longer conceived as a mere establishment of hierarchy: rather, it was the appropriation of culture as a collective creativity and as a resistance to commodity fetishism.

In spite of these aims, Burian's project could not eliminate subjection to a different and no less formidable authority. The director's subjectivity conceived as the focus of resistance against the present social order was also defined by the Marxist ideology of class struggle. The director as well as the actors were constructed as the representatives, the virtual "vanguard," of the working class in their millennial fight for emancipation. But their privileged position was limited to the theatrical space of their own creation: beyond its limits they were just ordinary soldiers on the ideologically demarcated battlefield. As a result, the texture of the subjective rhetoric of Burian's productions is sometimes disfigured by ideological violence. This aspect is also suggested by the epigraph to his *Hamlet* adaptation, which uses Heine's poem "Enfant perdu" ("The death of one man does not break the ranks; / My weapons can be used. I die of a broken heart") to thematize the clash between the author's subjectivity and the ideology of revolutionary class struggle. Heine's ironic lines ask the fundamental question whether ideological violence against the subjectivity of poetic language is necessary. Burian asks this again in the context of political theater.

Burian's Hamlet play—*Hamlet III, the Prince of Denmark, or To Be or Not to Be, or Thrones Good for Timber* (Hamlet III, kralevic dansky, anebo Byt ci nebyt cili Truny dobre na drevo, 1937)—rejects the "strong" notion of tradition based on the authority of the canonical text and of the Elizabethan epoch, in favor of intertextuality and stagecraft. Shakespeare's text is not handed down as a sacred gift of the great age in which the ideals of humanism were born, but grafted on an entirely alien text, Jules Laforgue's story entitled "Hamlet, or the Consequences of Filial Love." Burian rewrites the text in a Brechtian way with regard to its patent political meaning. He underlines the relationship between the actors and gravediggers as representatives of the creative working class and its closeness to the material basis of all being. Yet there is one important departure from the Brechtian approach. *Hamlet III* takes up Laforgue's richly varied theme of the conflict between the biological and social nature of man, to rewrite it in the familiar rhetoric of *mancipatio*, based on the father-son relationship.

Laforgue's Hamlet is conceived as a biological, sexual, and emotional other and contrasted with the authority of a social system vested in the biological powers of heredity and sexual drive. Unable to assert himself by means of philosophical reasoning, he turns to playwriting. Yet his play (reproducing the plot of *The Murder of Gonzago*) is inauthentic and full of poetical clichés. Only by identifying himself with the actors and finding his other in the theatricality of a beautiful actress (who also makes his text work on stage and destroys the power of the regicides, Fengo and Gerutha) can he achieve an illusory fulfillment of his desire for identity and freedom. Too proud to accept his authentic social identity (from the gravediggers he learns that he is a bastard and brother of Yorick, the clown) or to understand the subjection of the poor and marginalized (proletarians and actors), he sees the solution to his predicament in making his whole life theatrical. On his escape to Paris with his beloved actress he meets his death while pretending grief on the grave of Ophelia: he is killed by Laertes, a successful populist politician and an "idiot of humanity," who has only too late realized his longing to become the "theatrical" hero of the story.

Burian approaches Laforgue's text via the themes of playwriting and acting. In his preface he stresses the transformative function of stage metaphor, its ability to disrupt the accepted relationships between sign and object, signifier and signified, and its power to generate new signs. The prototype of this activity is not human labor, but the play of the child. In this play, relationships between signifier and signified become dehierarchized and inverted. Thus, the *Hamlet* text in its canonical form may be extricated from its habitual context and made to represent empirical and historical reality as something utterly alien, disrupting the play. Whereas Laforgue's concept of *Hamlet* is based on the crisis of identity and the vain attempt to solve it by acting, which collapses into theatricality, Burian represents the crisis of tradition conceived as the logocentric authority of the text and the economic, political, or ideological power of "social formation."

This crisis is especially apparent in the representation of Hamlet's father. Deprived of his ghostly persona, he exists only as an authoritarian text, which, however, has no subjectivity. His lines are taken up by the voices of living Laertes and dead Polonius. Thus he can be identified both with the authority of the social order based on the ideological use of traditional values and with the violence committed in the name of these values.[27]

In this situation, Hamlet's action cannot be prompted by the rhetoric of filial duty. Its dramatic function is weakened and overshadowed by the gesture that attempts to transpose the language game, with its constantly slipping signifiers of traditional social values ("constancy, thy name is woman, / vanity thy name is throne, / slavery, thy name is change, / . . . heroism—thy name is fear"), into forceful acting nurtured by the violence done to the language.[28] This acting is then represented as Hamlet's unsuccessful effort to transform his textual violence into historical action ("to scan several lines with my sword ripping the history of Denmark") and remains unredeemed even by the stagecraft of the actors who perform Hamlet's play.[29]

The conflict closes in the double failure of *mancipatio*: in art as well as in politics. In overestimating the possibility and value of violence done to the text and by means of the text, Hamlet has willingly cut himself off from the creative potential of art. The country is overrun by Fortinbras's troops and Hamlet drags himself toward his death, burdened by "the mammon," his father's only legacy.

All this is negotiated in the text produced by the stage signs. Here the discourse of "poetic theater" asserts itself in spite of the failures of the artistic hero. Ophelia's song and dance transforms the figures of folklore art into a kinetic metaphor of molested and maimed Mother Nature.[30] Her art revolts against the crude grotesque of the court scenes. The bizarre, monstrous, and puppetlike acting of other characters forms a contrasting theatrical gesture suggestive of the violence of dictatorial regimes, both Nazi and Stalinist.[31]

But the meaning of this gesture is deferred in the play and becomes evident only in further developments of Burian's stagecraft. His injunction concluding the epilogue, "Put away the book and redeem yourselves by some lie,"[32] was duly observed by the communist regime, which elevated the rigid Marxist aspects of Burian's aesthetic ideology. This also led to the monstrous revival of Burian's idea of the Theater of Labor, in the form of the Palace of Culture whose huge white pile, nicknamed "Moby Dick," now towers above Vyšehrad, the first legendary center of the Czech state. The empty core of this building is occupied by the badly designed Communist Party Congress Hall.

IV   "The Power of the Powerless": Macbeth in the Living Room

After the force of Soviet and Warsaw Pact tanks checked the progress of democratic changes in 1968 and safeguarded the installation of a hard-line communist regime in 1969, intellectuals, artists, and creative workers in general were soon made to feel the weight of new domination. The regime was not at all interested in Marxism as an aesthetic ideology of creativity and a new "sensuous appropriation of reality." It required manifestations of uniformity, obedience, loyalty, and expiation for "right-wing deviations" or "antisocialist attitudes." Most people complied: some because of fear for their careers and jobs or the intrusion of the secret police into their private lives, others to improve their chances of promotion. Only a small group was strong enough to repudiate the regime's authority and to undergo the trials of exclusion from society: loss of their jobs, secret police interrogations, serious restrictions of personal freedom, and even imprisonment.

Society was thus split into two parts. On the one hand, there was the docile majority. The loyalty of these subjects was not judged, as one might expect, chiefly according to political activities and capacities, such as their willingness to inform for the secret police or their oratorical skills and principled stances at meetings. Rather, it was evaluated with respect to their essential passivity and ability to demonstrate formal support for the government's policy of "normalization" and for communist ideology. Thus, the people were manipulated to maintain an appearance of public political life, and in fact to contribute to the smooth operation of an impersonal mechanism driven by reciprocating powers: fear of the secret police, and the benevolence its officers would show to duly awed and submissive subjects. According to Václav Havel this operation was made possible only because of the growing indifference of people to this general duality of public life, indifference to the split between rhetorical and ceremonial manifestations of state power and the "hidden agenda" of private struggle for advantage and political influence.

The presence of this impersonal mechanism in the public space manifested itself by means of signs, namely emblems, slogans, or ceremonies, whose political and moral content was immaterial to most people. Yet this emptiness of meaning had deepened the gulf between public and private behavior and posed a serious threat to moral integrity and the identity of individuals.[33] This process was effectively opposed only by the handful of "the powerless" who had decided to persist in their pursuit of personal identity as the only firm ground for their political attitudes.

Because of the surveillance of society and its general demoralization, many public spaces had lost their meaning and function. On 17 April, the anniversary of the 1969 pro-Soviet coup, National Security Day was celebrated by a meeting of selected police officers in the National Theater. This significant ritual of the new regime had shown its effort to turn the people's collective identity and festive time into "sacred gifts" generously administered by the Communist Party and security forces. All other forms of giving and *mancipatio* were suspect, especially if they occurred in ritualized theatrical form. In this way, all culture and especially theater were *instrumentally* defined as "cultural heritage." In bureaucratic practice this act meant that everything shown on the stage had to be approved twice: by the magisterial authority of the Communist Party and by the ministerial organs of state power (the "National Committees"). Thus all creativity within the limits of tradition was made impossible because tradition itself had been identified with the power of the totalitarian state.

Among the people who refused to comply with this state of affairs were actors, dramatists, writers, and musicians. In spite of having been banned from the public sphere, they decided to pursue their creativity. In fact, their privacy had often been made public, not only by the growing popularity of the alternative "dissident" culture, but also because every consistent private pursuit (whether the creative work of the artist, or just a simple, morally consistent private life) was doomed to collide with the power mechanism of the system. In the course of this encounter, one could either lose one's identity in yielding to the system's pressure, or might assert one's independence by means of resistance to the power mechanism. Although the scope and aim of such resistance was often individual and private, its meaning became inherently public and political,[34] because the system, and especially the secret police, generally understood all meaningful activities as at least potentially subversive. In these circumstances, however, the old identity rooted in undisturbed private life would not avail, and so the individual had to embark on a dangerous pathway of personal reconstitution.

This gesture of resistance as the reconstitution of personal identity was an important feature of the activities of the "Living Room Theater," a small group of people staging private performances in the apartment of the actress Vlasta Chramostová and also in the homes or country houses of other "dissidents." The birth of this unusual institution can be traced back to the days before the foundation of the "Charter 77" movement, but similar events were recorded much earlier, during the Nazi occupation. From its beginnings in 1976 to the early eighties (when performances became impossible owing to increasing harassment and pressure) the shows took place under close surveillance. Some of them were even gate-crashed by the police, and actors as well as their audiences were detained, interrogated, or just brought in cars to deserted places some fifty miles from Prague and left there. (Such a scene, of gate-crashing a performance of *Macbeth*, became the theme of Tom Stoppard's play *Dogg's Hamlet, Cahoot's Macbeth*.) Evidently, the state security feared this private and apparently unpolitical activity might become a genuine public event.

Despite its progressive political significance, the repertory of the Living Room Theater was fairly traditional. No absurd dramas or avant-garde experiments were staged: the first performance was a recitation of the poems of Jaroslav Seifert (1983 Nobel Prize winner) who was also one of the initiators of the project. The last production was a one-actor performance of the dramatized letters and diary entries of Božena Němcová, a prominent nineteenth-century woman writer. The only partially political production was a collage from Rostand's *Cyrano de Bergerac* and speeches from the 1977 trial of Václav Havel and his colleagues from "Charter 77."[35]

This anti-avant-garde quality in the Living Room Theater implied a new concept of tradition, completely devoid of the hierarchical relationship between giver and receiver. According to Jan Patočka, a leading Czech philosopher, such productions could be conceived as attempts to return to the origins of theater. This search for the sources was entirely different from E. F. Burian's project for the Theater of Labor. Burian envisaged the process as the rewriting of the "strong" tradition based on canonical texts into another "strong" discourse centered around the notion of stagecraft as a prototype of human labor and creativity. Instead of seeking some hypothetical origin of creativity, the Living Room Theater discovered the acting and watching of plays as a genuine communal activity, transforming one's own identity as well as the social function of the theater.

Havel's prison meditations in *Letters to Olga* provide us with the theoretical background to this discovery. In contrast to television and other media based on technological modes of representation, theater still retains some creative potentiality, inherent in the possibility of the ritual recreation of communal relationships, and in the individual's capacity for wonder. Creating an imaginary world, the playwright "finds himself miraculously caught up" in its rules, shaped by the collective nature of the event. He is forced to give up his authority and become "a humble subject . . . a mere handmaiden of the miracle of recreation."[36] Similar transformations, including the restatement of identity, are to be undergone by the actors as well as the spectators. In this way a community can be formed, giving new social meaning to the performed text. Therefore, theater performance is compared to "self-manifesting Being," which ceases to be a logocentric concept and is recreated in the form of an individual as well as a collective experience of identity.

Within this general framework, a number of questions arise concerning the poetics of drama. Pavel Kohout, the author of the *Macbeth* adaptation performed by the Living Room Theater, once said: "We must observe a genre which we do not yet know."[37] As his rendering of Shakespeare's text shows, this could be done with minimum cutting and pasting and with the preservation of most dramatic characters.[38] This approach is radically different from that shown in Tom Stoppard's *Dogg's Hamlet, Cahoot's Macbeth*, because the relation to Shakespeare as a "strong tradition" is not at all important in Kohout's adaptation, nor is the idea of resistance expressed by the encoding of language.[39] What is seminal for Kohout's rendering is the theater space, number of actors, and—to borrow Havel's idea from *Letters to Olga*—the enactment, or ritual presentation, of a *social bond* by means of the collective effort of the actors and the public, accompanied by the reconstitution of personal identities in the existential present, the "here-and-now" of the performance time.[40]

In Kohout's *Macbeth* theater space is purely imaginary, and so the stage directions are read aloud and in a very expressive way. Rather than just helping the audience to imagine dramatic spaces, these notes serve as a means of articulating dramatically the general rhythm of the performance. Because almost no articulation of space by bodily movement is possible in the living room, all nondramatic dialogues (for instance the exchange between Macbeth and Lennox preceding the moment when Macduff discovers the murdered king, 2.3.52–65) are cut, to emphasize the *performative* character of dramatic language. Omissions of minor characters (such as Old Man in 2.4) also provide chances for discarding nondramatic passages. Because all actors but those representing the main heroes have to change roles constantly, the monstrous integrity and isolation of the tyrant and his wife are highlighted by their separation from the general rhythm of the performance.

This also helps to create a theatrical metaphor of dynamic community by using the voices of other characters. The voices that have several identities exert stronger and stronger pressure on the tyrant. Such a representation of the collective solidarity of dissidents based on reconstituted personal voices/identities is fully consonant with Havel's thought about the "invisible pressure" that can be exerted on the state by various alternative movements.[41]

Moreover, a frequent use of passages put to music (and performed by a banned singer, Vlasta Třešňák) underlined the supra-individual meaning of some speeches, as for instance the monologues of Captain and Ross in 1.2 and the "choric commentaries" in 3.6 and 4.3. In the latter case the emphasis was on Ross's lines: "Alas, poor country, / Almost afraid to know itself! / It cannot / Be call'd our mother, but our grave . . ." (165–73).

Apart from its power to bind and harmonize the whole community in the course of the performance, this musical voice had several other functions. First, it represented the possibility of reconstituting personal identities for viewers afflicted and depressed by the harassment of the system (it ritualized individual experiences much as the songs at the mass rallies did in the late 1980s). Second, the rhythm of the sung passages accompanied by guitar asserted itself against the spoken blank verse by stressing authenticity over artificiality, favoring enjambments and suppressing metrical impulses. Thus it introduced an alternative temporal structure that could be ritually authorized by the voices of the audience joining the chorus. This collective identification with the temporality of broken rhythms and fragmented meter contrasted with the inauthentic relation to speech and acting of the central pair of heroes. Their inauthenticity was conspicuously thematized by Macbeth's "asides" ("My thought, whose murther yet is but fantastical . . ." 1.3.140–44) and Lady Macbeth's injunctions ("to beguile the time, / Look like the time; bear welcome in your eye . . ." 1.5.62–64). Thus the authority of dramatic representation was presented as the power originating in the collective, ritualized temporality of language.

Third, the focus of this enactment of authenticity was the part of Malcolm, which was sung throughout. Malcolm lacked the "green" nature of Shakespeare's hero. Instead he was stylized as the innocent victim of the tyrant's cruelty, a "dissident" forced to emigrate and seek foreign help to overthrow the regime. His victory over Macbeth, therefore, was not interpreted as the reestablishment of the old authority of sacred kingship and the reenactment of the traditional ceremony of giving and *mancipatio*. It was the utopian gesture, reversing the ceremony of the gift: the closing lines of Malcolm's last speech were sung as a chorus of the new community formed in the course of the performance. This community could then also function as a new donor, giving Malcolm his royal authority—authorizing his *pluralis maiestaticus*. (This was also suggested by Kohout's omission of reference to Malcolm's divine kingship—"by the grace of

Grace"—and of his promise to confer new titles and privileges.) In turn, Malcolm was able to articulate his relationship to the whole group (including the audience) in terms of *mancipatio* and thus to confirm the ritualized performance of the play as a source of supreme authority.[42]

Apart from the ritual, the establishment of political authority was also enacted *dramatically*. The most important instance is Kohout's adaptation of 4.3, discovering dramatic qualities in this most tedious and incoherent part of Shakespeare's text. The longest scene of *Macbeth* was heavily cut. All that remained was closely linked to three main themes: the fear of Macbeth's spies, the suffering of the country under the tyrant, and the contrast between Macbeth's individualist apostasy and Malcolm's nonviolent authority. The vagueness of Malcolm's personal identity in Shakespeare's text was not acknowledged. Instead, Malcolm was made to represent the reconstituted personal identity, based on the responsibility of the individual for the quality of communal life. In his exchange with Macduff, Malcolm derived his royal authority solely from this source. As a powerless exile and potential ruler of the country he impersonated "the power of the powerless" wielded by the dissident community.

V   Conclusion: Gestures of Resistance and Traditional Institutions

In all these examples of the use of Shakespeare's texts by Czech resistance movements, the meanings of gestures of resistance have been modified by two different traditions. The first introduced Shakespeare as a "universal value," "affirmative culture," "cultural capital," or "cultural heritage." The latter was embodied in various theater institutions that were the focus of the nation's cultural and political life. The traditional justification of institutional authority (in the paradigm of *mancipatio*) influenced the artists' efforts and often prevented them from articulating a clear pattern of resistance.

Thus, in the case of the Patriotic Theater, *Macbeth* could acquire an overt political meaning with respect to the peasants' rebellion against feudal authority, but this was dangerous in a theater whose repertory was expected to contribute to the reorganization of the absolutist state. To avoid associations with the revolt, the play was soon incorporated as a text and as an educational instrument into the program of peaceful cultural emancipation, respecting feudal order as well as foreign rule.

Similar shifts in the pattern and objectives of resistance occurred in the case of the 1916 festival, which sought to transmute Shakespeare into "cultural capital," thus revaluing Czech culture as the source of national identity in the fight against the Austrian Empire. This gesture was partially ineffectual because of the institutional character of the National Theater, based on the notions of cultural and political identity as "sacred gifts."

In its attempt to define theater space as "communal ownership" and the locus of collective resistance against the forces of the market or the progress of totalitarian dictatorships, Burian's stagecraft produced an opposite, alienating effect. In the adaptation of *Hamlet* in particular the creation of this space failed, because of the clash between the efforts at a "deconstructive" rewriting of the canonical text and the dogmatic ideology of class struggle inherent in the project of the Theater of Labor.

In contrast to these institutions based on the "strong" tradition, the Living Room Theater managed to link a successful political gesture of resistance (based on the ritualized act of identification of communal life) with Shakespeare as a part of the humanist and democratic tradition. It was certainly violent in some aspects of its treatment of Shakespeare's text, but this violence was very mild in comparison with Burian's "Theater of Labor" or any of the previous institutionalized Czech uses of Shakespeare. Moreover, in contrast to the official power structures whose representations of authority and power were emptied of meaning and made absurd (like the police festivities in the National Theater), this gesture articulated Shakespeare's existence in other forms than those of a "cultural capital" or of an instrumentalized and carefully administered "cultural heritage."

Notes

1. Herbert Marcuse, "The Affirmative Character of Culture," in *Negations: Essays in Critical Theory*, trans. Jeremy Shapiro (Boston: Beacon Press, 1968), 95.

2. In my previous attempts to write on Shakespeare in Czechoslovakia I worked within this general framework. The humanist representation of Shakespeare appealed to me as an alternative to the absurd ideological, political, and social divisions enforced by the totalitarian regime. But on the other hand, to pursue Shakespearean scholarship in this direction meant also to be relatively safe from harassment, as the ideological "facade" of the system had been designed in a similar way. The revolutionary changes of 1989 made me reconsider this ambivalence. The experience of the collective ritual of liberation enacted at the rallies led me to question the interpretation of revolution as a *spontaneous* renewal of the sacred. I became especially concerned with the relationship of

this "renewal" to the internalized world of humanist values. Moreover, the way in which these gatherings were organized and "directed" induced me to consider the role of theatricality in political changes and the function of the theater as an institution representing paradigms of tradition and heritage in the discourse of resistance against state power.

3. Cf. Michael Bristol, *Shakespeare's America, America's Shakespeare* (London: Routledge, 1990), 39–41. Bristol uses Mauss's discussion of the gift as a feature of a different value system from that based on the rational value exchange typical of political economy. See Marcel Mauss, *The Gift*, trans. Ian Cunnison, introd. E. E. Evans-Pritchard (New York: Norton, 1967), 50–51.

4 *Makbeth, vůdce šottského vojska* [Macbeth, the general of the Scottish army] (Jindřichův Hradec: I. V. Hilgartner, 1782).

5. Nicholas Brooke stresses the influence of the operatic witch scenes adapted and added by Davenant to the Restoration opera, quoting the example of Dryden's and Purcell's *King Arthur* (1684). Here (as well as in another transposition of the heroic epic theme, Purcell's *Dido and Aeneas*), "the musical parts centre on the witches who also control the main action" (Brooke, ed., *The Tragedy of Macbeth* [Oxford: Oxford University Press, 1990], 37).

6. The most important of these pieces was produced in 1785 under the title *Štěpán Fedinger*. In this translation of the German play by a Viennese author, Paul Weidmann (a zealous supporter of the emperor's reform policy), the leader of the revolt is confronted with an imperial general, a dogmatic defender of aristocratic privileges. There is no hope of a peaceful solution to their strife, because the general refuses to acknowledge the peasants' claim that feudal power has its origin in their daily toil and not in the divinely instituted social order. The only way out is envisaged in the intervention of the emperor's authority. Thus the power of Divine Mercy as well as the authority of the social order can be mediated for the peasants by means of the emperor's clemency. The traditional social bonds can then be renewed by the change of feudal allegiance: the play concludes with a solemn oath, which the peasant rebels swear directly to the emperor.

7. In the play entitled *The Grateful Son* (Vděčný syn, 1785), the ties binding the peasants to their land and giving concrete meaning to the filial bond are redefined in terms of the relation of the subject to state power, represented by the army. A faithful subject, the dutiful "son" of the state, is rewarded for his allegiance and promoted by the monarch to the rank of officer, a rank previously available only to aristocrats. Because of the ruler's "gift" establishing his new social status he can rescue his peasant father vexed by a corrupt servant of the state.

8 *Dějiny českého divadla* [A History of Czech theater], ed. František Černý (Praha: Academia, 1969), 2: 64–66.

9. Bristol, *Shakespeare's America*, 123ff., argues that for R. W. Emerson Shakespeare's originality represents literature as "a social institution in which collective understanding and practical consciousness are sedimented" (126).

10. Instead of fulfilling the promise of the constitution, the Viennese government enforced a police regime, similar in some aspects to pre-1848 absolutism. This regime was called Bach absolutism (after the prime minister) and lasted less than a decade. But even after the parliamentary system started to operate in the 1860s, Czech representatives had serious difficulty in asserting their political claims, because of their basically loyalist stance in such central issues

as Czech-German relations and the transformation of the empire into a federative state.

11. The festival consisted of an introductory lecture by the renowned Czech critic F. X. Šalda, and of fifteen productions staged between 27 March and 4 May 1916: *Comedy of Errors, Richard III, Romeo and Juliet, A Midsummer Night's Dream, The Merchant of Venice, The Taming of the Shrew, Much Ado about Nothing, As You Like It, King Lear, Twelfth Night, Hamlet, Measure for Measure, Macbeth, Othello*, and *The Winter's Tale*. All plays were performed in the fairly recent and at that time unusually good translations of Josef Václav Sládek.

12. The censors objected mainly because Shakespeare was a writer from a "hostile nation." To pacify them Kvapil produced an invitation to the *Shakespeare Tage* in Weimar. The authority of Kaiser Wilhelm of Germany and the Deutsche Shakespeare-Gesellschaft evidently had some weight. Cf. Rudolf Deyl, *O čem vím já* [Memoirs] (Praha: Melantrich, 1971), 236.

13. Cf. Bristol, *Shakespeare's America*, 51, using Pierre Bourdieu's term from *Distinction: A Social Criticism of the Judgement of Taste* (Cambridge: Harvard University Press, 1984).

14. The reviewers mention the emphasis on the relationship between Macbeth's "milk of human kindness" and "tyrannical logic," between "the profound humanity of King Henry IV, whose princely virtues are traced to their very origin" and his "dangerous insidiousness": O. F. [Otokar Fischer], "*Makbeth*," *Národní listy*, 29 February 1916: 4; -jv- [Jindřich Vodák], "Shakespearova historie" [Shakespeare's history play], *Lidové noviny*, 7 November 1916: 1.

15. The fact that the audience included all classes and strata of Czech society was duly recorded by F. V. Krejčí, the reviewer of a social-democratic newspaper, *Právo lidu*. The festival had a noticeable impact on the cultural activities of the Czech workers movement. *A Midsummer Night's Dream* was chosen as the first Shakespeare play for the traditional amateur May Day Theater Show (Zdeněk Stříbrný, *Shakespeare* [Praha: Orbis, 1964], 97).

16. Attempts to form an anti-Austrian coalition of Czech political parties (called the National Party, *Národní strana*) failed, and subversive activity remained restricted to the illegal organizations, whose most prominent members were still in prison. See Otto Urban, *Česká společnost 1848–1918* [Czech Society: 1848–1918] (Praha: Academia, 1982), 599.

17. O. F. [Otokar Fischer], "Národní divadlo," *Národní listy*, 7 November 1916: 4.

18. O. F. [Otokar Fischer], "Národní divadlo," *Národní listy*, 4 November 1916: 4.

19. -jv- [Jindřich Vodák], "Shakespearova historie," 2.

20. One of the reviewers praised the actor playing Falstaff for playing the part in a smooth, elegant way and with benign good humor (-jv- [Jindřich Vodák], *Nová doba*, 24 [1917]: 151–52). Apparently, Falstaff's stylization followed both the *Biedermeier* tradition of Viennese farce and the later vogue of French "drawing-room comedy."

21. Prince Henry is seen as detached from the "treacherous, insidious, and vile" environment of his associates, as a prototype of the "modern politician" and a careful student of the nature of common people (-jv-, *Lidové noviny*, 7 November 1916: 2).

22. Jaroslav Hilbert, "Několik poznámek po ukončení Shakespearova cyklu"

[Some remarks in the wake of the Shakespeare festival], *Venkov (Národní hospodář)*, 6 May 1916: 9.

23. Ibid., and Bristol, *Shakespeare's America*, 23–24.

24. E. F. Burian, "Divadlo práce" [Theater of Labor], *O nové divadlo* [In pursuit of new theatre] (Prague: Orbis, 1947), 39. Burian defines the Theater of Labor as an "ensemble of arts" (*Kunstensemble*). The activity of this ensemble is to serve society in shaping its functions by representing an ideal functional whole.

25. Bořivoj Srba, *Poetické divadlo E. F. Buriana* [E. F. Burian's poetic theatre] (Prague: SPN, 1971), 199–205.

26. Maintaining that this tradition as social agency (institutionalized at the level of the whole community) is scarcely operative in modern societies, Bristol takes into account only personal, and not institutional, forms of traditional authority (*Shakespeare's America*, 41–42). My argument however points out that a mere distinction between orality and literacy, or the personality and the text, as sources of authority is not sufficient for the discussion of different theatrical appropriations of Shakespeare.

27. Traditional values are invoked in the "Laertes context" of the ghost's words (which roughly correspond to Shakespeare's lines in the first act). Laertes assumes the rhetoric of filial duty only to hide his disapproval of the "oppressive and suffocating" regime in Denmark. The "Polonius context" of the ghost's second speech (modeled after the passage in the "bedroom scene" of *Hamlet*) motivates Hamlet's resistance by invoking the horrors, cruelties, and grotesque absurdity of the regime, which is a caricature of Hitler's Germany and all other dictatorships, including Stalin's Russia. Polonius, who is an architect of this dictatorship, also plays a buffoon to entertain the mentally retarded monarch, King Fengo. The inhuman monstrosity of the state is typified in the machine- or puppetlike body of the virtual ruler, Queen Gerutha.

28. E. F. Burian, *Hamlet III* (mimeographed typescript with Burian's marginalia, Library of the Theater Institute, Prague, call no. P 1244), 1:27. In reply to Ophelia's complaints about his violence and her pleas to speak "only one word [of kindness]," Hamlet says a nonsensical word, "*Virunkahtyuratye*." His explication, "It could have been a sound of sunray hissing as it sets into frosty sea," is a metaphor for the synaesthetic nature of Burian's theater, and converts the childish nonsense play with the sounds of speech into a figure anticipating the death of Ophelia, who later drowns herself in the sea (*Hamlet III*, 1:49–50).

29. *Hamlet III*, 1:45.

30. Burian used a lot of material from the oral and mimetic tradition of folklore. He even staged several performances based exclusively on Czech folklore sources.

31. The antitotalitarian and anti-ideological bias of Burian's project in *Hamlet III* did not remain unnoticed by communist reviewers. To them he addressed his dismissal of the emulation of Stalinist manners in contemporary Russia and his assertion of the high standard of Czechoslovak culture (Burian, *Pražská dramaturgie* [Prague, 1938], 86–91).

32. Burian, *Hamlet III*, 2:114.

33. Václav Havel, "The Power of the Powerless," in *Living in Truth*, ed. Jan Vladislav (London: Faber, 1989), 41–52.

34. Ibid., 61–62.

35. "Bytove divadlo Vlasty Chramostové," an interview with Vlasta Chra-

mostová, František Pavlíček, and Karel Milota, Czechoslovak Television, Federal Channel (F 1), 23 December 1990, 11:20 P.M..

36. Václav Havel, *Letters to Olga*, trans. Paul Wilson (New York: Alfred Knopf, 1988), 283.

37. "Bytove divadlo Vlasty Chramostové" (see n. 35).

38. Pavel Kohout, *Hra na Makbeta* [Play on Macbeth], *Macbeth* text translated by Erik Adolf Saudek, Living Room Theater, Prague 1979, private audiotape. Kohout omitted "nondramatic" or archaic passages from Shakespeare's text; for instance, the Porter's speech (2.3.1–19) is omitted because of difficulties with the historical references in the "equivocator" passage. Sometimes the cuts are more radical: the omission of a considerable part of 4.1 is motivated by the demands of the "stage" and "company," consisting of five actors. Kohout tends to omit some metaphors, partly because of their "baroque" effects, underlined in the Czech translation, and also because they might retard the dialogue or produce inconsistencies: for example, "And pity, like a naked new-born babe . . ." (1.7.21–26), or "I have given suck . . ." (1.7.55–58). Of characters, the only major omission is Hecate (and the whole of 3.5, which, however, is also missing in the Czech translation that is Kohout's source); others are Old Man (partially supplanted by Macduff), Siward and his son, Lennox, Menteith, Angus, Caithness, son of the Macduffs, Doctor in 4.3, and one of Banquo's murderers.

39. In the title of his play Stoppard makes a pun on the last name of Pavel Kohout to whom the play is dedicated. See Stoppard, *Dogg's Hamlet, Cahoot's Macbeth* (London: Faber, 1980), 9: "Cahoot is not Kohout, and this necessarily over-truncated *Macbeth* is not supposed to be a fair representation of Kohout's elegant seventy-five minute version."

40. Havel, *Letters to Olga*, 260.

41. Václav Havel, *Disturbing the Peace* (New York: Alfred Knopf, 1990), 183.

42. In Kohout's adaptation, the line "We will perform in measure, time and place" (5.7.104) was to articulate the final utopian gesture of the victory of the "dissident" movement over the totalitarian system. In contrast to the preceding passage sung by the chorus, the next line ("So thanks to all at once, and to each one") was sung by Malcolm alone to mark him not as a *donor* but as a *receiver* of authority.

Brecht's *Hamlet*

Michael Morley

I

In the late 1930s, while in exile in Denmark, Brecht wrote a number of what he described as "literary sonnets." The epithet was deliberately and ironically selected, for these sonnets offer, in a self-consciously "literary" form, a series of critical glosses and ironic reflections—deconstructions and reconstructions *avant la lettre* on well-known works from the German and European literary canon. The second of these poems is entitled "On Shakespeare's Play Hamlet":

> Here is the body, puffy and inert
> Where we can trace the virus of the mind.
> How lost he seems among his steel-clad kind
> This introspective sponger in a shirt.
>
> Till they bring drums to wake him up again
> As Fortinbras and all the fools he's found
> March off to battle for that patch of ground
> "Which is not tomb enough . . . to hide the slain."
>
> At that his too, too solid flesh sees red.
> He feels he's hesitated long enough.
> It's time to turn to (bloody) deeds instead.
>
> So we nod grimly when the play is done
> And they pronounce that he was of the stuff
> To prove "most royally," "had he been put on."[1]

Although this sonnet was far from Brecht's last word on the play, it can stand as a useful starting point for this survey of his attitudes to Shakespeare's drama and to its principal figure, presenting as it does a number of points that consistently recur over the years in scattered remarks and more extended commentaries. First, there is the deliberately antiheroic view of the principal figure: it is difficult to imagine this Hamlet as a sweet prince, with a noble heart cracking at the moment of death. Casting an eye over the list of German and English interpreters of the role in the twentieth century, one would be hard put to think of a performer who would bring to the part the necessary solid and inert fleshiness that Brecht seems to have in mind—a point to which I shall return.

Second, there is the view of a reflective Hamlet, lost in an alien world of arms and action: not all that radical a reading this, but notable nevertheless for the provocatively dismissive view of the man of introspection "born to put the times right." Then, in the second quatrain and the first half of the sestet, we have Brecht the director clearly declaring his choice of the crucial turning point in the play's action—the moment that prompts Hamlet to set out on the path of action. As Eric Bentley was subsequently to point out in correspondence with Brecht, this selection of 4.4 (what Brecht refers to as "A plain in Denmark," with Fortinbras and his army marching off to fight the Poles, and Hamlet delivering the monologue "How all occasions do inform against me") as the scene that marks a change in Hamlet's attitude is contentious.[2] Nevertheless, over the years, Brecht consistently and insistently pointed to this scene as providing a new and important signpost for the actor playing Hamlet; and his reasons (which will be spelled out in detail) are worth considering.

Finally, there is the response of the audience—though hardly Brecht's ideal audience. What he is implicitly criticizing here is that audience which is so conditioned and comfortable in its traditional view of Hamlet, that, even after a production that might present an against-the-grain reading of the play similar to that suggested in the first eleven lines, it still reverts to the clichéd "Aristotelian" response in which the empathetic confirming and reaffirming grim nod can take the place of any critical attitude toward both the action and the sententious comment on it provided—on what evidence?—by Fortinbras at the end.

The main point about this sonnet and Brecht's view of the play—and this is the central element in all his comments on *Hamlet* over the years—is that his approach to the work is not primarily that of the literary critic, but that of the director and member of the audience. The implied question that precedes this sonnet is: how can what he elsewhere refers to as the layers of plaster of Paris[3] that have been slapped on the classics by generations of uncritical directors and audiences be chipped away so that the work can be looked at for what it is rather than what it has become? One hesitates to drag in the overfamiliar concept of Brechtian "alienation"; but there is little doubt that the sonnet is a concise, if somewhat elliptical expression of Brecht's approach to making the familiar strange and the strange familiar. And linked to this is the attempt to nudge the audience toward a response that is somewhat different from the easy, almost Pavlovian reaction to the staged events that he satirizes overtly in the poem "Theatre of Emotions," dating from the same period as the Hamlet sonnet:

> Between ourselves, it seems to me a sorry trade
> Putting on plays solely
> To stir up inert feelings. You remind me of masseurs
> Sinking their fingers in all too fatty
> Flanks, as in dough, to knead away sluggards'
> Bellies. Your situations are hastily assembled to
> Excite the customers to rage
> Or pain. The audience
> Thus becomes voyeurs. The sated
> Sit next the hungry.
>
> The emotions you manufacture are turbid and impure
> General and blurred, no less false
> Than thoughts can be. Dull blows on the backbone
> Cause the dregs of the soul to rise to the surface.
> With glassy eyes
> Sweaty brow and tightened calves
> The poisoned audience follows
> Your exhibitions.
>
> No wonder they buy their tickets
> two by two. And no wonder
> They like to sit in the dark that hides them.[4]

II

In a diary entry for September 1920, Brecht, prompted by a visit to a clown performance and by his own dissatisfaction with the entire contemporary theater (a piece of typical Brechtian hyperbole) sets down his idiosyncratic plan for a theater and its repertoire:

> Once I get my hooks on a theatre I shall hire two clowns. They will perform in the interval and pretend to be spectators. They will bandy

opinions about the play and about the members of the audience.
Make bets on the outcome. Every Saturday the theatre will have a
Deuxième. The hit of the week will be parodied. (Up to and including
Hamlet, Faust.) For tragedies the scene-changes will take place with
the curtain up. Clowns will stroll across the stage, giving orders:
"He's about to go under, see. Dim the lights. That staircase gives off
an aura of tragedy. Bankruptcy is inevitable with caryatids like that.
He'll have to catch flies. That was good, the way he put his hands in
his trouser pockets. The way he said 'One must be as idle as a quail.'
Excellent! It's at this point that the principal scene takes place.
There's going to be some real crying. The Heroine's got her hanky
ready. Oh, how I wish it was over . . ." (They say all this sadly, with
absolute seriousness, they are sad fellows lit in a green light, green
angels preparing the Fall . . .) The clowns will laugh about any hero
as about a private individual. Absurd incidents, anecdotes, jokes. . . .
The idea would be to bring reality back to the things on the stage.[5]

The significance of this casual diary entry for the development
of Brecht's later theories on the theater is obvious: in a crude
and basic form—and, incidentally, one full of splendid theatrical
potential—we have a number of the elements of what is later
developed and refined into anti-illusionist and "epic theater."
But the Shakespearean connection has, to date, been passed over.
It is not, I would suggest, too capricious to see in this preliminary
study for a "metatheater" an inverted version of Hamlet's Mouse-
trap as it might apply to and through an entire performance. And
the models for the two sad, serious clowns—for whom there is
virtually no precedent in the German theater—might be readily
found in the graveyard scene from act 5. Moreover, although
Brecht sees their function in the context of parodying the hit of
the week, it is clear from the tension he suggests between the
comments they make and the way they make them that mere
travesty or caricature is not his sole intention. The hoped-for
response and attitude of the audience to what it is watching
would be more ambivalent and complicated than that—in exactly the same way as the clown who moves unpredictably from
seriousness to laughter and back again will be subverting the
familiar expectations of the viewer.

This dialectic of the serious and the comic is to reappear in
various guises over the years in Brecht's discussion of Shakespeare in general and of *Hamlet* in particular—along with a series of further oppositions and contradictions to which Brecht
was temperamentally attached. Thus, in his next, more extended
gloss on *Hamlet*, we find a collection of theses and antitheses

on which Brecht seizes in order to support one of his major concerns at the time—the conviction that art must be "cheerful" (the "noncheerful," negative example he gives is of the dilettante who measures the impact of an impression by whether it causes his pipe to go out). Against this, Brecht sets Shakespeare—to whom he refers as Wilhelm (not William)—clearly and humorously suggesting that in his view, Shakespeare was not (or was not only) English:

> A good play needs many shoals, nontransparent parts, a fair amount of gravel, and a surprisingly large dose of irrationality; and it must be alive, before aspiring to be anything else. . . . I reckon that at the point where, in *Hamlet*, all art seemed in vain, Wilhelm's artistic sense had its greatest triumph. It was a question of turning inside out an old, crude play with the theme "Cleaning out the Augean Stables," which derived its brilliant, but already worn out impact, from the rattling *furioso* of its Hamlet . . . of turning this all inside out for an actor who was fat and asthmatic, and had created the role of Richard III. For three acts they got by with hesitation, and then they started sticking in some nuances, and the play was deader than a dog carved out of wood. But the Augean stables, of course, had to be cleaned, and Wilhelm brought along a little scene which he'd written at home and which was barely distinguishable from a few others that had already been tried out (which had moreover been left in, because double stitching holds much better), but which was a real cheat . . . and the asthmatic was saved. The scene is that one which we, with nice consistency, always cut, where Hamlet sees Fortinbras's army marching by and makes a meal of the idea that fighting need not have a point for it to be extremely bloody just at the right moment . . . that is, half an hour before the audience is due to leave the theater. It is a really great moment in the history of the Germanic drama, and an extremely cruel one. And it is, in addition, what we are pleased to understand by "cheerfulness." (GW 15:121)

The tone of these remarks indicates that Brecht, far from feeling overawed by Shakespeare, deliberately reduced his size to something more approachable and accommodating—not only "Shakespeare, my contemporary" but also "Wilhelm, my fellow playwright." Such a degree of familiarity was intended as a provocation by the then barely thirty-year-old playwright. The later Brecht was more circumspect when speaking of his great predecessor (though Charles Laughton could write in a letter to Eric Bentley from 1948: "This is pretty strong and you could never print this, but I believe there is Shakespeare and then Brecht").[6] The young Brecht's contrived mateyness was partly a response to the "Shakespeare on a pedestal" approach of a large section of the German theater (even including Max Reinhardt), but also a reflection of his own views on the "material" value of Shakespeare's plays. Just as Shakespeare used material ready to hand, Brecht was also prepared to take Shakespeare's works and see how they could be utilized for the non-Aristotelian, "epic" drama.

The structural similarities between Shakespeare's drama, and Brecht's plays with their radical departure from the "well-made play" model and their deployment of a loose scenic structure, has been noted by many critics.[7] It is, however, worth remembering that English audiences and readers are in a more advantageous (or disadvantageous, depending on one's point of view) position vis-à-vis Brecht's work than their German counterparts—since, especially in performance, the division into scenes is a familiar and accepted structural pattern. That Brecht felt he had to defend Shakespeare against possible critics who might still cling to notions of a logically proceeding, organically evolving drama that derives from Ibsen, and, indirectly, from Freytag and his triangle, is clear from the 1927 essay on *Macbeth* with which Brecht introduced his radio adaptation of the play. Although in this essay he does not refer to *Hamlet*, it is appropriate to single out a number of comments he makes about the form of Shakespearean drama in general, as similar views are to be found in some of his later comments on *Hamlet*. Setting out to provoke the listener, Brecht asserts:

As a play for the theater, this drama offers little evidence of a gradated structure and it is certainly not concise. . . . Above all, I should like to direct your attention to [its] horrifying lack of logic . . . a crazy arbitrariness that calmly accepts all the technical consequences of scenic decentralization. This certain lack of logic in the incidents, this constantly interrupted course of a tragic event, is not peculiar to our theater, it is only peculiar to life. . . . Shakespeare has no need to *think*. He also has no need to *construct*. In his plays it is the audience that does the constructing. . . . In the disconnectedness of his acts, one recognizes again the disconnectedness of a human fate. . . . There is nothing more stupid than to stage Shakespeare in such a way that he is clear. He is by nature unclear. He is absolute material. (GW 15:116–19)[8]

Four years after this essay and the radio adaptation of *Macbeth* comes Brecht's radio adaptation of *Hamlet*, broadcast on 31 January 1931. As in the case of *Macbeth*, no text or recording of the adaptation has survived, while the materials in the Brecht-Archiv are sketchy and make it difficult to reconstruct the adaptation with any certainty. However, some scattered texts give an indication of the tenor of the adaptation and of how Brecht introduced into Shakespeare's "epic" form further elements characteristic of his own work at the time that were intended to reinforce this "epic" quality and also to prevent the listener from uncritically wallowing in the production.

The opening text, spoken by the announcer, sets the tone from the outset:

> We begin with the presentation of the tragedy *Hamlet, Prince of Denmark* by William Shakespeare, a jewel of the medieval drama, telling "Of carnal, bloody and unnatural acts / of accidental judgements, casual slaughters / of deaths put on by cunning and forced cause / and in this upshot, purposes mistook / fallen on the inventors' heads" as it says in the play. The ending of the work, representing as it does a family mass murder, is, of course, no longer suitable for the modern theater because of its complicated and preposterous content. The tragedy is set in motion by the following piece of information which, two months after his death, and after the remarriage of the queen to his brother, the ghost of the dead king imparts to his son Hamlet on the castle battlements at Elsinore by night.[9]

There then follows a long speech from the ghost which concertinas the three separate speeches from 1.5, ending with "Leave her to heaven."

What can be inferred from this introduction of Brecht's is a reading of the play that prompts him, as one critic put it, "to reject the feudal elements—above all the bloodbath at the end—as irrational, and no longer capable of being performed in the modern theater without some critical attitude" (Symington, 97). Moreover, the closing lines, penned by the author himself as a postscript to the broadcast, are a clear expression of his deliberate and cold refusal to view the bloody events divorced from any possible contemporary associations:

> And so, making heedful use
> Of the fortuitous flourish from a drum
> And the war cry of unknown soldiers,
> He slaughters, through such a chance encounter
> Finally freed of his human and reasonable inhibition,
> In a single moment of running amok
> The King, his mother and himself.
> The assertion of his successor

"He was likely had he been put on
To have proved most royal"
Consequently appears as no exaggeration.

(BBA, 344/40)

And a slightly later comment of Brecht's from the thirties spells out the lesson to be drawn from these lines:

> In Hamlet's famous hesitation, the Middle Ages may have seen weakness, in the final carrying out of the deed, however, a satisfying conclusion. We see precisely this hesitation as an act of reason, and the atrocity of the ending as a relapse. Such relapses, to be sure, still threaten us, and their consequences have intensified. (GW 15:334)

Though such a reading of the play may seem antihistorical to the Elizabethan scholar (and the literary historian might well object to Brecht's somewhat cavalier blanket use of the term "Middle Ages"), it is certainly not ahistorical, seeking as it does to establish some connection between the events of the play and the social and historical environment in which it is to be performed. And one might even find support for Brecht's interpretations in Hamlet's line at the end of act 1: "The time is out of joint—O cursed spite, / That ever I was born to set it right!" As Margot Heinemann puts it, in her stimulating and wide-ranging essay "How Brecht Read Shakespeare": "Shakespeare is a great realist, firstly because he is a great observer, because of his ability to embody so much contradictory material . . . this material is not tidied up or harmonized in accordance with a preconceived idea."[10]

But to return to the radio adaptation. For this, Brecht relied on the published Schlegel-Tieck translation, working from two editions, cutting and pasting, and occasionally inserting his own texts, either in verse or prose. Such prose insertions were a logical consequence of the form of the radio drama—the announcer introducing the broadcast—but also provided Brecht with the opportunity to work against any conventional semblance of a seamless dramatic flow; as always, the new technology and form was viewed as something that could be refunctioned for artistic purposes. The clearest and most provocative instance of this among the extant material suggests that the adaptation may have jumped straight from the closet scene, omitting most of act 4, to the following:

Speaker: At this point we interrupt the progress of the tragedy, showing Hamlet in the graveyard, on account of the extraordinary report which the queen gives of Ophelia's death. (BBA, 351/38)

There then follows Gertrude's speech from the end of act 4. Predictably, this type of affront to the sensibilities of listeners accustomed to their familiar dose of Shakespeare was singled out for special mention in the reviews: one reviewer labeled the adaptation "disrespectful" and Brecht was compared with "an adolescent who, for the purposes of melodramatic amusement, runs round the garden lopping off flowers" (Symington, 98).

The only study that to date has looked at the scanty material—Symington's thorough and perceptive *Brecht und Shakespeare*—concludes from the apparent lack of material that, after this speech, the rest was more or less silence and that the whole of the remainder of the play from 4.5 to 5.2 was not transmitted. Now although Brecht may have been strolling through the Shakespearean garden with a pair of pruning secateurs, it seems hard to accept that these were replaced by a scythe for the last five scenes of the play. The evidence of the extant material is not quite as unequivocal as Symington suggests: the announcer's introduction to the account of the death of Ophelia specifically refers to the graveyard scene and, by implication, suggests it is to come. Yet it also appears from Brecht's own underlinings in the edition from which he worked that other remaining speeches definitely intended for broadcast were the monologue in 4.4; Hamlet's dying words to Horatio; five lines thereafter; and the epilogue referred to earlier. *Hamlet* without the melodrama of the duel with its switched blades, poisoned cups, characters dropping down dead in all directions? Well, one can guess what Brecht's aim might have been in denying the listener the frissons of this particular *scène à faire*, while having some doubts about the shortcuts involved.

The only remaining material among Brecht's papers that relates to this adaptation is not discussed by Symington at all. This is a page of musical sketches, draft translations, and reworkings of Ophelia's songs in 4.5, which show that Brecht replaced the last three lines of the first one ("Larded all with sweet flowers / Which bewept to the grave did not go / With true-love showers") with three of his own; and that he omitted the last two stanzas of "Tomorrow is Saint Valentine's Day" and ignored "They bore him bare-faced" and "For bonny sweet Robin" entirely (BBA, 122/40–41).

III

The next chapter in Brecht's reading of *Hamlet* is marked by some scattered comments and references from the thirties that occur in those theoretical writings where he develops some of the concepts central to his own theory and practice. What is interesting here is not the reinterpretation or adaptation of Shakespeare, but the fact that Brecht, in giving dramaturgical examples that are intended to clarify his theoretical descriptions, regularly chooses instances from Shakespearean rather than from German drama.

For example, in a crucial passage, he discusses one of the central ideas of Brechtian theater—the notion of *Gestus* (translated by John Willett as "gist" and the obsolete "gest"). For Brecht, *Gestus* means "a complex of gestures, mime, and, usually, statements, which one or more people direct toward one or more people" (*GW* 15:409). He then goes on: "A man calling on his God only becomes, in terms of this definition, a 'gestus' when this occurs with reference to others or in a context where relations between people emerge (e.g.; the king praying in *Hamlet*)" (409). Perhaps not such an earth-shattering theatrical insight. But more provocative and indicative of Brecht's directorial approach to bringing out the meaning of a scene is the following throwaway comment:

> The elementary gestic content of the first scene of *Hamlet* can be expressed by the following title: *In the Castle of Elsinore a Ghost Is Sighted*. The scene presents the theatricalization of the reports circulating in the castle about the king's death. Any staging in which the ghost evokes horror *qua* ghost naturally detracts from the main issue. (*GW* 15:335)

(It is worth noting that the "title" articulates an observation with which Stanislavsky and other proponents of the "major action" theory might well have concurred.) The comment is an instance of Brecht at his best: precise and demonstrating the need to concentrate on the more difficult essentials rather than on the easier and more obvious theatricalities. As a counter to that, and as a real quarry for the textual and historical critics, there is the following longer passage from the collection of dialogues on the theater entitled the *Messingkauf Dialogues*. I think there is sufficient evidence here of Brecht's quirky and individual—though still stimulating—slant on the play to prompt considerable disagreement:

THE DRAMATURG: Shakespeare's plays are extraordinarily full of life. Apparently they were printed from the prompt copy, and took in all the changes made at rehearsal and the actors' improvisations. The way the blank verse is set down suggests that it must in many cases have been done by ear. *Hamlet* has always interested me specially for the following reasons. We know it was adapted from a previous play by a certain Thomas Kyd that had had a great success a few years earlier. Its theme is the cleansing of an Augean stable. The hero, Hamlet, cleans up his family. He seems to have done so quite without inhibitions, and the last act is evidently meant to be the climax. The star of Shakespeare's Globe Theatre, however, was a stout man and short of breath, and so for a while all the heroes had to be stout and short of breath; this went for Macbeth as well as Lear. As a result the plot was deepened for him; and probably by him, too. Cascades and rapids were built in. The play became so much more interesting.[11]

While some of Brecht's propositions in this passage are at best speculative, at worst untenable (cf. Symington 108–12), they nevertheless are consistent in their statement of his attitude to questions such as the relationship between written and performed text, and the physical characteristics of the lead actor. At the end of the thirties when he started work on the *Messingkauf Dialogues,* Brecht was also experimenting with what he called "parallel scenes," or "intermezzi," which could be used in rehearsal as contemporary glosses on well-known classical dramas. Generally, these "alienating" practice scenes were intended to replace what he saw as the theater's fondness for playing not so much the incidents themselves but rather the outburst of temperament that these incidents allow, whereas the particular practice scene for *Hamlet* was intended to prevent a "heroicized" portrayal of Hamlet. Brecht introduces the scene with the following comment:

This ferry scene, to be inserted between the third and fourth scene of act 4 and the recitation of the closing report is intended to prevent a heroicized presentation of *Hamlet.* Bourgeois *Hamlet* criticism usually sees Hamlet's hesitation as the interesting new element in this play, but considers the carnage of act 5, that is the throwing aside of reflection and the transition to "the deed" as a positive solution. But this carnage is a relapse, for the deed is an atrocity. Hamlet's hesitation is given an explanation through the little practice scene: it corresponds to the new bourgeois code of behavior, which is already quite widespread in the political-social sphere. (GW 7:3014–17)

The action of the scene can be summarized as follows. We find Hamlet and a companion at the ferry: Hamlet asks the ferryman about a building overlooking the coast, and learns that this had earlier been a fort for the coastguard, but is now used for salting the fish that are exported to Norway. The argument with Norway over the stretch of coastline has been sorted out: the land has been ceded in return for the permission to export fish to Norway. Moreover, an insult to the Danish ambassador at the Norwegian court has been forgotten. Hamlet defends the resolution of the argument: "New methods, friend. You come across it everywhere. Blood no longer smells good, tastes have changed." Economic politics determine human actions: war is set aside in favor of the export of fish; the ambassador has to forget the insult, Claudius is considered to be a good king because of his economic policies, and, last but not least, Hamlet receives his portion of honor because he does not seek revenge on the murderer who has led his country toward a sound economic policy (cf. Symington, 160).

At the end of a lengthy prose speech Hamlet finally concludes: "and so, the best thing is to go to bed, lest the fishing enterprise be disrupted." But then, within the space of twelve lines of very regular iambic pentameters, he opts in favor of—action:

> And so Trade prospers, the ornate grave decays.
> How louder sounds its decay th'accusing cry.
> . . . .
> And you, tear down what's now built up, because
> It stands on ruins (and flourishes and bears rich fruit!)
> Fill once more the fort with slaughterers, turn back
> To bloody deeds, since he [i.e. Claudius] began with them!
> Oh, had he then only wavered, all were well!

(The last line is an ironic comment on what we learn earlier in the scene—namely that Claudius *had* hesitated to sign the treaty, but, of course, had—apparently—*not* hesitated to kill his brother!)

In a detailed analysis of this scene, Symington tends to reduce the dialectic to an oversimplified "does Brecht see the new bourgeois thinking of Hamlet as a sickness or a strength, and is his hesitation to be seen as a positive or a negative factor?" (161–64). The answer—or rather an answer—to these questions he might have found in a lengthy diary entry from 11 December 1940 which, for some reason, he does not consider. It is crucial to an understanding of Brecht's view of *Hamlet* because it represents

an extended discussion of the problems of the play as they need
to be addressed *in production*.

> Went to see the Swedish Theater's *Hamlet*. What a combination of
> touches of finesse and crudeness. The older play keeps on peeping
> out all the way through, yet the clumsy acts of butchery probably
> have a doubly clumsy impact because the bits of intrigue have appar-
> ently been cut in order to make space for all the moments of reflec-
> tion. It's more or less the roughest plot Shakespeare has adapted
> (*Titus* doesn't really count); he has inserted into it his most sensitive
> hero. His vulnerability causes wounds for everybody. I don't believe
> that later critics are correct in their interpretation that the sense of
> the play lies in the representation of the hesitating intellectual—
> even if its significance may lie in that. Hamlet is simply an idealist
> who is thrown off course by the collision with the real world, the
> idealist who becomes a cynic. It's not: to act or not to act that is the
> question but: to be silent or not to be silent, to approve or not to
> approve. Nothing is more comical than the serious way our theaters
> stage Shakespeare. He may be theatrical, but he is never representa-
> tive. Our Philistines simply cannot imagine naiveté and complexity
> side by side. Shakespeare wrote for a small theater with great sig-
> nificance, an intimate beer garden. His greatness is not to be meas-
> ured by the yard. His stage was what we call surrealistic—without,
> of course, the shock effect that surrealism is after, it's an innocent
> surrealism. (The commanders' tents of two enemy armies on one
> stage, simultaneous action, etc.) *Hamlet* is even for Shakespeare's
> time a folktale, a tangled and bloody one, with ghosts, poisoned
> sword hilts, armies wandering round, etc. The end, even if it is a
> compromise with Kyd's Hamlet-drama, is a prodigiously bold stroke
> on Shakespeare's part: all this thinking and planning, all these
> spasms of conscience end in uncertainty, fortuitously, in a chaos of
> intrigues and aimlessness. Still awaiting confirmation of the suspi-
> cion that his life is threatened, Hamlet dies, himself a multimurderer.
> This melancholy massacre without a moral, self-annihilation of a
> clan could only have been produced by a theater like the Elizabethan.
> The production itself, very provincial [i.e. representative], showed
> me, by the way, just how much depends on the actor cast as Hamlet
> playing the action and not only offering the exhibitionistic and re-
> flective aspects. It's here that most Hamlets fail.[12]

All that needs to be added to this critique is that the production in question—according to one critic—occupies a position
in the Finnish theater history analogous to Gielgud's and Olivier's Hamlet in the English-speaking theater![13]

IV

Brecht was to return to some of the issues in *Hamlet* once more in his treatise *A Short Organum for the Theatre*. From his remarks in section 68,[14] it is clear that he has not substantially altered that view of the play that determined his reading of sixteen years earlier, or of the Finnish production. The Fortinbras scene is still seen as crucial, the resolution of the dramatic conflict as "barbaric carnage." Brecht's assertion that Hamlet's "meeting" with Fortinbras prompts his decision to "turn back" and that he then "butchers his uncle, his mother and himself" prompted Eric Bentley to write, suggesting that this view needed modification.[15] Brecht readily conceded the latter point, though the translation of the relevant passage in the English edition of the letters obscures the distinction when Brecht is made to write "It must be changed to 'puts his uncle, his mother and himself to death.'"[16] What Brecht actually wrote was: "You are right: . . . it must be changed to 'and in a barbaric bloodbath brings about the death of his uncle, his mother and himself.'"[17]

But Brecht disagrees with Bentley's view that Hamlet turns back later and for other reasons. And although Bentley and others have maintained that Brecht was wrong, I feel both his interpretation and the way he expresses it warrant closer attention. What is really at issue here is an argument between the textual scholar and the dramaturg-director. The crucial point in Brecht's argument is *what the actor playing Hamlet can show to an audience.*

> We take act 4, scene 4 ("A plain in Denmark"), in which we encounter Hamlet for the last time before his return "in the flesh" and where he speaks the great monologue in which he gives himself over to the wardrums of Fortinbras's army to be the turning point. ("O, from this time forth, my thoughts be bloody or be nothing worth.") True, the letter to Horatio two scenes later announces that Hamlet nevertheless takes ship for England, but there's nothing there that can be played; and the account he gives Horatio of the King's plot against him (5.2) does not give the actor the moment in which to take the decision.
> This interpretation of *Hamlet* is only an example of *interpretation.*

And when Bentley writes again, still disagreeing with Brecht's line, the playwright spells out his reasons in more detail:

> Re *Hamlet* and *Organum*, I think I am staying within the limits of interpretation. Few textual changes are needed. It is true that Hamlet . . . after his "storing up (of) warlike spirit" during the meeting with

Fortinbras, still needs the discovery that his own life is threatened for his final offensive. But this is only spoken of; after the monologue (in praise of action) the actor has nothing more that he can show on stage. And so the emphasis automatically falls on this monologue. (And the other aspects can definitely be included in performance.) In short (and put somewhat pointedly): it can be argued that *without* the meeting with Fortinbras, the subsequent discovery of the king's plot would still not induce Hamlet to clean out the Augean stables.[18]

Unfortunately, Brecht did not live to stage his own production of *Hamlet*—though his pupil Benno Besson has staged no fewer than five productions of the play in which, while some of the ideas derive from Brecht, the interpretation of the central character is not at all the same. It is reasonable to assume that it would have combined the vigorous theatricality and irreverence of his version of Goethe's *Urfaust* with the dialectical view of the (in)-dispensable hero incorporated into his adaptation of *Coriolanus*. For all the occasionally forced and, perhaps, perverse readings of aspects of the play and of the Elizabethan theater that one finds in Brecht's comments over the years, one feature remains constant: his fascination with the work and the conviction that the contradictions, and what he saw as the play's essential dialectic, needed to be brought out as emphatically as possible.

In 1948 after reading Hegel on the play, he writes:

What a piece of work this *Hamlet*. The interest in it over the centuries probably comes from the fact that a new type, fully worked out, comes forward—in a type of A-effect—in an environment that still has medieval clutter lying around in it. The cry for revenge ennobled by the Greek tragedians, then disqualified by the Christians, is, in the drama of *Hamlet*, still loud enough, reproduced with enough infectious power, to make the new doubting, testing, planning appear surprising and strange.[19]

In the same way that the two clowns Brecht thought of engaging for his theater would comment on the incidents and issues of the play, the mature playwright is still looking askance—though not too askance—at the work and seeking to shake out of it the sense that a modern audience needs to receive. In his planned production of the play he had already cast the one actor who would have combined all those aspects which remain constant over the years: the sickliness of the pale cast of thought; the fat and, in both senses, unfit hero; the pathological aspect (on which he never really comments but which is clearly there in the theatrical persona of his Hamlet); the combination of melancholy and clownishness described in the diary entry of 1920; the capacity to switch suddenly from morbid inactivity into frenzied mental and physical activity.

In 1950 Brecht offered the role of Hamlet to an actor who had been one of the most gifted and versatile performers on the German stage prior to 1933. He had starred in a number of stage productions and films—one of which still stands as one of the masterpieces of the German cinema—before going into exile in America where he continued, alas, to be typecast in Hollywood movies. After the war he returned once to Germany and made one little-known, yet powerful, film as both actor and director.[20] In 1950, suffering from jaundice, he turned down Brecht's offer. His name? Peter Lorre.[21]

Notes

For permission to quote copyright archival material thanks are due to the Bertolt-Brecht-Heirs and Suhrkamp Verlag. © Stefan S. Brecht 1992. I should also like to acknowledge the assistance of Dr. Marc Silberman and Dr. Erdmut Wizisla (Bertolt-Brecht-Archiv) in obtaining photocopies of the relevant passages.

1. Bertolt Brecht, *Poems 1913–1956*, trans. John Willett and Ralph Manheim (London: Methuen, 1987), 311.

2. Eric Bentley, *The Brecht Memoir* (New York: PAJ Publications, 1985). Also in Brecht, *Letters 1913–1956*, trans. Ralph Manheim, ed. John Willett (London: Methuen, 1990).

3. Brecht, *Gesammelte Werke* (Frankfurt: Suhrkamp, 1967), 15:108–11. Referred to hereafter as *GW* followed by the relevant volume and page number. Unless otherwise indicated, all translations from Brecht's writings are by the author.

4. Brecht, *Poems 1913–1956* (London: Methuen, 1987), 309–10.

5. Brecht, *Diaries 1920–1922* (London: Eyre Methuen, 1979), 32–33.

6. Bentley, *Brecht Memoir*, 35.

7. Cf. Rodney K. Symington, *Brecht und Shakespeare* (Bonn: Bouvier, 1970), referred to hereafter as Symington; Ute Baum, *Bertolt Brechts Verhältnis zu Shakespeare* (Berlin, 1981); Margot Heinemann, "How Brecht Read Shakespeare," in *Political Shakespeare*, ed. Jonathan Dollimore and Alan Sinfield (Manchester: Manchester University Press, 1985), 202–30.

8. This lack of logic to which Brecht refers is a point to which William Redfield, in his fascinating study of the rehearsal process of Burton's Hamlet under John Gielgud's direction, also draws attention. He puts it in even more general terms: "Riding roughshod over logic has never been unusual in the theatre. Shakespeare himself cared little for the logic of time and/or geography. Shakespeare was a bit like a magician. No card sharp can do his trick slowly and still fool the observer. It is much the same with Shakespeare. Since he is neither a novelist nor a painter, one cannot notice his oversights or jerrybuilding unless one reads him with the utmost care. A theatrical performance

moves swiftly, and I defy any audience member . . . to catch Shakespeare at his occasional shell game" (Redfield, *Letters from an Actor* [New York: Limelight Editions, 1984], 125–26).

9. Bertolt-Brecht-Archiv, 361/34–35. Referred to hereafter as BBA.

10. Heinemann, "How Brecht Read Shakespeare," 206.

11. Brecht, *The Messingkauf Dialogues*, trans. John Willett (London: Methuen, 1965), 59–60.

12. Brecht, *Arbeitsjournal* (Frankfurt: Suhrkamp, 1973), 210–11 (author's translation). The Swedish theater spoken of is actually located in Helsinki.

13. Cf. Clas Zilliacus, "*Hamlet*, Brecht and Besson," in *The Brecht Yearbook* 15 (Madison: University of Wisconsin Press), 73–82.

14. John Willett, ed. and trans., *Brecht on Theatre* (London: Methuen, 1987), 201–2.

15. Bentley, *Brecht Memoir*, 93–94.

16. Brecht, *Letters 1913–1956*, 481.

17. Brecht, *Briefe* (Frankfurt: Suhrkamp, 1981), 621. While some might argue with this view of Hamlet's involvement in the deaths of the other characters, it is interesting to note that Mallarmé had the same view, remarking in an essay from 1896: "Hamlet kills with unconcern—or at least people die. The black presence of this doubter causes this poison—that all the characters die: even without him bothering always to run them through, behind the arras" (Mallarmé, *Œuvres Complètes* [Paris: Gallimard, 1945], 1564).

18. Brecht, *Briefe*, 621, 622. Although these passages occur in the English edition of *Brecht's Letters* (481), the translation is at times so odd that Brecht appears to be even less familiar with the play than is actually the case. Consequently, the author's own translation is used.

19. Brecht, *Arbeitsjournal*, 861.

20. *Der Verlorene* [The lost one], 1950.

21. Brecht, *Arbeitsjournal*, 936.

Shakespeare and the German Imagination: Cult, Controversy, and Performance

WERNER HABICHT

"SHAKESPEARE in Germany" has a history that, though it has become fossilized into a cultural stereotype, at times in the past assumed the quality of a myth. Occasional references to the possessive slogan "Unser Shakespeare" even at a conference as remote from the field of action as the one in Adelaide, Australia, in 1992 can serve as an appropriate reminder of this cumbersome heritage. The myth can be briefly described as follows: in eighteenth-century Germany, between the ages of rationalism and romanticism, young intellectuals began to "discover" Shakespeare, and in doing so they miraculously discovered themselves, a national identity, the German spirit, and the potential for a national literature of the future. As a consequence, Shakespeare legitimately achieved the status of a German classic.

This, at any rate, is how the process was stylized and glorified a hundred years later, from the mid-nineteenth century onward, when it was narrated, elaborated, streamlined, and recapitulated over and over again, until it was at last persuasively confirmed and theoretically buttressed by the authority of the *Geistes-geschichte* practiced in Friedrich Gundolf's cult book *Shakespeare und der deutsche Geist* (1911). Cultivating a myth, however, meant disregarding the cultural contexts and controversies out of which it arose. And it could also lead one to underestimate the distortions the appropriated Shakespeare image has suffered and the dubious uses to which it has been put. Reconsidering and rewriting the history (rather than the myth) of Shakespeare's reception in Germany is, indeed, a considerable yet necessary task, and one still to be accomplished. I can only hope here to evoke some of the intricacies inherent in it.

Even in the eighteenth century, German involvement with Shakespeare had more paradoxical facets than some late nineteenth-century priests of the Shakespeare cult were prepared to acknowledge. Complexities resulted from such diverse and yet interrelated factors as debates on the aesthetics of drama in general, the politicization of both the debates and the Shakespearean interest by which they were propelled, and discrepancies between intellectual and theatrical approaches. For instance, it is well known—since it has been repeated so often—that G. E. Lessing in his *17. Literaturbrief* (1759) recommended Shakespeare, and English drama in general, as being a more appropriate paradigm for the German theater and more suited to German literary taste than what had been imposed by the tyranny of French classicism. It is equally well known that Lessing was soon bypassed by J. G. Herder, who praised Shakespeare's art and its roots in Nordic popular poetry more rhapsodically, sensed Shakespeare's consanguinity with the Germans more deeply, rejected French drama more passionately; indeed he felt himself to be closer to Shakespeare than even to the Greeks epitomized by Sophocles. And it is no less well known that, partly under the influence of Herder, the self-declared young geniuses of'the *Sturm und Drang* movement—such as F. M. Klinger, J. M. R. Lenz, and the young Goethe—were encouraged by the precedent of Shakespeare to produce their powerfully unrestrained plays, which defied Aristotelian aesthetic rules; these indeed were stage sensations in the 1770s, again accompanied by anti-French polemics.[1]

Hence from the late nineteenth-century perspective the German "discovery" of Shakespeare, productive as it turned out to be, could be considered as a sort of spiritual prefiguration of the Franco-Prussian wars—even if this meant ignoring the demonstrable fact that a comparable process of Shakespeare reception had taken place in France itself (from Ducis to Le Tourneur), and that it was via France that many eighteenth-century Germans first came to know about the Bard—even before Lessing, whose traditional designation as the first promoter of Shakespeare in Germany has long been proved to be untenable.[2] And, of course, Lessing's own ideas evolved from those of Voltaire and drew on English critics from John Dryden to Henry Home. But Voltaire, because of his anti-Shakespearean diatribe in his *Lettre à l'Académie* (1776), was also a convenient scapegoat and was xenophobically attacked as such—by Ch. M. Wieland, for instance, who was the first to translate as many as twenty-two complete Shakespeare plays into German prose (curiously, in Paris and with the help of an English-French dictionary when he could not get hold of an English-German one), and, naturally, by the *Sturm und Drang* dramatists, whose anti-French belief in original genius was largely derived from Young and Macpherson. But then the adverse criticism to which the unwieldy *Sturm und Drang* plays were subjected even in Germany was in keeping with Voltairean arguments. Eighteenth-century explorations of Shakespearean drama, far from being the specifically German phenomenon that would befit a national myth, were in fact debated in European dimensions.

On the stage, the unruly explosiveness of the *Sturm und Drang* dramas imitating and supposedly justified by Shakespeare coincided with the earliest productions of Shakespeare's own plays. These, however, were almost dogmatically considered to be in need of refinement and regularization in order to be acceptable to theater audiences. When in 1776 the actor-manager Friedrich Ludwig Schröder staged the first German Shakespeare series of note in Hamburg, beginning with *Hamlet*, his treatment and arrangement of the tragedy followed Garrick's example, and the script he used was his own adaptation of Heufeld's adaptation of Eschenburg's revision of Wieland's prose translation. Schröder himself made thorough changes to his adaptation for subsequent *Hamlet* productions, always being careful to have both Hamlet and Laertes emerge unharmed from the final duel. He seems to have been bolder with his first *Othello*, which followed two months after the Hamburg *Hamlet*. Perhaps he had taken a point made two years earlier by Christian Heinrich Schmid, who had claimed that this was Shakespeare's only play of which practically unaltered performances might be ventured—though even in Schmid's stage version the Moor is deprived of his blackness and turned into a white Venetian of lowly birth.[3] Schröder, on the other hand, retained even the color of the Moor's skin; but the result was devastating, if one is to believe what a chronicler of the Hamburg theater recorded eighteen years after the event:

The demonic passion of the African, the satanic malice of his ensign, the cruel slaughter of innocent Desdemona—all exceeded by far what the nerves of the men of Hamburg, and even more those of the women of Hamburg . . . could bear. The closer the performance approached the catastrophe, the more uneasy the audience grew. "Swoons followed upon swoons," reports an eyewitness. "The doors of the boxes opened and closed. People left or, when necessary, were carried out; and, according to trustworthy reports, the miscarriages suffered by various prominent ladies were the result of seeing and hearing the overly tragic play."[4]

Some of this may be exaggerated, considering the chronicler's
reference to an anonymous "eyewitness" who in turn relies on
unidentified "trustworthy reports." Even so, Schröder learned
his lesson, hastened to rewrite the script, removed or replaced
objectionable expressions, and again substituted a more edifying
"music of the close," which kept both Othello and Desdemona
alive. The second performance was announced as "*Othello* with
changes," so that, as the chronicler was pleased to add, Hamburg's coming generations were preserved from untimely theatrical accouchements.

While, then, in the theater progressive German plays strove to
outdo the power of Shakespeare's original genius in the name of
both Shakespeare and the future of German drama, Shakespeare's own plays were domesticated to suit the sensibilities
and intellectual horizons of German middle-class audiences. The
pattern is familiar from Shakespeare's stage history in England;
but in Germany the question of stage adaptations was also colored by the national context. Its literary locus classicus, which
reflected the debate and contributed to its perpetuation, occurs
in Goethe's *Wilhelm Meisters Lehrjahre*. The hero of this novel,
one will remember, comes under the spell of Shakespeare by
reading his plays, *Hamlet* in particular, in a remote room of a
duke's residence, where he is a guest and where, like Hamlet
himself, he becomes involved with a company of actors. Wilhelm
undertakes to prepare a performance; in order to do so he must—
as he is taught by Serlo, the impresario of the troupe—come to
terms with theater conditions and objectify the subjective reading experience. The result is Wilhelm Meister's studiously
adapted performance of William Shakespeare's *Hamlet*, which,
though applying Serlo's principles with an independent mind,
brings the play closer to the very model of French classicism
which Wilhelm had emphatically rejected under the impression
of reading the original. The fictional theater director Serlo is
modeled on none other than the real Friedrich Ludwig Schröder,
who had first staged *Hamlet* in Hamburg and had had to put on
"*Othello* with changes" to avoid the alleged swoons and miscarriages. Interestingly enough, even if by coincidence, the chronicle reporting on Schröder's seminal performances was published
at about the same time as the first version of Goethe's novel. Later
on, in 1815, Goethe, with much of his own experience as theater
director in Weimar behind him, was even more explicit, considering the idea that Shakespeare should be played "word for
word" a "prejudice" and "nonsense," which, if implemented,

might well lead to his immediate disappearance from the German stage.

This warning, which occurs in Goethe's essay "Shakespeare und kein Ende!"[5] was directed against the romantics of Jena, one of whom, August Wilhelm Schlegel, had by then provided his metrical translation of seventeen Shakespeare plays, which was published around 1800. Based on the romantic recognition of the autonomous nature and "organic poetry" of Shakespearean drama, it paid sensitive attention to the formal and functional details of Shakespeare's verse, style, and construction as well as to semantic meaning. Hence adherents of the romantic school took to pleading for performances as faithful to the "organic" texts as were Schlegel's translations. In practice, however, such pleas were seldom heeded; for the contrary verdict of Goethe continued to exercise its authority and to provide justification for the adjustments that were a common routine of the theater anyway. A theater historian in 1882 was still essentially right in pointing out proudly that in Germany it was "only through adaptations that it had become possible for Shakespeare's works to be played more often than the plays of any other serious dramatist."[6]

And yet it was because of the recognition of Shakespearean drama as autonomous, "organic," and ironic art that the romantics' achievement came to be celebrated as the second truly German discovery of Shakespeare—its similarity with what Coleridge lectured on in England notwithstanding. A. W. Schlegel himself, and also his brother Friedrich Schlegel, were not entirely innocent in suggesting as much. Both commented repeatedly on the special German (or at least Germanic) affinity that existed with the romantically conceived Shakespeare and made him a better inspiration for the German imagination than, say, Calderón, who otherwise might have been as good a paradigm. "One may boldly assert," wrote A. W. Schlegel in Schiller's journal Die Horen in 1796, "that there is no nation besides the English to whom [Shakespeare] belongs so particularly as to the Germans, because nowhere else . . . is he studied so deeply, loved so warmly, admired so judiciously."[7] In private A. W. Schlegel, not a particular Anglophile, was even more explicit; in 1797 he wrote to Ludwig Tieck, alluding to the latter's plan to write a book on Shakespeare: "I hope you will prove, among other things, that Shakespeare was not an Englishman. How did he possibly come among the frosty, stupid souls on that brutal island?"[8] Moreover, the romantics' Shakespeare, too, became af-

fected by implicit anti-French attitudes, which turned him into
a kind of spiritual counterhero to Napoleon, Germany's martial
conqueror.[9] At the same time the particularly romantic interest
in historical drama enkindled by Shakespeare's histories—for
K. W. F. Solger, for instance, "Shakespeare was the first author
ever to create true historical drama, and so far he alone has been
completely successful in doing so"[10]—suggested what the growing national consciousness of the Germans was in need of: universalizing dramatizations of the national past.

Ideologically, however, the romantic fascination with Shakespeare's ironic mode was coming under attack by 1830, when
Napoleon was dead and when an intellectual avant-garde had
started to rebel against the reactionary tendencies that followed.
When in 1827 the dramatist Christian Dietrich Grabbe—himself
an author of historical plays inspired by Shakespeare—in his
essay "Über die Shakespearo-Manie" (1827) inveighed against
the immobilizing tyranny of Shakespeare's excessive German admirers in order to expose what had become a "Shakespeare ma-
nia," he explicitly blamed partly the romantic school, in whose
aesthetic criticism he diagnosed a lack of philosophy, and partly
Shakespeare himself, of whose aesthetic faults he compiled a list
that reads like a parody of what Dr. Johnson had already discussed in the Preface to his edition. Nor was Grabbe convinced
that Shakespeare could have a national impact. Politically, he
was more likely to offer role models of a negative kind—Hamlet
in particular, the tender soul so dear to Goethe and the thought-
ridden hero so dear to the romantics, whom in the 1830s revolutionary poets of the Young Germany movement such as Börne,
Freiligrath, and Heine singled out for the purpose of turning
him into a symbol of German political inactivity and national
disunity, and to disparage him ostentatiously as such.[11] All this
was obviously polemical, besides betraying "anxieties of influence." The Shakespeare skepticism that thus surfaced was
henceforth also to be reckoned with; at any rate it redirected and
polarized responses to Shakespeare's inescapable German
presence.

To remedy the philosophical deficit of Schlegel's romantic
criticism as diagnosed by Grabbe and also by Heine,[12] scholars
such as Ulrici and Gervinus, who were indeed philosophers by
profession, came to the fore. Their sizable books on Shakespeare,
which went into several editions both in German and in English
translation, set out, partly in the wake of Hegel, to initiate a third
stage in Shakespeare's German "discovery" by determining the

aesthetic laws and the unifying ideas underlying his plays. This, too, was impossible without accusations being leveled against the romantics, whose attempts at understanding Shakespeare's greatness had, Ulrici maintained, simply left them in awe of his mysteriousness and inscrutability.[13] Significantly, such pronouncements originated in the context of the political events leading up to the revolution of 1848. Gervinus was one of seven professors of Göttingen University (the others included the brothers Grimm) who in 1837 were dismissed from their positions in retaliation for their public protest against the suspension of the constitution decreed by King Ernst August of Hanover—an incident that did much to strengthen the liberal cause. The 1848 revolution itself failed, but the ideas and the idealism derived from Shakespeare continued to be held up in order to inspire new courage. Once again the importance of Shakespeare's histories, both English and Roman, was stressed. For adequate German historical drama had not yet been born; Ulrici declared its generation to be not merely a literary concern (as the romantics had thought), "but also an ethical-political, national, and universal [one]."[14] Gervinus, who considered his two-volume work Shakespeare, published immediately after the 1848 events, "a necessary completion" of his previous, severely critical multi-volume history of German literature,[15] recommended the histories as providing lessons in historical progress and necessity, patriotism, political responsibility, and heroic leadership. The cue was taken up by Franz Dingelstedt, who in 1864, to celebrate Shakespeare's tercentenary in the Weimar theater, produced (for the first time ever) a cycle of all ten English history plays.

Not everyone, however, was ready to embrace the Hegelian objective ideas distilled from Shakespeare by Ulrici, or the patriotic idealism infused into them by Gervinus. In fact, this produced another wave of skeptical comment. The dramatist Franz Grillparzer, for example, confided to his diary what he thought of scholars such as Gervinus, calling them "vain schoolmasters," "half-wits," and "idiotic art philosophers," and was in turn led to rethink his own position: "Shakespeare is tyrannizing my mind, but I would prefer to remain free."[16] Eventually even a martyr of the Shakespearean tyranny became available for public sympathy—Otto Ludwig, a gifted author of realist plays and novellas, whose self-abandonment to the admiration and copious annotation of Shakespeare's works was said to have caused the premature extinction of his own creativity and probably also his death in a mental institution.

In the mid-nineteenth century such unease appears to have been no less common than the current of mythical consolation, partly because both the idealist and the romantic image of Shakespeare obstructed the quest for realist drama. Even historical drama would have to have a realist basis, as Hermann Hettner explained in 1852, telling authors and critics not to rely on the great model of Shakespeare, not to assume "that his historical plays represent the necessary inner form of the genre itself."[17] A realistic, demythicized, and rehistoricized approach to Shakespeare was indeed advocated by Gustav Rümelin, political scientist and chancellor of Tübingen University, who in 1864 published, in a widely read cultural journal, a series of articles entitled *Shakespeare: Studies of a Realist*.[18] Shakespeare, he declared, had not written his plays for nineteenth-century German professors to test their aesthetic systems on, but for a practical theater within the social context of sixteenth-century England. If in his discussions of individual plays he pointed out weaknesses, it was to suggest that these were determined by real conditions and conventions rooted in Shakespeare's personal experience and in the imaginations of his original audience— hence, no one in Germany ought to expect from him spiritual edification and national leadership. Response to Rümelin's argument was divided, especially in as much as it, too, affected the national cause. A Shakespeare firmly placed in his Elizabethan English environment could hardly be acclaimed as Germany's spiritual leader, especially in a more advanced culture and a time that was experiencing the belligerent lead-up to German unification and the foundation of the Second Reich in 1871. Indeed Rümelin's articles reinforced the views of those who tended to object to the cult of a foreign author when in fact excellent German classics were available.[19]

But Shakespeare's spiritual admirers eloquently came to and indeed organized the Bard's defense. They founded the Deutsche Shakespeare-Gesellschaft in Weimar in 1864, and from this public forum poured vituperation on the dilettantism of Rümelin and his like. They insisted on an idealistic view of their idol and were ready to excuse and remedy Shakespeare's faults, such as indecent puns and euphuistic mannerisms that were attributable to the primitivism of his own age and nation.[20] As a consequence, the German appropriation of Shakespeare was considered to be a more truly patriotic enterprise than was his xenophobic disparagement. Was not Bismarck himself known to be ardently devoted to Shakespeare, often quoting from his plays in his political speeches?[21] Professor Ulrici, presiding at one of the first annual meetings of the Deutsche Shakespeare-Gesellschaft, proclaimed what was to be a major objective of that organization: "We want to de-Anglicize the Englishman Shakespeare, to Germanize him in the widest and deepest sense of the word; we want to do everything in our power to make him even more and in the truest and fullest sense what he already is—a German poet."[22]

It was in those founder years of the Second Reich that numerous books and articles both learned and popular (not to mention the Deutsche Shakespeare-Gesellschaft's own *Jahrbuch*) stylized the story of the eighteenth-century German "discovery" of Shakespeare into a national myth. This obviously required more than merely evoking the Germanic heritage that permitted England and Germany to have their national poet in common, and which had already been sensed by Herder and the romantics. A more powerful Shakespearean discourse was needed, one adorned with compelling metaphors derived from nature, law, and war. For example, Shakespeare was described by Gustav Liebau as a tree, which, because transplanted onto German soil, had been able to take firm root and to bear glorious blossoms; or, by F. A. Leo, as Germany's adopted son, who as such had a right of abode. Germany's right to Shakespeare was declared to be both one of ownership ("Shakespeare's works have, ever since Herder, been the property of our nation," wrote August Koberstein in 1853), and one of conquest: "Certain it is that we have conquered the great poet for ourselves," said Gervinus, "just as the English have conquered our Händel."[23] (One could add dozens of similarly embarrassing quotations.) Some of the discourse grew aggressively anti-British as well. Since Shakespeare—so it ran— had been mishandled, misunderstood, and betrayed by his own countrymen, first by the Puritans, later by materialist liberals, Germany was a more adequate place for him to flourish in, a point that was reiterated and further elaborated in the early twentieth century. Gerhardt Hauptmann's notorious manifesto uttered at the beginning of the First World War to justify performances of the enemy's dramatist did no more than throw the weight of authority behind current slogans: "There is no nation, not even the English one, that has acquired a right to Shakespeare as the Germans have . . . and if he was born and buried in England, it is in Germany that he truly lives."[24] His words were later to be remembered and ruthlessly quoted at the beginning of the Second World War.

However, Rümelin's plea for a demythicized view of Shakespeare was not without its nationalist repercussions either. Eru-
dite scholars, even if they disdained Rümelin's dilettantism,
began to do exactly what he had recommended: to study and
explicate Shakespeare in the context of his original historical
and theatrical conditions, to collect the evidence and provide
the tools needed for that purpose. Such activities, too, could be
turned into an argument justifying the annexation of Shakespeare: it was the industry and thoroughness of German scholarship that had conquered the real Shakespeare.[25] The question of
what Shakespeare's appropriation should be primarily ascribed
to—the Bard's own Germanic background or the superior insight
of his German explicators—became itself a matter of debate.[26]
But there was little hesitation in yoking together both explana-
tions, despite their logical incompatibility, in daring metaphors.

In many respects it was, indeed, the synthesis of opposing
views that allowed Shakespeare to be installed in the pantheon
of German classics, as in fact he was—at least verbally—by 1900.
Gundolf's grandiose image of him, propounded in 1911, as a
catalyst of the German spirit was exactly this: a retrospective
symbiosis of conflicting views, an accommodation and welding
together of rationalist thinking, preromantic exuberance, romantic subjectivism, and Goethean classical control. But in creating
that image, Gundolf dismissed as insignificant the actual
nineteenth-century debates, battles, and inconsistencies, which
in fact he was summarizing.

The same is essentially true of the "Schlegel-Tieck" translation, that much-admired product of the romantic era, which
around 1900 was standardized and canonized and thus became
the concrete basis of Shakespeare's status as a national classic.
As the dramatist Ludwig Fulda, himself a Shakespeare translator,
summarized the general opinion in 1901: "The Schlegel-Tieck
Shakespeare has become our Shakespeare [unser Shakespeare],
a German poet as close to us as our own classics. . . . Who would
dare to change texts that, as they are, ring in every German's
ear?"[27] Homage had been paid to the translation, especially its
early Schlegel part, throughout the nineteenth century, not only
because it was, as even Grabbe and Heine admitted, the finest
fruit of romantic aesthetics, but also because its language and
rhythms were similar to those of the classic German plays by
Schiller and Goethe. But at the same time the translation had
been challenged by more than a hundred competing nineteenth-
century translators. Some of them (such as J. H. Voss and sons

as early as around 1820) confronted Schlegel's embellishments with rougher alternatives; others (such as Dingelstedt in the 1860s) replaced what they considered the roughness of Schlegel's own translations by more polished and more actable versions. Others again (such as a scholarly team headed by Ulrici) tried to improve on and emend the "Schlegel-Tieck" texts themselves, notably the plays omitted by Schlegel and translated under the supervision of Tieck, which were felt to lack Schlegel's primordial luster. And yet toward the end of the nineteenth century the Deutsche Shakespeare-Gesellschaft itself insisted—albeit not without a fierce debate on the matter first[28]—on the publication of the unaltered Schlegel-Tieck translation, both as a cheap one-volume edition (edited by Wilhelm Oechelhäuser, who had previously subjected many of the texts to severe revisions for the stage) and as a multivolume library set (edited by Alois Brandl, then the Shakespeare-Gesellschaft's president), both of which were unprecedented successes on the book market. The wealth of creative insight and critical understanding contained in, and the reception history reflected by, all those numerous translations competing with Schlegel-Tieck and with each other—products of an activity that has continued undiminished in the twentieth century—tended to become buried beneath the standardized idol, and still waits to be unearthed.

I do not here have time to pursue this in further detail. Nor shall I discuss (because I have done so elsewhere) the political and propagandistic use to which the canonized German Shakespeare—and the Shakespeare myth—was put in critical periods of the twentieth century, especially during the Third Reich.[29] It may be pointed out, however, that the German appropriation of Shakespeare was of a symbolic (or, if you will, discursive) nature. "Unser Shakespeare," Shakespeare the German classic, the tutelary god with his place alongside not only Goethe and Schiller, but (as the learned author of a Shakespeare Grammar insisted) alongside Luther and Bismarck as well:[30] this general notion may have gratified nationalist instincts, but it did not greatly affect even the writing of histories of German literature, an activity that itself began to flourish in the second half of the nineteenth century. For the very concept of national literature propagated by histories of German literature such as the ones by Wilhelm Scherer, Richard M. Meyer, or Adolf Bartels after all required Shakespeare to be treated as a foreign author and permitted no more than marginal references to his "influence," summary recapitulations of his eighteenth-century "discovery," and the occasional dropping of his name to confer distinction on some German dramatist considered less than inferior. By contrast, the genuine German classics were treated at great and even excessive length. Literary historians were more inclined to deplore the absence of a full-fledged German equivalent of the British dramatist, or else to prophesy the messianic advent of a second Shakespeare, a real German this time, to be the founder of a German dramatic art even greater than that of Goethe and Schiller and Kleist. "We Germans," wrote Adolf Bartels in an appendix to the fourteenth edition (1934) of his *Geschichte der deutschen Literatur* (originally published in 1901), "have without doubt the strongest hopes and yearnings—nowhere else does anyone wait in such anticipation as we do for the future dramatic Messiah, the new Shakespeare" (604). But that greater German dramatist, for whom the Shakespeare appropriated from the British was only a temporary substitute, was a dream that was bound to dissolve under the pressure of changing historical realities, and the German Shakespeare myth hardly survived the Second World War, which crushed the cultural nationalism by which that myth had been fostered.

To some extent, however, the myth had always been subverted by the very real energies of the theater. It is true that Shakespeare's tragedies (especially *Hamlet*) and histories, on which the intellectual discourse dwelt with especial emphasis, were the object of frequent—if adapted—performances as well. But even nineteenth-century actors were perfectly capable of contributing an experience and a sensitivity of their own. As a reviewer remarked apropos of Emil Devrient's impersonation of Hamlet in 1856, two ways of playing the Danish prince were in evidence: there were, on the one hand, actors who were trying to fathom the secrets of every speech, emulating the noble efforts devoted to them by philosophers; these performances, however, tended to leave their audiences dissatisfied—whereas, on the other hand, by their command of emotion and technique, the "roughest naturalists" among actors elicited the most enthusiastic response.[31]

It is perhaps because of its independent imaginative approach that the theater also favored the comedies, which at that time were still relatively unmolested by literary theorizing. There had always been an emotional predilection for some of them, quite independent of national concerns. It is surely no coincidence that the first two major Shakespeare translators, Christoph Martin Wieland and A. W. Schlegel, both approached their task and clarified their principles by first rendering A Midsummer Night's Dream, and that Ludwig Tieck, doubtless influenced by Friedrich Schlegel's concept of romantic irony, in his essay on Shakespeare's use of the marvelous (Shakespeares Behandlung des Wunderbaren, 1793) began to develop, on the basis of A Midsummer Night's Dream and also of The Tempest, his understanding of the way Shakespeare simultaneously and paradoxically builds up and breaks down dramatic illusion—an illusion that totally replaces the reality on which it nevertheless depends. Tieck was to apply this principle in his own ironically satirical comedies, which in fact are more genuine Shakespearean offshoots than any one of the nineteenth-century plays that strove to transplant the Shakespearean sense of history onto German soil. And in 1843 in Berlin Tieck directed what was the first "unaltered" production of A Midsummer Night's Dream. (It coincided with the comparable effort by Elizabeth Vestris and Charles Mathews in London.) Even if much of the popular success of Tieck's production may have been attributable to its lavish choreography, painted setting, and Mendelssohn's music, he did convey a sense of the Shakespearean dramaturgy of continuous performance, which he had grasped better than the scholars. It was of course with sheer delight that audiences of this and subsequent productions of the Dream responded. Even a realist such as Rümelin had nothing to object, thinking of A Midsummer Night's Dream as being "not a profound or substantial, but the most delightful and original work of our poet."[32] Max Reinhardt in 1905 exploited the techniques of realist theater to create the fantastic illusion, thus undercutting the German Shakespeare myth at a time when its canonization had reached its most dogmatic stage. And A Midsummer Night's Dream was to remain a source of inspiration that allowed many theater directors to develop their practical approaches to the staging of Shakespeare. For Reinhardt's own theater work this comedy was, of course, a permanent test case: his thirteen productions of it included one in the park of the Palazzo Pitti in Florence as well as the Hollywood film. The Dream was no less central to Otto Falckenberg's achievements in Munich; in his four productions the comedy progressively changed into a nightmare, revealing what he described as "a dangerous play with the power of the darkness of human nature"; that revelation was, moreover, assisted by R. A. Schröder's robust new translation and by the partly dissonant music of Carl Orff, which replaced the more harmonious Mendelssohn tunes.

Postwar productions of the *Dream* moved further in this direction, especially in the 1960s when some of them exhibited the anarchy and the dangerous drugs of a green world to which young people rebelling against law and order were exposed. In the 1970s Peter Brook's Royal Shakespeare Company production set a new standard; for the next decade hardly any German production remained unaffected by its impact—a fact that also proves that the theatrical exploration of Shakespeare had by then become an international affair. This occurred when, in the early 1970s, the iconoclastic treatment of Shakespeare and other classics was well under way, when Shakespeare performances released a free play of fragmentation and association, when the act of retranslating the text became part of the productions, when Jan Kott became a major influence, when progressive directors separated Shakespeare productions from the opulence of conventional stages—Peter Zadek in Bochum had *King Lear* performed in an old cinema and *Hamlet* in a factory hall; and Peter Stein produced *As You Like It* in a huge Berlin film studio, where the audience were made to share the characters' theatrical hardships in the Forest of Arden. None of this required a nationalist impulse or a specifically German imagination. One could conclude that "unser Shakespeare" has indeed proved to be no more than a "myth."

Notes

1. Recent documentations include Hansjürgen Blinn, ed., *Shakespeare-Rezeption: Die Diskussion um Shakespeare in Deutschland*, 2 vols. (Berlin: Erich Schmidt, 1982, 1988), and Wolfgang Stellmacher, ed., *Auseinandersetzung mit Shakespeare*, 2 vols. (Berlin: Akademie-Verlag, 1976, 1985).

2. From a comparative point of view the relativity of Lessing's importance as "discoverer" of Shakespeare has been pointed out repeatedly; see, for example, Roger Bauer, ed., *Das Shakespeare-Bild in Europa zwischen Aufklärung und Romantik* (Bern: Lang, 1988), 9; and Kenneth E. Larson, "Traditions and New Directions in the Study of French and German Shakespeare Reception," *Michigan Germanic Studies* 15 (1989): 103–13.

3. See Rudoph Genée, *Geschichte der Shakespeareschen Dramen in Deutschland* (Leipzig: Engelmann, 1870), 218.

4. Johann Friedrich Schütze, *Hamburgische Theatergeschichte* (Hamburg, 1794), quoted in Jocza Savits, *Shakespeare und die Bühne des Dramas* (Bonn: Cohen, 1917), 31. Translations of this and subsequent quotations from German sources are the present author's.

5. Goethe, "Shakespeare und kein Ende!" in Stellmacher, *Shakespeare*, 2:65.

6. Gisbert Frhr. von Vincke, "Zur Geschichte der deutschen Shakespeare-Bearbeitung," *Shakespeare Jahrbuch* 17 (1882): 84.

7. A. W. Schlegel, in Stellmacher, *Shakespeare*, 2:125.

8. See Karl von Holtei, *Briefe an Ludwig Tieck* (Breslau, 1864), 3:227.

9. Cf. Jonathan Bate, "The Politics of Romantic Shakespeare Criticism: Germany, England, France," *European Romantic Review* 1 (1990): 4ff.

10. In K. W. F. Solger's review of A. W. Schlegel's *Vorlesungen über dramatische Kunst und Literatur*, rpt. in Solger, *Erwin. Vier Gespräche über das Schöne und der Kunst*, ed. W. Henckmann (Munich: Fink, 1971), 445.

11. See Walter Muschg, "Deutschland ist Hamlet," *Deutsche Shakespeare-Gesellschaft West, Jahrbuch* 1965: 32–58.

12. In *Die romantische Schule* (1835); see Heinrich Heine, *Historisch-kritische Gesamtausgabe der Werke*, ed. M. Windfuhr (Hamburg: Hoffmann und Campe, 1979), 8/1:168.

13. Hermann Ulrici, *Shakespeares dramatische Kunst*, 2nd ed. (Leipzig, 1847), 3:211.

14. Ulrici, *Shakespeares dramatische Kunst*, 3:216.

15. G. G. Gervinus, *Shakespeare* (Leipzig: Engelmann, 1849–50), quoted from 4th ed. (1872), 1:xi; Gervinus, *Geschichte der deutschen Dichtung* (Leipzig, 1841–42).

16. Quoted from Edgar Gross, "Grillparzers Verhältnis zu Shakespeare," *Shakespeare Jahrbuch* 51 (1915): 6f.

17. Hermann Hettner, *Das moderne Drama* (1852), rpt. in *Dramaturgische Schriften des 19. Jahrhunderts*, ed. Klaus Hammer (Berlin: Henschel, 1987), 1:586.

18. Published in book form: Gustav Rümelin, *Shakespearestudien* (Stuttgart: Cotta, 1866).

19. This point was particularly emphasized by Roderich Benedix in his *Shakespearomanie* (Stuttgart: Cotta, 1873).

20. See Hermann Ulrici, "Über Shakespeares Fehler und Mängel," *Shakespeare Jahrbuch* 3 (1868): 1–19; Wilhelm Oechelhäuser, "Shakespeares Werth für unsere nationale Literatur," *Shakespeare Jahrbuch* 5 (1870): 148–53.

21. Bismarck's Shakespeare quotations were collected in Arthur Böthelingk, *Bismarck und Shakespeare* (Stuttgart: Cotta, 1908).

22. Ulrici, "Jahresbericht," *Shakespeare Jahrbuch* 2 (1867): 3.

23. Gustav Liebau, *William Shakespeares Leben und Dichten* (Gera, 1873), 50; F. A. Leo, "Rückblick," *Shakespeare Jahrbuch* 24 (1889): 4; August Koberstein, *Vermischte Aufsätze zur Litteraturgeschichte und Ästhetik* (Leipzig, 1858), 221; Gervinus, *Shakespeare*, 1:viii.

24. Gerhardt Hauptmann, "Deutschland und Shakespeare," *Shakespeare Jahrbuch* 51 (1915): xii.

25. See, for instance, Karl Fulda, *William Shakespeare: Eine neue Studie über sein Leben und Dichten* (Marburg: Ehrhardt, 1875), 125.

26. See B. Tschischwitz, *Nachklänge germanischer Mythe in den Werken Shakespeares* (Halle, 1865), 1.

27. Ludwig Fulda, *Shakespeare Jahrbuch* 37 (1901): xliii.

28. Cf. W. Wetz, "Zur Beurteilung der sogenannten Schlegel-Tieckschen Shakespeare-Übersetzung," *Englische Studien* 28 (1900): 321–65.

29. Werner Habicht, "Shakespeare and Theatre Politics in the Third Reich," in *The Play out of Context*, ed. Hanna Scolnicov and Peter Holland (Cambridge: Cambridge University Press, 1989), 112–20.

30. Wilhelm Franz, *Shakespeare als Kulturkraft in Deutschland und England* (Tübingen: Kloeres, 1916), 40.

31. Quoted in Wilhelm Widmann, *Hamlets Bühnenlaufbahn* (Leipzig: Tauchnitz, 1931), 219.

32. Rümelin, *Shakespearestudien*, 125.

Shakespeare's Comic Locations

ANN BLAKE

In this century of collapsing empires and breaking nations, questions of national identity become metaphorically as well as literally sites of conflict. What Terence Hawkes wrote in *That Shakespeherian Rag* in 1986 about world events having "to some degree brought into focus the matter of the definition, limits and specific character of 'Englishness'" is even more true now than it was then. Shakespeare's role as national poet and emblem of England is under vigorous reexamination. Hawkes has argued that the establishment early this century of the academic study of English was for some Britons a response to a perception of national emergency—the natural order of things was under threat. Shakespeare, a "powerful ideological weapon, always available in periods of crisis," was invoked to give prestige to a study designed to promote a conservatively defined "Englishness."[1] A related collection of essays, edited by Graham Holderness, describes how what he calls a "Shakespeare myth" functions in contemporary culture to sustain false notions of "unity, integration and harmony" within British society.[2] Cartelli's essay "Prospero in Africa," one of many that consider the relation of Shakespeare and "Englishness" abroad, argues that Shakespeare's *The Tempest* has itself contributed to colonialist ideology.[3] It is well known that performances of the plays have been shaped to serve perceived national needs. Olivier's patriotic *Henry V* (1944) was seen, and funded, as part of the war effort. On the other hand, Adrian Noble used his 1984 RSC production of the same play to make a protest against the government's Falklands campaign. Currently in England, the fury of the protest at the reduction of the amount of Shakespeare in the new National School Curriculum is (according to some) a response to the perceived threat to national sovereignty posed by the prospect of imminent closer ties between the United Kingdom and the European Economic Community. Letters to the newspapers invoke the name of Shakespeare as if he were John Bull.

Arguments about the cultural importance of Shakespeare to the construction and manipulation of ideas of "Englishness" depend first on his acknowledged position as the greatest English writer or, in the language of a postcolonial critic, the author of "culturally privileged texts."[4] The second essential factor is that Shakespeare wrote massively about England. He is Poet of England as well as England's poet. Not only did he write ten plays of English history but there is also a wealth of reference to English places and to the material details of English life contained in his plays: the landscape, trees, flowers, animals, customs, work, pastimes, and the weather. "Elizabethan England is reflected everywhere in Shakespeare's works," says the preface to *Shakespeare's England*.[5] To the great, and often sentimental, gratification of the natives of England, Shakespeare is seen as a recorder and celebrant of English life and thus a creator of a sense of continuity with the glorious past. But what can be said of his attitudes to other nations and places? Is it only possible to construct Shakespeare as a national emblem, to quote him (selectively) as a patriotic poet, because the plays have little engagement in a "world elsewhere"?

Since much of the evidence that might be adduced to answer that question suggests either an indifference to "abroad" or a neglect of the otherness of other countries, it is important to recollect first how powerfully the plays dramatize the experience of anyone separated from their native land, England or any other place. The bewildering experiences of Antipholus of Syracuse in Ephesus depend in part on the existence, unknown to him, of his twin brother, but as far as he is concerned this is what happens when one is abroad in a strange country. He wonders who he is, and when he meets and falls in love with Luciana, he invites her to redefine him in any way she pleases. For Sebastian in *Twelfth Night* there is a happier sense of liberation and erotic reward when traveling in strange places. However, though he rejoices to lose himself in a world in which he finds Olivia, the most moving episode is his reunion with Viola and thus with the world he knows. When Mowbray in *Richard II* receives the sentence of banishment he sees his fate as "speechless death," (1.3.172), the loss of his language more painful than physical absence: "My native English, now I must forgo" (1.3.160). Coriolanus, who acknowledges no ties, responds to banishment by declaring "There is a world elsewhere" (3.3.135). Mowbray, to whom banishment from where people speak his language amounts to the loss of himself, also finds no distinction to be

made: "now no way can I stray; / Save back to England, all the
world's my way" (1.3.206–7).

Mowbray's judgment that, since all places other than England
are foreign they are inferior and much the same, is not the impression given by Shakespeare's plays, though at times he is remarkably careless about his exact location. Certainly he exhibits
none of the simple patriotism that made certain of his contemporaries' plays so popular. His *Henry V,* unlike *The Famous Victo-
ries of Henry V,* can be made to carry either a jingoistic or a
skeptical reading, or both.[6] Katherine's English and Henry's
French are both objects of amusement. Another contemporary
dramatist interested in other nationalities and their languages
was William Houghton. He too shows himself capable of resisting stereotypical thinking about other nationalities. In his
contribution to *Patient Grissil* (1599), as well as airing his knowledge of Welsh, he includes the foolish courtier, Emulo, who tries
to push the blame for his folly onto Italy:

> Emu: Oh patience be thou my fortification: *Italy* thou spurnest me
> for vttering that nutriment, which I suckt from thee.
> Far[nezie]: How *Italy*? away you ideot: *Italy* infects you not, but your
> own diseased spirits: *Italy*? out you froth, you scumme, because
> your soule is mud, and that you have breathed in *Italy,* you'll say
> *Italy* haue defiled you: away you bore, thou wilt wallow in the
> sweetest countrie in the world.[7]

But in his own play *Englishmen for My Money,* that cheap English nationalistic dealing in European stereotypes—which, by
analogy with Said's "orientalism," deserves perhaps to be called
"continentalism"—runs riot. The villain here is a London usu-
rer, a Portuguese Jew, the heroes three young Englishmen who
intend to marry his three daughters to escape paying their debts
to him. Meanwhile the father has an un-English desire to marry
his daughters to a Dutchman, a Frenchman, and a Spaniard. But
these three, gullible, awkward, and unattractive, are no fit husbands for the sisters. The foreigners are mocked when they speak
their own languages, mocked when they speak broken English,
and subjected to a series of uncomfortable practical jokes no
doubt to the delighted applause of much of the audience. The
play was very popular.[8] Shakespeare treats the nations and natives of Europe more evenhandedly than this. All but one of his
comedies are set outside England (or two if *Cymbeline,* set in
Britain, is counted as English) and in them a Portia will ridicule
the English along with the rest. Similarly, Dromio of Syracuse

gives England no special privilege in his topographic analogies for the body of Nell the kitchen wench in *Err.* 3.2.114–39.

I cannot consider here the presentation of England's various enemies in the history plays and must content myself with one remark. Although some recent productions of *Henry V* might suggest that Shakespeare consistently ridicules the French with their flowery speech and overconfidence, by the end of the play they emerge with some dignity and respect for their suffering. If it is easy to see that Shakespeare avoids the blatant nationalism of some of his contemporaries, it is less easy to define how far he travels imaginatively outside England. He evinces little obvious enthusiasm for the achievements of the voyagers and explorers of his century: "Shakespeare did not write of the new-found new world or the new-found old world as momentous additions to the world in which his characters lived and moved," wrote J. D. Rogers in *Shakespeare's England.*[9] In spite of the "brave new world" of *The Tempest*, there is not in Shakespeare's works that excitement which manifests itself in the poetry of Donne. Shakespeare's reference to the new map of 1600 "with th'augmentation of the Indies," as Rogers points out, "like most of his passages referring to 'the beyond,' is little more than an aside," a joking reference to the lines on Malvolio's face when he smiles. Shakespeare's world is centered on Rome and Athens, in what Rogers calls the old Mediterranean plays, and in Italy in the new Mediterranean plays. Beyond Europe Shakespeare, unlike his contemporary, Hakluyt, saw a misty region that "contained islands only, not continents." It was, Rogers concludes, Europe that fascinated Shakespeare: "his real living and working world consisted of the fifteen or more kingdoms of Europe" (173).

If this is so, he was careless and disengaged in his evocation of it. The notorious blunder in *The Winter's Tale* of giving Bohemia a seacoast has been excused by editors as copied from the source, Greene's *Pandosto*. For whatever reason, Shakespeare did not correct him. In *Two Gentlemen of Verona*, Verona is "misdescribed as a tidal port" (Rogers, 171), and there is no explanation of how Helena in *All's Well* sets out from Rossillion for the shrine of St. James of Compostella and arrives at Florence. Details of physical geography are immaterial: his imagination is not traveling across a map of Europe. This impression is confirmed by the standard authority on Shakespeare's references to place, E. H. Sugden, compiler of *A Topographical Dictionary to the Works of Shakespeare and His Fellow Dramatists.*[10] This remarkable volume, which records and annotates all place names in Shakespeare, four hundred contemporary plays, and a considerable number of important nondramatic works, including *Paradise Lost*, is one of those monumental volumes of Shakespeare scholarship compiled in the first part of the century, as a tribute to and affirmation of the national poet. This particular huge labor is of special interest since it was produced, virtually singlehandedly, "outside England," in that far-flung part of the empire, Melbourne, where Sugden was the first master of Queen's College. And in common with other Shakespeare works published during or soon after the war, it pays tribute to a poignant sense of "Englishness" since it is dedicated to the thirty members of Queen's College who died in the Great War.

Sugden must have known more about Shakespeare's sense of place outside England than anyone, but sadly his modesty led him to leave the dictionary entries to speak for themselves. He provided no overview of his labors, except a brief description of his methods. Valuable general remarks can however be found in the entries for countries. Under "Italy" Sugden notes that a quarter of all Elizabethan and Jacobean plays were set in Italy. In them there is, says Sugden authoritatively, "hardly any local colour" (278). The substantial entry on "Rome" points to the one location outside England in Shakespeare's plays where the sense of place is developed, and which has therefore attracted scholarly discussion. Those who argue for a particular Shakespearean understanding of Rome have much to go on, names of places, buildings, institutions, practices, festivals, food, clothes, that large body of detail attached to Plutarch's narratives of the Noble Greeks and Romans, and to Latin sources. When he turned to the plebeians, Shakespeare found that the social bias of history left him ill-informed. The result was, in *Julius Caesar*, an "English" Roman crowd of tradesmen, led by a punning cobbler who speaks English proverbs.

The fullest impressions of actual places outside England are to be found in Shakespeare's more serious plays. Rome, Egypt in *Antony and Cleopatra*, Scotland in *Macbeth* are significant as places of a distinctive culture. What makes this possible is a wealth of consistent reference to physical features, weather, place-names, and familiar historical events.

The comedies, on the other hand, have only the lightest definition of place. In giving them a foreign setting, however sketchy, Shakespeare goes against the practice of much contemporary English comedy. A vogue in the last years of the sixteenth century for middle-class comedies set in an English town may partly explain why *The Merry Wives* is set in England.[11] With all the rest set in foreign countries, Shakespeare's practice stands out sharply against that of Ben Jonson, who moved his one non-English comedy, *Every Man In His Humour*, back to London from Italy. The contrast is just as noticeable between Shakespeare's romantic comedies of the 1590s, which look back to Greene and Peele, and those of the early 1600s by Dekker, Middleton, and others, some satirical, some sentimental, but all set in England and usually London. (Sugden's figure of a quarter of all plays in the period being set in Italy is bolstered by the numerous English tragedies of Italian vice and some satirical comedies set in Italian courts, such as Marston's *The Fawn*.)

In choosing a setting Shakespeare is most often led by his source, if he has one. Sometimes a more familiar place is substituted for an unusual one. Thus Epidamnum in the *Menaechmi* becomes Ephesus in *The Comedy of Errors*, better known and also associated with witchcraft and sorcery. "Julio," the setting of *Promos and Cassandra*, which, Sudgen explains, is Gyula in Hungary (289), becomes Vienna in *Measure for Measure*. The plays thus acquire "a local habitation and a name," but rarely more than that. Rather than tying the dramatist down, the named setting becomes a license to enter what, in a phrase rather worn after the 1980s' preoccupation with nationalism and literature, we call "countries of the mind."

The location of Shakespeare's comedy establishes itself as a country of the mind above all by its eclecticism. These lightly identified foreign places easily accommodate episodes of distinctively English life. Dogberry, Verges, and the Watch are found in the streets of Messina, Bottom and the mechanicals, as English in detail as the recruits in Shallow's Gloucestershire, in the wood near Athens. An English country schoolmaster and curate appear in the park of Navarre. Launcelot Gobbo and his father keep a "fill-horse" called Dobbin in Venice.[12] The forest of Arden in *As You Like It* may be originally the Ardennes, but when the sheep farmer Corin is on stage, it is a Warwickshire forest (Sugden, 28). Creatures of romance, lions, and serpents live there, along with Mediterranean olive trees, but the hunting and sheep are English, and so, intermittently, are the scenery and weather.

In this century some critics have praised certain of the comedies set in Italy for authentic Italianness, identifying them as "Italianate." Admirers of Shakespeare's Italian local colour quoted by Mario Praz include one who finds "'a pure Paduan atmosphere' hanging about *The Taming of the Shrew*" (Praz, 96).

F. P. Wilson quotes Stopford Brook's assertion that *Much Ado* is
"Italianate 'in sentiment, in morals, in evil and good passions,
in its high honour and villainy, in its scenery, pageantry and
love of war'" in order to dismiss it as inaccurate, and "a little
highhanded" in repudiating responsibility for villainy (Wilson,
87). Wilson rightly exposes the naive "continentalism" of the
impulse to define Italians as passionate, extreme, sensationalists.

Here the Italian Mario Praz's account of Shakespeare's Italy,
along with his comments on others' opinions, is a valuable
counter. He agrees with G. K. Hunter that in English comedy
before 1600 Italy presents a "traditional romantic image," derived from Ariosto and Castiglione (Praz, 96). Hunter calls it a
courtly place: "This is the Italy of the *Cortegiano*, of courtship
in both senses of the term, and of Euphues' proverb, 'If I be in
Crete I can lie, in Greece I can shift, if in Italy I can court it.'"[13]
This defines the Italy of, for instance, *The Two Gentlemen of
Verona*, though admittedly it is hard to distinguish it from the
places that Shakespeare calls Navarre or Paris. With English trav-
elers excluded from Spain by the hostility of the Inquisition,
Italy, then the most cosmopolitan of European countries, was the
most attractive destination, and the plays offer a golden image
of the young man on a grand tour of courts and universities.

Praz's study of the Italian detail in Shakespeare's comedies
underlines their thoroughly eclectic principles. Though Shakespeare certainly had some knowledge of the northern Italian
towns Verona, Padua, Milan, and more of Venice, extending to
acquaintance with the forms of government and customs, the
comedies demonstrate no interest in maintaining a sense of national differences. In Italian towns the taverns have English
names, and the people sing English ballads. As for "the curious
problem of Shakespeare's Italian geography," when Shakespeare
writes of traveling between these cities his imagination turns to
London. Verona is a city on a tidal waterway, Milan is "in a
waterway communicating with the sea." Shakespeare is "using
Milan and Verona as mere labels."[14]

In a comedy set in London, the London audience enjoys hearing reference from the stage to the familiar places of their day-
to-day life. This pleasure was combined in the satirical comedy
of, for instance, Jonson and Middleton, with the ridicule of exaggerated local types. The audience is doubly flattered, by a presentation of its own world, and by being positioned where it may
look down on other people's follies. In Shakespeare's romantic
comedy, that distance between audience and play, which comedy

needs to thrive, is established differently and with distinctive effects. His audience is shifted from the London theater to a foreign place, but one with a reasonably familiar label. There, rather than face a version of its own world, the audience finds itself at once positioned at a distance from the foreign figures. In this setting anything can happen, any human behavior becomes plausible. Freed by the setting from the expectations of satirical comedy to provide a cast of recognizable types, the satirical figures in this landscape, such as Malvolio and Parolles, can be woven into the wider concerns of the comedy. Moreover, here Shakespeare has the liberty to incorporate, with casual ease, the strange, even the supernatural, for within the multiple dimensions of the foreign settings are found what Anne Barton describes as "fantasy worlds, places that never were on sea or land, where life has something of the qualities of a dream." These include Portia's house over the sea at Belmont, forests in *The Two Gentlemen of Verona*, *A Midsummer Night's Dream*, and *As You Like It*, and the park of Navarre. Even in *The Comedy of Errors*, *The Taming of the Shrew*, *The Merry Wives of Windsor*, and *Much Ado about Nothing*, there are, Barton finds, "shadowy traces of this pattern of movement from an ordinary world to a second, somehow magical, environment in which characters are transformed."[15] The fantasy world is the place where wonder is made familiar. It promotes a temporary illusion of belief in extraordinary good luck, fortunate coincidences, and, most important, the possibility of self-realization and happy transformation to which Barton refers, and which has been explored in recent critical writing on these comedies. These places are versions of pastoral, not limited by the conditions of the everyday, and marked off by two boundaries, one only in *Twelfth Night* and *The Tempest* where fantasy world and foreign setting coalesce. Northrop Frye's influential analysis of Shakespeare's romantic comedy traces a movement into and back from "the drama of the green world," which he describes as having "affinities with the medieval tradition of the seasonal ritual play."[16] Records now being gathered and published from the south of England establish the persistence of these traditions into the sixteenth century. In these romantic comedies the public theaters mirrored those summer festivals, associated with church ales, morris dancing, and Robin Hood plays, all distant descendants of pre-Christian summer rituals celebrating fertility. From one angle nothing could seem more quintessentially English than festivals of morris dancing and Robin Hood plays. Yet in those surviving forms of ancient ritual the participants enter into a place and time of celebration, distinct and set apart. To this Shakespeare's comedies with their foreign settings offer an interestingly close analogy: they too transport their audience to a place that, nominally foreign, both is and is not England.

Notes

1. Terence Hawkes, *That Shakespeherian Rag* (London: Methuen, 1986), 122, 68.

2. Graham Holderness, preface to *The Shakespeare Myth*, ed. Holderness (Manchester: Manchester University Press, 1988), xiii.

3. Thomas Cartelli, "Prospero in Africa: *The Tempest* as Colonialist Text and Pretext," in *Shakespeare Reproduced: The Text in History and Ideology*, ed. Jean E. Howard and Marion F. O'Connor (New York: Methuen, 1987), 99–115.

4. Cartelli, "Prospero in Africa," 100.

5. *Shakespeare's England*, 2 vols. (Oxford: Clarendon Press, 1917), 1:vi.

6. This position is most impressively presented in Norman Rabkin's account of the play, "Either/Or: Responding to *Henry V*," in *Shakespeare and the Problem of Meaning* (Chicago: University of Chicago Press, 1981), 33–62.

7. Thomas Dekker, Henry Chettle, and William Houghton, *Patient Grissil*, in *The Dramatic Works of Thomas Dekker*, ed. Fredson Bowers (Cambridge: Cambridge University Press, 1962), 1:248.

8. William Houghton, *Englishmen for My Money: A Select Collection of Old English Plays*, ed. W. Carew Hazlitt (1874–76; rpt. New York: Benjamin Blom, 1964), 5:469–564. The play, first acted in 1598, was published, according to "The Preface to the Former Edition," no less than three times, in 1616, 1626, and 1631 (Houghton, 471).

9. J. D. Rogers, "Voyages and Exploration: Geography: Maps," *Shakespeare's England*, 2 vols. (Oxford: Clarendon Press, 1917), 1:174. Hereafter referred to as Rogers.

10. Edward H. Sugden, *A Topographical Dictionary to the Works of Shakespeare and His Fellow Dramatists* (1925; rpt. Hildesheim: Georg Olms, 1969). Hereafter referred to as Sugden.

11. F. P. Wilson, *Shakespearian and Other Studies*, ed. Helen Gardner (Oxford: Clarendon Press, 1969), 89–90. Hereafter referred to as Wilson.

12. Mario Praz, "Shakespeare's Italy," *Shakespeare Survey 7*, ed. Allardyce Nicholl (Cambridge: Cambridge University Press, 1954), 99. Hereafter referred to as Praz.

13. G. K. Hunter, "English Folly and Italian Vice," in *Jacobean Shakespeare*, ed. John Russell Brown and Bernard Harris, Stratford-upon-Avon Studies 1 (London: Edward Arnold, 1960), 93.

14. Praz 98, 98, 100. Praz (96–98) reports that Bardolators have been at work ingeniously explaining away these errors, but not to his satisfaction.

15. Anne Barton, introduction to *Twelfth Night*, *The Riverside Shakespeare*, ed. G. Blakemore Evans (Boston: Houghton Mifflin, 1974), 405.

16. Northrop Frye, *The Anatomy of Criticism: Four Essays* (Princeton: Princeton University Press, 1971), 182.

Shakespeare Outside England: "Much More Monstrous Matter of Feast"

Trevor Code

"A miracle is a monster." R. W. Emerson: (miracle . . . theatre/ carnival . . . monster . . . miracle)

I

"Much more monstrous matter of feast": this piece of heavy alliteration is articulated by that quintessential Roman cynic, Enobarbus, when questioned in Rome about the excesses of Alexandrian feasting:

> Ay, sir, we did sleep day out of countenance, and made the night light with drinking.
> *Maecenas:* Eight wild-boars roasted whole at a breakfast, and but twelve persons there; is this true?
> *Enobarbus:* This was but as a fly by an eagle; we had much more monstrous matter of feast, which worthily deserv'd noting.

And then Maecenas makes the transition, as if it is not transition but the most natural consequence in the world—or is he drawing Enobarbus on?

> She's a most triumphant lady, if report be square to her.
> (2.2.177–85)

There follows, of course, the passage many readers find to be the most memorable in the whole of *Antony and Cleopatra*, Enobarbus's evocation of the erotic, overwhelming, myth-associated Cleopatra, a passage that has often been anthologized as a separate poem, and which became the model for T. S. Eliot's famous parody in *The Waste Land*.

111

The much more monstrous matter of feast in which Enobarbus is engaged is concerned with, first, the confirmation of a wild life of parties, of extreme hedonism and gluttony, eight roasted boars to twelve men at breakfast, of which we may see the court of Cleopatra as the great provider. In addition to this, the extended presentation of the lady herself is given in terms of beauty, sexuality, and what appears to be almost a religion of sensual excess. But the main element of feast, here, is the feast of information, of gossip, tale, rumor, or report. Such feasting depends on ambivalence of perception, or ambiguity in the display itself, and on the various textures of moral judgment. There is always a gap between the event and the telling.

It has often been seen as a problem of the play that this over-the-top piece is presented to the audience by the outspoken cynic who has been ordered to keep silent earlier in the same scene, when he had sought to utter warnings against the marriage.

> Go to then—your considerate stone.
>
> (110)

But one obvious interpretation of Enobarbus's speech is that here is the description of how Antony fell and was trapped, why the luxury of the Egyptian world is so attractive, and why Antony will inevitably return to it. The description comes at the end of the scene in which Antony has made an uneasy and mechanical peace with Caesar, and has agreed to a loveless and mechanical marriage of convenience to the widow Octavia, and there is no doubt that it counterbalances what is ominous in that scene with its most eloquent release of poetry.

Yet there are several further comments to make about this set piece. First, it is delivered in Rome among a group of Roman soldiers, within the rules of a male club with its ribaldry and distortion. Second, quite obviously the speech depends upon absence, and raises important theoretical questions about the nature of presence in literary texts and play texts. The highest levels of presence in a prose fiction are created by just such memorable word pictures. The reader creates the vision: we think we see Cleopatra, and countless critics of this scene have apparently attested they have done so, just as many readers, particularly in the nineteenth century, preferred Shakespearean play texts as private reading. Third, a close reading of the scene will show how it mirrors theater with its attention to trappings and analogy: the mystique is created by telling us that "For her own person, / It beggar'd all description" (197–98), and that she is comparable to the classical Venus. There is no direct portraiture of Cleopatra in the scene: in a significant way, she is not there, even in the speech. This is followed in turn by Enobarbus's memorable judgment:

> Age cannot wither her, nor custom stale
> Her infinite variety.
>
> (2.2.234–35)

This is really about male attitudes and male genital sex. Cleopatra is stereotyped as gypsy-whore and as captive-queen. Our aesthetic pleasures in the play are confounded or confused with moral explorations that appear to be foregrounded in Plutarch, and which have bedeviled the story in later hands, whether Dryden's, who effectively rewrote this play in his *All for Love*, or various later interpretations, including film.

The opening of the play is a comic love scene, where the tension of civic business is held against the passion of the lovers' affairs, but where trouble in turn is caused by Antony's wife, Fulvia, as *general*, a factor too easily forgotten when one encounters Cleopatra's fatal efforts at leadership. The Roman world is mainly one of soldiers and bureaucrats. Cleopatra's world in contrast is a freak show, almost a *Commedia* display. Alexandria is a play world of changeability, her play with him, set within a filmic technique within the scenes themselves. There is a tension between Antony's duty and his play world. Is Cleopatra's world really the theater?

Of course, it is a well-worn truth that art is about absence, and even exists because of absence. The event is narrated because it happens elsewhere; the character is described because absent; the picture is hung on the wall to stand for an absent entity. Poetry and prose fiction are constantly about what is not present, a point that Paul de Man brought to bear as a critique of romantic epiphanies.[1] But here we are discussing theater, Shakespearean theater, and this focuses the question in terms of the way in which information is transmitted in the theater. What is an action? What do we see? What happens? Clearly a character may tell or narrate an event, whether it be one of those essential messengers in Greek drama, or whether it be such a powerful set piece as the drowning of Ophelia, that absent event that so many painters have found it necessary to fill. Such absence is not theatrical illusion: "Is this a dagger that I see before me?" Nor is it the imaginary vision that underlies theater: "When we speak of horses, think that you see them." It is, instead, the confirmation of absence. What takes place away from the stage may be part of the story, may even herald presence or display, but it might also be testimony to remoteness, to the essential gap that exists in time and place between the character with her setting and the stage where the narration takes place, as in this case. Cleopatra is not in Rome. The play itself is very much concerned with these gaps in information.

Antony and Cleopatra is a play in which little action happens on the stage, but where a large amount of information is carried by the various reports, rumors, and reminiscences. It is also a play with great ebbs and flows of fortune and with considerable instability in main characters. There are discrepancies within the play itself, not only between the accounts of different characters, but also within the speeches of the principal roles, not to mention the significant gaps between this play and *Julius Caesar*.

One of the problems of the barge scene must be its embarrassing fidelity to Plutarch. In Shakespeare's text, presented at a time when a large proportion of the audience would have recognized the closeness to Plutarch, this scene gives a very recognizable reading, almost book-in-hand. In spite of the wonderful scholarship of Adelman and others,[2] I don't think of Will Shakespeare spending hours on scholarly research for this play. But how does one dramatize North's Plutarch? How does one turn it into a major theatrical piece, even if it is one that is so apparently misunderstood in production? Which scenes have to be given to a character as narrator? Which are to be played out as a presence? How will these decisions change the reception and the actual information that is delivered? Film directors have inevitably been attracted to the barge scene as visual image. One can't escape the clear-cut textuality of the speech.

And in a play where identities themselves are so fragmentary, Cleopatra cannot be a presence in Rome. Hypothetically, she may be brought to Rome as a captive, to be led in Caesar's triumphs before patriotic mobs. A major preoccupation of act 5 is the plotting and the escape from this possibility. Denying her presence in the one sense, she may be presented in the theater by a boy.

> and I shall see
> Some squeaking Cleopatra boy my greatness
> I' th' posture of a whore.

> (5.2.219–21)

But this, if we accept Shakespeare's attribution to the conventions of his theater, is what his Jacobean audience has been viewing: the transgression or discrepancy of Cleopatra as impersonated by a boy actor. Here is the centralist sideshow by which the monstrous may be exhibited rather than simply reported, becoming a presence through the expedience of that transgressing group close to the town and outside the town, close to the court and outside the court, by the whorehouse, bearbaiting world that disports itself alongside the seat of power, the carnival outside the citadel.

Caesar's need to bring Cleopatra to Rome for exhibition is significant: he is clearly willing to use various strategies and treachery to achieve this. And yet he boasts of his rectitude and his true "writing." The appearance of the presented Cleopatra is more important in his triumph than any diminution of image created by lies or tricks.

In *The Tempest* Trinculo and Stephano discuss bringing Caliban from the island for exhibition also—as a sideshow. The verbal slip, a comic and necessary one, is to propose exhibiting him in England, not Milan or Naples. Once again we are reminded: Caliban is not to be a presence in England except as a kind of sideshow, as presented through the medium of the theater. And in this character one encounters the discrepancy between a splendid poetic rhetoric in much of his speech, and the monster or mooncalf description given by those around him.

II

Now, in an essay supposedly concerned with Shakespeare outside England, it here appears that I have been led into a trap. That "much more monstrous matter of feast" may turn out to be the feast of the theater as presentation, even as sideshow presentation, of the monstrous, and therefore dehumanized and quintessential, other; but we seem to be engaged in a process of inevitable convergence or centripety, where the things are drawn to the center of power, and seen from its point of view. One even notes this in *Hamlet* in the equivocation over journeys to England, where the men are as mad as Hamlet is, the joke of the English actor-gravedigger. There is no doubt that Shakespeare's plays are firmly lodged in this English context. The current historicist researches are energetically directed to filling out more of the pattern of political and social events and discourses which surround their inception and early reception. There even seems the assumption that in this lies the meaning of the plays, giving to this supposed anulus of context an unexpected transcendence of its own.

In Renaissance England, the various Roman texts, Plutarch for example, were clearly read as a pattern of classical Roman antiquities and in turn as texts through which English society itself could be read. Automatically, Rome often came to stand for the political state, and hence for an analogy with the realm of England. So Shakespeare's Roman plays in turn were applicable to the English political scene concerning class, order, good government, and the role of empire. The analogy was all the more trenchant when one considers the costuming available for the plays. Not for Shakespeare the togas and tunics and fancy dress of a Hollywood epic of ancient Rome. Wearing the cast-off clothes of the deceased wealthy, Shakespeare's actors, including those portraying foreigners and those of other times, appeared as Elizabethan gentlemen and ladies. This is no mere historical byway, but a point of significance in considering presentation. Julius Caesar, Mark Antony, and Brutus appeared before an Elizabethan audience as Elizabethan nobles or generals, indeed, with the distinct possibility that the clothes might have been worn a short time before by now deceased members of their audience. We cannot really duplicate the identity this creates, either by playing in Elizabethan dress, or by our forced efforts in modern dress. How can the actors before us appear with but little gap, as ourselves?

Whether or not Gonzalo was mistaken in declaring "this Tunis . . . was Carthage" (Tempest, 2.1.86), it is much more certain that this Rome was their London. Analogically at least, the city in which a captive Cleopatra would have to be displayed if alive, and played by a boy actor if not, was London, and similarly the returning journey of Prospero and coterie was effectively to England also. We should note in passing how Italian or other European characters and plots gave the playwright license, through distancing, caricature, and assumed decadence, together of course with that special factor that the story be extant and writ in choice Italian and thus touch us not, as in Hamlet. This is all grist to the English political and creative mill—an English manufacture now exported along with worsted cloth and Rolls Royce engines (or ironware and cheap tin trays) to a waiting world.

Shakespeare in Australia has been an industry based on the provincial and colonial, or English, positioning of both players and audiences in this country. For example, the first Shakespeare I saw, the 1948 Antony Quayle *Macbeth*, was simply a tour of the English production. When our short-lived Arrow Theatre in Melbourne challenged the Stratford *Othello*, it was inevitably an English repertory challenge to a major British touring company, even though it used the Australian actors Frank Thring, Zoe Caldwell, and Alex Scott as its principals against Anthony Quayle, Barbara Jefford, and the expatriate Leo McKern. Peter Brook's *Midsummer Night's Dream* used that play to comment on contemporary Britain, and this version was played throughout Australia. Furthermore, in terms of values the plays may be seen as repeating a hierarchically structured map, template, imprint, or formula, displaying power and relationships in society—masked paradigms that may be put down in Germany, Russia, America, Japan, or Australia. "If you do the same thing, the outcome will be the same."

So who owns the Shakespearean text? American institutions traditionally have seen literature in English in two major groups: major British authors and major American authors. For some administrators, Shakespeare is not in either category, but is *Shakespeare*. As it has been explained to me, "We think of him as one of our own. We brought him to New England with us." Certainly the Jonsonian epithet of a man for all times is supported by thinking of immigrants with the collected Shakespeare in their luggage alongside that other book with black covers bringing their "real" English tradition to bear in this new English commonwealth. I am not sure whether Shakespeare is, in fact, an immigrant text in Australia in quite that sense.

In terms of this, *The Tempest* becomes a special case. No one these days seems to envisage Prospero's place of exile in *The Tempest* as a Mediterranean island. The play moves on a north-south axis between Europe and Africa, the courts of Italian civilization and the world of the dark king of Tunis to whom Claribel has just been married—shades of the marriage of Proserpina to Hades, and apparently for no reason of love, wealth, or diplomacy. The magical island inhabits an east-west axis too between Asian or Greek mythological islands with half-human creatures in the east and a new world with "such creatures in it" in the west.

It is momentous, and yet entirely predictable, that people who regard the author as theirs and who are situated at the western end of such an axis will read the play from its western extremity, placing the island perhaps in the vicinity of Bermuda, or even in New England, but certainly not in the Mediterranean Sea. In that sense, *The Tempest* has been seen as the first American play in English, and it was first a novelty, later a cliché, to present the play in just such American terms, with Caliban as American Indian, or black slave, or both. This is really quite significant in terms of the geography of the play. The American point of view has to be appreciated and assimilated.[3] It sees the play on a map between England and America but places the emphasis or viewpoint in America and thus judges the play to be about its own colonial period. So, according to one much repeated reading, Prospero has to give up his unjustly acquired power as his colonial conquest, and surrender Caliban's supposedly rightful kingdom. This is, after all, a strange reading to come from the descendants of these colonial venturers who stayed, and one intent on bending the play text to a new set of ideas, manifestly a postcolonial ideology in an imperial world—rather (I observe) like Claudius's attempts at prayer in *Hamlet*.

Such readings have in turn fed into English research on both sources and context of the initial writing, so that even from England the cartography spans the Atlantic, and we discover that the play partakes of colonial discourse. This attractive and now well-worn approach tends to highlight Caliban, turn attention away from much of the thematic court plotting and dispute, and significantly reposition us as audience somehow at this colonial end. The ship departs from us and our island. It is a simplification, but it produces a different place from which to view events, a late twentieth-century exercise of conscience, by an interpretation in the direction of the film *Dances with Wolves*. In considering the journeys that make *The Tempest* an American play, we might be perceiving it within a form of interrupted rite of passage: Milan/island/Milan, but with our focus only on the island as we are led to see the world from the undergrowth rather than as the court, a virgin space to which these outsiders come, and from which they depart. It is possible to view the play from that new world vantage, and if we do, some radical and even subversive changes are imposed on the centrality of all these discourses—that is, other plays too. More than that, we become caught up in a series of ongoing problems in assigning analogy to the whole text. Similarly, and by extension, *Antony and Cleopatra* is a play set in Alexandria, permeated by the atmosphere of the Alexandrian feast, and partaking of excursions to Rome (therefore England) in the process. While it appears to be about two worlds and while the Roman world invades the perspective in Alexandria at the outset, Alexandria is clearly the base and atmosphere of the location, clashing with the Roman viewpoint. We are positioned to view the action, and initially to judge from a Roman point of view. Alexandria is the margin or periphery away from Rome and its version of civilized or ordered power, and there is agitated movement back and forth on that axis. So although its power structure is Rome/Alexandria/Rome, the play appears to be structured: Alexandria/Rome and other fields/ Alexandria.

In *The Tempest* the power structure of the megasociety is actually drawn to the periphery, neutralized and reformulated. In *Antony and Cleopatra* the victory of Cæsar is seen as trivial, inevitable, and the victory contains both its defeat and the triumph of the alternative set of values. In *Othello* we may see that, although the Venice/Cyprus/Venice trek is completed, and is clearly centralist, the focus of action is on Cyprus as an exotic world in which the tragedy is possible.

What happens then if we take up the mental maps that such cartography makes available, and see the plays from the margin far flung from the center? How can we do this without being false to the supposed authenticity of the plays? In one sense such authenticity, if that is the word, is an expression of the centralist assertion, and is embodied in one view of the works as unproblematic schemata. But in another sense, the plays do it to themselves, certainly as the location begins to talk back within the plays. This is one of those senses in which the text is unstable and differs from itself. Furthermore, play texts are essentially incomplete, by definition so, to a degree that is beyond prose fiction. It depends on what one chooses to do in completing them. We have merely the record of the words that were spoken, and words are a minor part of the apocryphal or nascent completed text. Many more factors contribute to what happens in theatrical production, let alone the events that are deputed to be happening off stage as well. The fallacy of centralist structure is to delve into the image or word, seeking for its true meaning, and even for a cosy range of ambiguities, whereas the meaning of the play often resides in what we put around or alongside the text. And these decisions are often quite independent or arbitrary. There is no necessary causal interpretative reason within the text for the decisions taken to complete it.

If we take these cartographical plays and decide to look at what is outside England, what do we perceive in terms of reality and unreality, presence and absence, narration and illusion, lies and deception? If we read *Antony and Cleopatra* through the character of Cleopatra and her ambience or *The Tempest* possibly through a Caliban, we commit ourselves to fresh invention in a host of ways.

However, the American appropriation of *The Tempest* is in itself deceptive. Had such a position been proposed in, for example, 1650, that would have been one thing, but to appropriate the play in the second half of the twentieth century is simply doing so when the center of colonial or imperial power has shifted, when the power center or citadel might not be England, but might indeed be that America; or when England and America as Milan and Naples might play venturers to some other third world "island." America equally is the citadel of power, and even the excellent discussions in Howard and O'Connor's *Shakespeare Reproduced* show how neatly the imperial world of Shakespeare studies is divided between these two imperial edifices.[4] Both represent the centralist or power position of the plays and both are thus represented in turn by the London/Rome/Milan center. By simple analogy the citadel may equally be that governmental position or power in any society such as Germany or Russia, so that fresh or touring productions may simply repeat the same political imprint wherever placed. But the island, or Alexandria, or even Cyprus, is always on the outside. Such locations of otherness define themselves as quasi-colonial, or quasi-provincial, not by declaring a new center, but by proclaiming their alterity.

III

In 1978 I wrote a discussion of *The Tempest* in which I suggested that Prospero, after the epilogue to that play, moves like the rest of us out of the theater into the London street.[5] I had never been to England, but having unwittingly positioned myself and my readers as honorary English, I later rewrote the passage to make the outside street more general. The message is there, however. We are positioned by the English and class assumptions of these texts, and we move within their ideologies.

Yet the country in which we read or perform, and hold these debates, is Australia, a country not part of Shakespeare's map at all. A later British writer, Jonathon Swift, was accidentally to use these latitudes for his own fantasy island, Lilliput. Furthermore, plays, even those of past ages, must be performed in the present tense. We can only comprehend them through our own present, and with our own constructions of a past that includes Shakespeare's possible worlds.

But our consciousness may also include our knowledge of a range of histories and geographies that impinge on the plays. Actors and audience of The Merchant of Venice do know of the Holocaust. A very spiritual people, the Australian Aborigines, whose world was peopled by spirit beings like Ariel, were pushed back and almost destroyed by the invasion here of the Europeans. Initially, these Europeans were, in turn, people who for the most part had been robbed of their lands and birthright, and who were sent into exile, partly as convicts, partly as settlers. They were expected never to return, and in some cases even their marriages were ignored or erased. Their consequent varied attempts at defining themselves, and at returning or relating to the old world, make up their own mythology. Throughout its European history this Australia has been a land of exiles, and of arriving "boat people."[6] We live in a world of electronic media. My own readings of Antony and Cleopatra are about discrepancy and subversiveness, the gulf between image and message, the fabric of lies, fallibility and misunderstanding, about the dislocation of message and the deception of static characterization, and the general instability of interpretation. Who or what is the Antony that Antony is supposed to be, when he is being Antony? Is he more than cloud shapes? If Cleopatra can be played by a boy, and is played by a boy, what then is this Cleopatra? How is she also the male product of film industry interpretations, and how other than that? In act 1 of The Tempest Prospero tells the male story of a lost dukedom, one of those most common myths or illusions of the Australian exile, full of vainglory, strutting pomposity, and self-deception. We recognize his myth from our own history, but can we believe him? And it is Prospero who defines and narrates the stories of both Caliban and Miranda for us. Caliban, whose relationship with Prospero exhibits the greatest tension of the play, is clearly from an antipodean point of view a wild colonial boy, or first-generation native, and certainly no indigen, but he is also mysteriously that "thing of darkness" which Prospero must belatedly and crucially decide to acknowledge as his own. If we insist on endowing him with Aboriginality, however, we cannot do so without a reminder of how foreign the concept of kingship would be to his people, and of the cruel joke of "lags," such as the drunken butler and jester, who might tie a tin plate around his neck and mock him as "king" of his tribe. In a play with an invisible population of spirit people who are barely acknowledged except when they play a classical, English, colonial, imported pastoral imposed by Prospero, we are led to a feast, which, "by a strange device," vanishes, as do all the revels and the cloud-capped palaces. If we read the plays in our place, then our anthropology and our history make at least some intellectual claim in the completion of the texts. This is a matter of consciousness of our location and history, and not the imposition of a forced relevance.

Our revels are thus ended. We are men of sin, and such stuff as dreams are made on. The play's the thing, writ in choice Italian, of which the text we are told is extant. But that text is far from home, and can only have a message that is, whatever it is, not what was built in by some lost author of The Murder of Gonzago. Perhaps, like this, the playscripts blur and run together in our antipodean world. If the play becomes our own, it becomes a different play. Even more than music on the original instruments, if it is genuinely English and Elizabethan, imported or reconstructed, then it belongs in a museum, and there is great value in museum studies here as elsewhere. But generally speaking, we are able to perceive a gap between a sixteenth-century construction in a museum and these spaces and perspectives where we live.

Hamlet spoke of holding up the mirror, as we are often told. But in the sideshow world "they do it with mirrors," as the saying goes. Many things are deceptive in the tradition. There never was a bard of Avon; that's a nineteenth-century apotheosis of the corpse in the monument. Speaking from my iconoclastic, provincial antipodean position, I do not seek a pageant, mimesis, or fidelity, but, instead of these, provocative carnival. I hope that rather than confining these verbal texts in the traditional academy, or sending them back to England, we will be able to set them free.

Notes

1. See Paul de Man, Blindness and Insight: Essays in the Rhetoric of Contemporary Criticism (New York: Oxford University Press, 1971), and The Rhetoric of Romanticism (New York: Columbia University Press, 1984).

2. Janet Adelman, The Common Liar: An Essay on Antony and Cleopatra (New Haven: Yale University Press, 1973).

3. The finest piece of scholarship to come out of this reading of Caliban as American Indian is Alden T. Vaughan and Virginia Mason Vaughan, Shakespeare's Caliban: A Cultural History (New York: Cambridge University Press, 1991). Drawing mainly on the resources of the Folger Library in Washington, a historian of Indian culture and a Shakespeare scholar combine forces to

document the Indian-European contacts, and the history of Caliban on the stage.

4. Jean E. Howard and Marion F. O'Connor, eds., *Shakespeare Reproduced: The Text in History and Ideology* (London: Methuen, 1987).

5. Trevor Code, in *Myth in Literature and Society: Shakespearean Mythmaking* (Geelong: Deakin University, 1978).

6. See Robert Hughes, *The Fatal Shore* (London: Collins Harvill, 1987), Thomas Keneally, *The Playmaker* (Sydney: Hodder and Stoughton, 1987), and Timberlake Wertenbaker, *Our Country's Good* (London: Methuen, 1988).

"That Map Which Deep Impression Bears": The Politics of Conquest in Shakespeare's *Lucrece*

MERCEDES MAROTO CAMINO

WHEN Lear placed the map before him, he was aware that his signs would effect an irreversible division of his kingdom. With this gesture he fragmented not only his state but also his psychic integrity. As the Fool notes, Lear's partition turned the world upside down:

> When thou clovest thy crown i'th'middle, and gav'st away both parts, thou bor'st thine ass on thy back o'er the dirt . . .

> thou mad'st thy daughters thy mothers . . . thou gav'st them the rod and putt'st down thine own breeches . . .

> thou hast pared thy wit o'both sides, and left nothing i'th'middle.
> (1.4.156–59, 168–70, 183–84)[1]

The divided map stands for Lear's emasculation, that is, for his loss of a sense of identity, which was given by his class, his gender (now he has "nothing in the middle"), and their power relationships. The prominent position the map occupies in this play is determined by the remarkable developments in cartography that stimulated and were stimulated by an age of exploration, discovery, and conquest.

The increase in the production of maps and chorographic descriptions in the early modern period was inextricably enmeshed with colonialism, the rise of nationalism, and bourgeois individualism. Countries were rendered meaningful and intelligible, their surfaces were fixed, and they were internalized as objects with a historical reality.[2] Significance was inscribed in the texts which stood for the emerging nations, and was in turn

124

reified in the "body natural" of the king whose physical being was assimilated to that of his territory.[3]

As texts, maps recorded and created geographical, religious, and political beliefs. The "mapping impulse"[4] was consequent upon a desire to decode the unreadable, to imprint every blank space, to efface the void, which would often become tragic for those to be colonized. This drive, as I see it, was not merely geographical or macrocosmic: the discursive fragmentation of the female body effected by blazons participated in the same dialectic. To borrow Peter Stallybrass's formulation: "as the nation-state was formed according to new canons of incorporation and exclusion, so was the female body refashioned."[5] My analysis of the relationship between the topological and the feminine in Shakespeare's Lucrece will be precisely aimed at reinscribing woman as terra incognita. In other words, I shall present "Lucrece" as a space framed by a patriarchal power in which sexual and political conquests are aspects of a particular definition of masculinity.

Renaissance princes, like Charles V or Henry VIII, used their full-length portraits as propaganda in a religious and nationalistic struggle. Their virility, emphasized by their prominent codpieces, was an aspect of this all-conquering thrust.[6] This masculine notion found, however, a stumbling block in the England of Elizabeth who, nonetheless, managed to become an "honorary man" by enshrining her chastity and crafting an icon out of it. Marion Campbell has summed up this interesting process as follows:

> Unlike the modern state, which is defined territorially with power vested in neither the ruler nor the ruled, the Elizabethan body politic was contained within the natural body of the Queen. . . . With its inviolable frontiers, moral purity, and unchanging physical state, virginity became the connecting link between the natural and political bodies. . . . Elizabeth . . . presented her virginity as the single most important guarantee of her country's safety, a personal virtue that was simultaneously a political asset.[7]

This was made apparent, for instance, when Phillip II sent his armada and she pursuaded her subjects that the defense of the English borders was the defense of her own body; that their honor rested upon preserving her virginity from Phillip's intended rape.[8]

The publication of Shakespeare's Lucrece in 1594, six years after the armada fiasco, would probably conjure up images of that frustrated attempt and its topical associations.[9] Lucretia's violation had marked the end of the Roman monarchy and the beginning of the republic. Her story was extremely popular and had been rehearsed by, among others, Chaucer, Gower, and Painter. Lydgate's *Serpent of Division*, written early in the fifteenth century and reprinted in 1590, used Tarquin's rape as a warning against the dangers inherent in tyrannical systems of government. A similar admonition was voiced in Sir Thomas Elyot's *The Boke Named the Governour* and in Holinshed's *Chronicles*.[10] That the rape of a woman's "body natural" could precipitate a positive change in the "body politic" of the country could not, however, pass unobserved. The Marian mythology evolved around the figure of the Virgin Queen might relate Elizabeth with Lucretia as a paragon of female integrity. The possibility that the absolutist Tudor rule could be overthrown would, however, place the Queen in Tarquin's position and therefore question this image. Shakespeare needed then to contend with the paradoxical political readings of a myth of female heroism and virginity already built into the language.[11]

Shakespeare's poem is preceded by a prose narrative, "The Argument," which follows closely the sources he used.[12] It begins on an evening during the siege of Ardea, a city some thirty miles away from Rome, when Tarquin and other warriors blazoned the virtue and beauty of their respective wives. Unaware of his effect upon Tarquin, Collatine "extolled the incomparable chastity of his wife Lucretia." Since martial words had to be supported by evidence and action, they went to see for themselves what their wives were doing and found that, other than Lucretia who was "spinning amongst her maids," they were all "dancing and revelling, or in several disports." The chastity and the beauty of the contest's winner, Lucrece, "inflamed" Tarquin's lust and after they returned to the camp he went back and "ravished" her. She then dispatched messengers to her father and husband, made them swear that they would avenge her, told them what had happened, and stabbed herself. Upon Brutus's suggestion, they paraded her corpse around Rome where the people rebelled against the tyranny of the Tarquins, who were exiled, and a republic replaced their monarchy.

The outline of events presented in the Argument allows Shakespeare to start the poem *in medias res*. The sequential order of events is altered and many a significant element of the traditional story is relegated to the background or removed. The beginning, as Tarquin posts from Ardea with the rape of Lucrece already in his mind, adds momentum to the initial pace and narrows its focus to Tarquin's oncoming sexual transgression. As we are soon informed of the previous events by a flashback, the role of Collatine's rhetoric in the tragedy to come is highlighted. This, as Richard Lanham has observed, is a telling departure from the main sources of the legend:

> Livy adds her chastity as an attraction. . . . But in Shakespeare's pamphlet . . . Tarquin falls in love from report only. . . . Not beauty but *envy* stimulates Tarquin to ultimate rashness. . . . He wants to rape Lucrece *because* she is pre-eminent in virtuous womanhood. . . . Shakespeare has so pointedly removed the obvious motive—sight of the beloved.[13]

The modification of the sources serves to foreground what in the poem is the motif that prefigures the tragedy to come. Not only are the wager and the sight of Lucrece absent, but it is explicitly Collatine's praise that "inflames" Tarquin's desire. That his bragging is the catalyst of the subsequent action is clearly stated by Shakespeare:

> For he the night before, in Tarquin's tent
> Unlock'd the treasure of his happy state;[14]
> What priceless wealth the heavens had him lent,
> In the possession of his beauteous mate;
> Reck'ning his fortune at such high proud rate
>   That kings might be espoused to more fame,
>   But king nor peer to such a peerless dame.
>
> . . . .
> Beauty itself doth of itself persuade
> The eyes of men without an orator;
> What needeth then apologies be made,
> To set forth that which is so singular?
> Or why is Collatine the publisher
>   Of that rich jewel he should keep unknown
>   From thievish ears, because it is his own?
>   (15–21, 29–35)

Lucrece's undoing is clearly the outcome of Collatine's initial textualization of the economies of her beauty and her virtue. To borrow Nancy Vickers's words:

> Lucrece thus reveals the rhetorical strategies that descriptive occasions generate, and underlines the potential consequences of being female matter for male oratory. . . . In Lucrece, occasion, rhetoric,

and result are all informed by, and thus inscribe, a battle between men that is first figuratively and then literally fought on the fields of woman's "celebrated" body.[15]

A rhetorical display is the primary cause of Tarquin's loss of self-control, of his failure to keep his passions under his own "rule." He, who should have framed his physical and his political bodies, surrenders to the drives of his "body natural" so that social disruption comes from him who should uphold law and order. Sexuality thus becomes politics when the king becomes "soft fancy's slave" (200):

> "Thou art not what thou seem'st, and if the same,
> Thou seem'st not what thou art, a god, a king:
> For kings like gods should govern everything.
>
> . . . .
> Hast thou command? by him that gave it thee,
> From a pure heart command thy rebel will.
>
> . . . .
> I sue for exiled majesty's repeal;
> Let him return, and flatt'ring thoughts retire.
> His true respect will prison false desire,
>   And wipe the dim mist from thy doting eyne,
>   That thou shalt see thy state, and pity mine."
>   (600–602, 624–25, 640–44)[16]

As with Lear, Tarquin is presented as the source and the consequence of the political upheaval that ensues.

Tarquin's conquest of Lucrece's body is, in Shakespeare's poem, an ambitious quest that contains the seeds of the conqueror's self-destruction:

> Those that much covet are with gain so fond
> That what they have not, that which they possess
> They scatter and unloose it from their bond;
> And so by hoping more they have but less,
> Or gaining more, the profit of excess
>   Is but to surfeit, and such griefs sustain,
>   That they prove bankrout in this poor rich gain.
>
> (134–40)

We are, nonetheless, made to understand Tarquin's conflict because we are offered in the first part of the narrative a vision of his hesitant self contemplating his victim and poised in a struggle to conciliate his erotic desire and his inability to satisfy it without destroying a part of himself. His sexual urgency and his guilt are simultaneous and the split subjectivity that results from this self-alienation is a sign of the exile from the interior coherence Tarquin loses by robbing his kinsman, Collatine, of his lawful property.[17]

It is precisely that relationship which informs Tarquin's inner "disputation," his fear of a dishonor that will be forever printed on his "golden coat [of arms]" (205). In his balance of prospective gains and losses Lucrece is but a blank space. Moreover, his "black deed" (226) is unjustified because Collatine has done no offense he wishes to avenge:

> "Had Collatinus kill'd my son or sire,
> Or lain in ambush to betray my life;
> Or were he not my dear friend, this desire
> Might have excuse to work upon his wife,
> As in revenge or quittal of such strife:
>   But as he is my kinsman, my dear friend,
>   The shame and fault finds no excuse nor end.
>
> Shameful it is—ay, if the fact be known.
> Hateful it is,—there is no hate in loving.
> I'll beg her love,—but she is not her own."
>
> (232–41)

Tarquin's "theft"[18] of his kinsman's property not only effectively breaks the male bonding they had formed in their military campaign, but puts in question the existence of boundaries between the political and the psychological selves.

Because Tarquin's society is centered upon men and their interests, "feminine" attributes (such as softness, diffidence, or cowardice) are, of course, devalued and their "masculine" military counterparts (such as aggressiveness, pride, or prowess) are celebrated for their own sake. Furthermore, since the rape of women seems to have gone hand in hand with the conquest of land throughout history,[19] it is the same masculinist mode of thought that made Tarquin identify with an all-male fellowship and that stimulated his wish to rape Lucrece. He therefore marches toward her accompanied by images of warfare:[20]

> Affection is my captain, and he leadeth;
>   And when his gaudy banner is display'd,
>   The coward fights, and will not be dismay'd.
>
> (271–73)

He progresses thus until he opens the door of Lucrece's chamber
with his knee. He then draws the curtain from the bed and
watches Lucrece's body, which lies "at the mercy of his mortal
sting" (364). It is from his position that we participate in a voy-
euristic exercise whereby the body he is to "sting" is dehumanized in a Petrarchan blazon:

> Her lily hand her rosy cheek lies under,
> Coz'ning the pillow of a lawful kiss,
> Who therefore angry, seems to part in sunder,
> Swelling on either side to want his bliss:
> Between whose hills her head entombed is,
>   Where like a virtuous monument she lies,
>   To be admir'd of lewd unhallowed eyes.
>
> Without the bed her other fair hand was,
> On the green coverlet; whose perfect white
> Show'd like an April daisy on the grass,
> With pearly sweat resembling dew of night.
> Her eyes like marigolds had sheath'd their light,
>   And canopied in darkness sweetly lay,
>   Till they might open to adorn the day.
>
> Her hair like golden threads play'd with her breath:
> O modest wantons, wanton modesty!
> Showing life's triumph in the map of death,
> And death's dim look in life's mortality.
> Each in her sleep themselves so beautify,
>   As if between them twain there were no strife,
>   But that life liv'd in death and death in life.
>
> (386–406)

Lucrece is here described as a "map of death": her head is "en-
tombed" and she is a "virtuous monument" covered by flowers
(marigolds, daisies, lilies, and roses);[21] she is a composite icon
of worldiness and vanity, surrounded by hills and arranged with
a lavish display of flowers. These flowers, as Shakespeare writes
in the sonnets, blossom and wither; they are at the same time a
memento mori and a celebration of life. Conventional though it
may be, this imagery is striking in this context because the whole
poem is set indoors and crowded with images of diverse enclo-
sures, dark houses, prisons, and fortresses. By contrast, "the sight
of Lucrece asleep is transformed into an apparition of spring and
fragile innocence."[22] In her sleep, she is a map on the *vanitas*
theme reminding Tarquin of the eternal presence of the great

leveler, death. Lucrece's "map of death" speaks about mutability and the worthlessness of material and sensual possessions, rather like the skull in the cartouche placed on North America by Hondius which warned explorers of the transitoriness of life and the futility of their ambition.[23]

The trope of the female body as a synecdoche of sexuality and death is thus reinforced not only by the image of the map but also by that of the garden, which represents the ability of humans to dominate their environment, and also, as Terry Comito notes, mortality and the meaninglessness of worldly riches: "The garden is an image of fruition, order, and completeness; and at the same time, and by the same token, it is an image of growth, process, and mutability. It is at once a privileged place and witness to the effects of time."[24] The recurrent cycle of birth, growth, decay, and death that corresponds to the seasons made gardens at the same time tropes of both worldly ambition and *contemptus mundi*. Lucrece's bucolic landscape is therefore further associated with the idea of death not only for its paradisal connotations but also because the presence of flowers and maps assimilates her body to a conquered plot of land that has been conveniently landscaped.[25] The classical "monuments" that figured prominently in gardens and in tombs further suggest an intricate relationship between gardens, *vanitas*, and women's bodies.

The description of Lucrece as a "map of death" follows the contemporary pattern of rhetorical conventions that are often grouped under the label "Petrarchism." Through her problematic relationship with various flowers, mountains, grass, marble, and metallic elements, Lucrece is drawn as a cartographic landscape where her body is effaced. Her "rosy cheek" is, in this figuration, like the wind rose of a map, the north of which is indicated by the "lily," which was often used to point the north in maps from the mid-sixteenth century.[26] The convergence between these mapping ornaments and the Petrarchan erotic description is not merely coincidental. Blazons mapped a body, that of a woman, to be appropriated, in the same way that the mapping of land served to facilitate its invasion. Lucrece is a colonial fortune, a "jewel" to be enjoyed by the conqueror. Her blazon is nothing other than the fragmented map of an alien landscape, of an impossible geography that had to be brought under control.

It is worth noting that the writer who popularized blazoning, Petrarch, was not only devoted to the study of maps but was also himself "the author of a Syrian itinerary and a map of Italy."[27] That maps and blazons were Renaissance artifacts that circumscribed land and women by reducing them to discursive and fixed coordinates is corroborated in the poem when Shakespeare explicitly refers to Lucrece's face as "that map which deep impression bears" (1712). And the same trope is deployed to describe as a "map of woe" Lavinia's face after she has been savagely raped and mutilated.[28]

For Patricia Parker this blazoning of Lucrece is already expressed as a potential rape. She analyzes the intricate relationship between "exploration, inventory and blazon" and concludes that

> The verbal display of a woman, opened up to view by her possessor; the narrative inventory of a feminized America . . . the Baconian description of the parts of nature . . . and the expansive display of an English owner's property . . . all participate in an imagery of opening and controlling something gendered as female before spectators and possessors gendered as male, in a process in which ostentatious display, copia, or "increase" is constrained within an economy of mastery and ownership.[29]

The image of a feminized America to which Parker alludes is a figure often represented as waiting to be raped by Europeans so that she would be made to "bear" the "impression" of civilization (Fig. 1). The similarity between the naked vulnerable bodies of Vespucci's "America" and Titian's Lucretia (Fig. 2) reinforce the notion that both bare "bodies" are reifications of conquest as a gendered process. These two images convey two sequential moments of a "rape": the conqueror's initial sense of wonder as he gazes at the body he is to conquer and his violent possession of the female body. The interpretation given by Michel de Certeau to Jan van der Straet's etching is worth quoting at length:

> Amerigo Vespucci the voyager arrives from the sea. . . . Before him is the Indian "America," a nude woman reclining in her hammock, an unnamed presence of difference, a body which awakes within a space of exotic fauna and flora . . . an inaugural scene: after a moment of stupor . . . the conqueror will write the body of the other and trace there his own history. From her he will make a historied body—a blazon—of his labors and phantasms. She will be "Latin" America . . . she is a nuova terra not yet existing on maps—an unknown book destined to bear the name Amerigo, of its inventer. But what is really initiated here is a colonization of the body by the discourse of power. This is writing that conquers. It will use the New World as if it were a blank, "savage" page on which Western desire will be written. It will transform the space of the other into a field of expansion for a

"America," from Stradanus, *Nova Reperta*. Reproduced by permission of the Burndy Library of the Dibner Institute for the History of Science and Technology, Norwalk, Ct.

system of production. From the moment of a rupture between a subject and an object of the operation, between a *will to write* and a *written body* (or a body to be written), this writing fabricates Western history. *The Writing of History* is the study of writing as historical practice.[30]

Like Vespucci, Tarquin, after a "moment of stupor" and estrangement, makes Lucrece's body his own possession; he makes her a map, the text where he writes the history of his tyranny.

The main argument Tarquin uses to persuade Lucrece to consent to her rape consists in threatening her with her husband's dishonor (514–25). She tries to make him aware of the consequences of his crime (568ff.) but he silences her appeal and departs,

> A captive victor that hath lost in gain,
> Bearing away the wound that nothing healeth,
> The scar that will despite of cure remain.
>
> (730–32)

Lucrece's rape is made to appear as Tarquin's emasculation. He has, in other words, lost forever an identity that was contingent

Titian, *Tarquino e Lucretia,* ca. 1570. Reproduced by permission of the Syndics of the Fitzwilliam Museum, Cambridge.

on a display of "macho" attitudes among other men. His error is not that he rapes a woman but that he rapes Lucrece, the private property of his kinsman, rather than, say, an Ardean woman.

Lucrece is then Tarquin's "newfoundland": a country to be invaded, a stronghold to be "taken," a "walled" city to be conquered, a map on which to place his shield, a body made to "bear" the colonizer's "impression."[31] To materialize such conquest Tarquin signs it with his own hand which he places upon her "turrets":

> His drumming heart cheers up his burning eye,
> His eye commends the leading to his hand;
> His hand, as proud of such a dignity,
> Smoking with pride, march'd on to make his stand
> On her bare breast, the heart of all her land;
> > Whose ranks of blue veins, as his hand did scale,
> > Left their round turrets destitute and pale.
>
> > > > (435–41)[32]

Lucrece's text bears Tarquin's impresa. His text is, however, hermetic for her before he forces his way into her room. Indeed, it is her innocence that prevents her from knowing his intentions:

> But she that never cop'd with stranger eyes,
> Could pick no meaning from their parling looks,
> Nor read the subtle shining secrecies
> Writ in the glassy margents of such books;
>
> > > > (99–103)

Contemporary theories about the different humoral composition of the sexes are of particular relevance for an understanding of the tropes deployed in those passages. Women's humors were considered to be cold and moist and this constitution was thought to retain the "impressions" made upon them. In contrast, men's harder makeup enabled them to inscribe women's bodies. These notions are clearly expressed in the Artistotelian digression on womanhood that surrounds the pathetic scene in which Lucrece's maid cries when she sees her mistress's distress:

> For men have marble, women waxen, minds
> And therefore are they form'd as marble will;
> The weak oppress'd, th'impression of strange kinds
> Is form'd in them by force, by fraud, or skill.
> Then call them not the authors of their ill,

No more than wax shall be accounted evil,
Wherein is stamp'd the semblance of a devil.

Their smoothness, like a goodly champaign plain,
Lays open all the little worms that creep;
In men as in a rough-grown grove remain
Cave-keeping evils that obscurely sleep;
Through crystal walls each little mote will peep;
    Though men can cover them with bold stern looks,
    Poor women's faces are their own faults' books.

                                        (1240–53)[33]

Woman was a field to be furrowed, the site where men wrote their own history; she was to reflect a man's identity by fulfilling the (re)productive role to which she had been assigned by a division of labor, which, some argue, became increasingly restrictive as cities grew and industries began to develop.[34]

The same discourse in which women were "maps" made to "bear" men's "deep impressions" made them often responsible for the very marks of those "impressions." Only through her suicide, Lucrece believed, could she oppose the deeply rooted tradition that questioned the testimony of raped women. Only by showing that she cared less about life than about her chastity would her contemporaries understand that she had neither enjoyed her rape nor consented to it willingly; she acted to preserve the honor of her men.[35] Her words, thus, had to be believed and ratified by her husband:

Here folds she up the tenure of her woe,
Her certain sorrow writ uncertainly.
By this short schedule Collatine may know
Her grief, but not her grief's true quality;
She dares not thereof make discovery,
    Lest he should hold it her own gross abuse,
    Ere she with blood had stain'd her stain'd excuse.

                                        (1310–16)

Lucrece's acceptance of such a paradigm is expressed therefore in an immolation aimed at preserving the patriarchal system that forced her to act in the way she did. Her final motto addressed to womankind corroborates the idea that her self-destruction is nothing more than partiarchy restored. In the name of the masculine code of honor she has championed, she affirms that she will not be the excuse of other women:

"No, no, quoth she, no dame hereafter living
By my excuse shall claim excuse's giving."

(1714–15)

Subject to textual determinism, Shakespeare's Lucrece turns the knife against herself in order to re-present Tarquin's conquest on the map of her body:

"Faint not, faint heart, but stoutly say 'So be it';
Yield to my hand, my hand shall conquer thee;
Thou dead, both die, and both shall victors be."

(1209–11)

With this gesture Lucrece effectively reinscribes Tarquin's rape with her own hand.[36] It is only in this final moment that she acquires power over those around her: the knife that was instrumental to her rape is now central to making a reversal in the relationship between the sexes. But this knife is both the symbol and the means of a masculine power: it is a visible weapon, the mark of which is engraved effectively upon Lucrece's body, the body of her text. The rape of Lucrece is both the physical violation of a "woman," Lucrece, and Lucrece's self-annihilation; that is, the violence she inflicts on her own body, on her text, and on woman. It is in a man's hand, Brutus's, that such a weapon will finally become the icon of Lucrece's power(lessness). All that she commands is the tragic victory of a doubtfully heroic death.[37] Brutus, the artificer of the political upheaval that would banish the Tarquins, can then become a hero who deposes a tyrant rather than a fanatic rebel, and he does so by virtue of vindicating the chastity and the castigation of a woman.[38] And Lucrece is finally made to be the loyal embodiment of a particular sense of femininity and holiness consisting largely in harming oneself for the love of others. Not surprisingly, then, men used her destroyed body in order to erect a paragon of female heroism on which they wished women to model themselves.

Lucrece's suicide breaches the symmetrical pattern normally obtaining in revenge tragedies. Brutus signals a possible alternative when he tells Collatine:

"Thy wretched wife mistook the matter so,
To slay herself that should have slain her foe."

(1826–27)

And it is precisely Brutus who breaks the lamentation over Lucrece's dead body and restores the potentially unending chain of revenge by aiming his wrath against Tarquin. He extracts the knife from Lucrece's wound and makes it the focus of an oath that will be reenacted in *Hamlet* and in *The Revenger's Tragedy*. His publication of her rape fuels the upheaval that deposes the Tarquins and, as Donald Cheney observes, recalls Collatine's initial praise of Lucrece:

> By publishing Lucrece's virtue, Collatine had diverted energy from war to lust; now it is for Brutus to publish her virtue in such a way as to provoke Tarquin's banishment and his own accession to power in Rome. Such publication makes Brutus a playwright of sorts, a rhetorician who knows how to show Lucrece to best advantage and win the applause of the people; but language is being used in the service of political rather than purely artistic, sentimental goals: history is being written, or revised.[39]

When Brutus draws the knife, Lucrece's blood flows out; and as the serum and the clot separate she is hemmed in by the polluted black blood of the terra incognita mapped by Tarquin's "discovery" and the "untainted" blood of her own landscape:

> And bubbling from her breast, it doth divide
> In two slow rivers, that the crimson blood
> Circles her body in on every side,
> Who like a late-sack'd island vastly stood
> Bare and unpeopled in this fearful flood
>   Some of her blood still pure and red remain'd,
>   And some look'd black, and that false Tarquin stain'd.
>   (1736–43)

Her divided blood surrounds a corpse that, like the newly conquered Caribbean islands, had been "unpeopled" and ravaged by ferocious colonization.[40]

    Shakespeare made Lucrece the locus where the contradictions of domestic and political conquest met. She is conquered territory beyond and within one's own borders. The Roman and the New World imperial enterprise merge in the conquest of the landscape of woman's body:

> Her breasts like ivory globes circled with blue,
> A pair of maiden worlds unconquered;
> Save of their lord, no bearing yoke they knew,
> And him by oath they truly honoured.
> These worlds in Tarquin new ambition bred;

Who like a foul usurper went about,
From this fair throne to heave the owner out.

(407–13)

Lucrece's breasts are a composite map made of two "ivory globes" hemmed in by the blue of the "Ocean Sea." The cartographic Petrarchan blazoning uses the conventional "ivory" to contrast Lucrece's dazzling white skin against Tarquin's Etruscan "foulness." It is precisely the purity of these immaculate "maiden worlds" that excites his ambition to encompass the globe, his urge to place his banner upon her body, his mimetic desire to rob the lord whose exclusive "yoke" Lucrece "bears." The blue ocean that surrounds the globe Tarquin is about to conquer turns red and black at the end as Lucrece's blood abandons her lifeless body. The cause of his ultimate banishment is his unfortunate choice of a "plot" that had already been discovered, mapped, named, and inscribed by another man.

Political and domestic conquests are thus made to converge in *Lucrece* as aspects of the discourse of tyrannical princes. To treat one as metaphor for the other not only reduces the scope of patriarchy's reach in this poem but also diminishes the devastating effects of the violence effected on the female body by sublimation. The rape of Lucrece was the imperial "achievement" of patriarchy: a structure of power that reaches all strata of society, not separating the geographical from the domestic realms.[41] Roman and Elizabethan Lucreces are mediums through which men communicate, fight, and effect political turmoils. Not surprisingly, the "new" regimes rest upon the foundation of woman's mutilated body;[42] so that woman is nothing other than the unlucky terrain where political struggles are fought and her sexuality the liminal space where a culture establishes its coordinates and fixes its boundaries.[43]

After Lucrece's suicide Shakespeare closed the narrative hastily.[44] Given the politically sensitive environment in which he lived, he would obviously be cautious when presenting a change from an absolutist monarchy to a republic achieved by breaching a woman's chastity. Elizabeth might be identified with Lucrece insofar as she had assimilated the integrity of her realm with her virginity. Such an association would come to an end if she were seen as a (to be deposed) monarch and a rapist. Like Tarquin's short-lived happiness, Elizabethan conquests entailed irreconcilable paradoxes. Nowhere are those contradictions more apparent than in a poem where conquest entails the alienation of the conqueror and the destruction of the conquered. The weapons used to construe the Elizabethan sense of nationhood were therefore the same that would be deployed to conquer strange worlds. But outside England and beyond the physical borders of the modern masculine "individual," all women and all landscapes were realms that could be opened to discovery: bodies the maps of which had to be drawn in order for them to be conquered.

Notes

I wish to thank Mac Jackson for his "peculiar" support. Carmen Maroto's help is deeply appreciated. Her own work for MAP (Medical Aid for Palestine) has helped me to see more clearly the pragmatics of map-making. For comments, suggestions and much else I am grateful to Louis Montrose, Roger Horrocks, and Christine Arkinstall. Above all, I am deeply indebted to Michael Neill. While I (re)produce some "graver labor," this article is dedicated to him.

1. All Shakespeare references are to the relevant Arden edition. Francis Barker analyzes Lear's gesture as a split in the interrelated domains of the self, the family, society, and the kingdom, in *The Tremulous Private Body: Essays on Subjection* (London: Methuen, 1984), 33.

2. It is significant to note that the name of America caught on when it was printed on a map included in Waldseemüller's *Cosmographiæ Introductio* (1507). See Djelal Kadir, *Columbus and the Ends of the Earth: Europe's Prophetic Rhetoric as Conquering Ideology* (Berkeley: University of California Press, 1992), 24–52. I am grateful to Kadir for letting me see this section of his book before its publication. On this topic see also my "Mapping *terra incognita*: The Reification of America in the Works of Cortés, Vespucci and More," in *Travellers' Tales, Real and Imaginary: The Hispanic World and Its Literature*, ed. Alun Kenwood (Melbourne: Voz Hispánica 1993) 169–87.

Richard Helgerson analyzes the relationship between the rise of nationalism in England and the Saxtons' atlas in "The Land Speaks: Cartography, Chorography, and Subversion in Renaissance England," in *Representing the English Renaissance*, ed. Stephen Greenblatt (Berkeley: University of California Press, 1988), 326–61.

3. See Ernst Kantorowicz, *The King's Two Bodies: A Study in Medieval Political Theology* (Princeton: Princeton University Press, 1957).

4. The idiom comes from Svetlana Alpers, "The Mapping Impulse in Dutch Art," in *The Art of Describing: Dutch Art in the Seventeenth Century* (London: John Murray, 1983), 119–68.

5. Peter Stallybrass, "Patriarchal Territories: The Body Enclosed," in *Rewriting the Renaissance: The Discourses of Sexual Difference in Early Modern Europe*, ed. Margaret Ferguson, Maureen Quilligan, and Nancy J. Vickers (Chicago: University of Chicago Press, 1986), 130. Stallybrass offers an expanded version of these Bakhtinian ideas in Stallybrass and Allon White, *The Poetics and Politics of Transgression* (Ithaca: Cornell University Press, 1986).

6. On the association of power and sexuality in those portraits, see Catherine Belsey and Andrew Belsey, "Icons of Divinity: Portraits of Elizabeth I," in *Renaissance Bodies: The Human Figure in English Culture c. 1540–1660*, ed. Lucy Gent and Nigel Llewellyn (London: Reaktions, 1990), 11–13; also Louis Adrian Montrose, "The Elizabethan Subject and the Spenserian Text," in *Liter-*

ary Theory/Renaissance Texts, ed. Patricia Parker and David Quint (Baltimore: Johns Hopkins University Press, 1985), 303–40.

7. Marion Campbell, "Inscribing Imperfection: Sir Walter Ralegh and the Elizabethan Court," ELR 20 (1990): 244–45.

8. This is clearly conveyed in the "Armada" portrait. See Montrose, "Elizabethan Subject," esp. 315, and Belsey and Belsey, "Icons of Divinity," esp. 11–15. The study of Elizabethan iconography has produced a copious literature. See especially Roy Strong, Gloriana: The Portraits of Queen Elizabeth I (London: Thames and Hudson, 1987); and Frances A. Yates, Astraea: The Imperial Theme in the Sixteenth Century (London: Ark, 1975).

9. The poem was written while the theaters were closed (1592–94) due to an outbreak of the plague, and was published as Lucrece. The title The Rape of Lucrece was first used in the 1616 quarto. Lucrece became extremely popular and was reprinted four times between 1594 and 1600 (E. P. Kuhl, "Shakespeare's Rape of Lucrece," Philological Quarterly 20 [1941]: 352).

10. See ibid., 354–55.

11. Ian Donaldson offers a comprehensive review of her "myth" throughout history in The Rapes of Lucretia: A Myth and Its Transformations (Oxford: Clarendon Press, 1982).

12. Shakespeare's main sources were Ovid's Fasti (2.721–852) and Livy's Historia (1.57–60). See T. W. Baldwin, On the Literary Genetics of Shakespere's Poems and Sonnets (Urbana: University of Illinois Press, 1950), 108–12.

13. Richard Lanham, The Motives of Eloquence: Literary Rhetoric in the Renaissance (New Haven: Yale University Press, 1976), 95–96. As Patricia Joplin puts it, "rape is the price Lucrece pays for having been described" ("The Voice of the Shuttle Is Ours," Stanford Literature Review [1984]: 102). See also René Girard, "Envy of So Rich a Thing," in A Theatre of Envy: William Shakespeare (Oxford: Oxford University Press, 1991), 21–28.

14. This line, for Girard, "sounds as if Collatine were undressing Lucrece in the midst of his fellow soldiers" (22). Eric Partridge gives some Shakespearean references for "jewel" used as a synonym for maidenhead. The citation in Lucrece is the only example Partridge notes in which "jewel" is equated with female married virtue (Shakespeare's Bawdy [London: Routledge, 1947], 128). See also Marlowe's use of "diamond" in The Jew of Malta, ed. Richard van Fossen (London: Arnold, 1965), 2.3.49ff.

15. Nancy Vickers, "'The Blazon of Sweet Beauty's Best': Shakespeare's Lucrece," in Shakespeare and the Question of Theory, ed. Patricia Parker and Geoffrey Hartman (London: Routledge, 1985), 96.

16. The same appeal is used throughout this speech (600–44) and also in 651–55, 659–60, and 666.

17. Tarquin is then precisely at the intersection between two modes of discourse and of being, at the threshold of modern "civilization." His conflict is at the crossroads between a "shame" culture and a "guilty" one. The guilt is, as Paul Ricoeur remarks, a "'means' used by civilization to tame aggressiveness" ("Psychoanalysis and the Movement of Contemporary Culture," in Interpretive Social Science: A Reader, ed. Paul Rabinow and William M. Sullivan [Berkeley: University of California Press, 1979], 309). Freud outlined this as follows: "The tension between the harsh super-ego and the ego that is subjected to it, is called by us the sense of guilt, it expresses itself as a need for punishment. Civilization, therefore, obtains mastery over the individual's dangerous desire for aggression by weakening and disarming it and by setting up an agency within

him to watch over it, like a garrison in a conquered city" ("Civilization and Its Discontents," in *Complete Psychological Works of Sigmund Freud*, ed. and trans. James Stratchey et al., 24 vols. [London: Hogarth Press, 1953–74], 21:84). Of course, as Sander L. Gilman argues, "Freud continues a discourse which relates the images of male discovery to the images of the female as object of discovery" ("Black Bodies, White Bodies: Toward an Iconography of Female Sexuality in Late Nineteenth-Century Art, Medicine, and Literature," in *"Race," Writing and Difference*, ed. Henry Louis Gates [Chicago: University of Chicago Press, 1985], 257).

18. Coppélia Kahn remarks that in *Lucrece* and in *Cymbeline* "the chaste wife is seen as a precious jewel which tempts the thief; in both works, the husband's boasts initiate the temptation, in effect challenging his peers to take that jewel" ("The Rape in Shakespeare's *Lucrece*," *Shakespeare Studies* 9 [1976]: 53). The word *rape*, from the Latin *rapere* meaning "to seize," meant originally "theft of property" (OED *sb.*[2]1). This meaning is complemented by that of the physical violation of a woman against her will in the early modern period.

19. See the remarkable review Susan Brownmiller offers in *Against Our Will: Men, Women and Rape* (New York: Bantam, 1976), 23–87.

20. An alternative reading of the significance of military metaphors in the poem is offered by Michael Platt in "*The Rape of Lucrece* and the Republic for Which It Stands," *Centennial Review* 19 (1975): 59–79.

21. The conventional symbolism of flowers and gardens used to describe Lucrece's body parts had been part of the Marian cult which was taken over by Elizabeth.

22. J. W. Lever, introduction to *The Rape of Lucrece* (Harmondsworth: Penguin, 1971), 10.

23. A reproduction of this cartouche can be seen in James A. Welu, "The Sources and Development of Cartographic Ornamentation in the Netherlands," in *Art and Cartography*, ed. David Woodward (Chicago: University of Chicago Press, 1987), 160. In the same volume Juergen Schultz's article, "Maps as Metaphors: Mural Map Cycles of the Italian Renaissance" (97–122), mentions some allegorical maps on the *vanitas* theme, among which

> The large thirteenth-century world map in Hereford cathedral in England . . . shows the *Last Judgement* above the map proper, together with inscriptions announcing the Day of Judgement and imploring mercy. Around the planisphere itself are inscribed the letters M-O-R-S, characterizing the earth as the realm of death. The map expresses the transitoriness of earthly existence and thereby reinforces our understanding of the finality and universality of the Last Judgement. (112)

The *vanitas* theme is also prominent on the title page of *Purchas his Pilgrimes*. A facsimile of this remarkable engraving, which includes, among various icons, Elizabeth's death monument, James sitting on a map of the British isles, and a globe encircled with the inscription *"vanitas vanitatis,"* is reproduced in Samuel Purchas, *Hakluytus Posthumus or Purchas His Pilgrimes* (1625; rpt. Glasgow: MacLehose, 1905), xxxvi. I am grateful to Michael Neill for bringing this engraving to my attention.

24. Terry Comito, "Caliban's Dream: The Topography of Some Shakespeare Gardens," *Shakespeare Studies*, 14 (1981): 40. John Roe compares this passage with a similar one in Ovid and reads the paradox of life in death as a contradic-

tion resolved in paradise. See his introduction to *The Poems*, ed. John Roe (Cambridge: Cambridge University Press, 1992), 28–30.

25. The obsessive landscaping and the recurrent colonialist trope of the "planting" of people, customs, and the like seems to me to illustrate a frantic desire to convert the whole earth (people included) into a domesticated set of symmetrical pot plants.

26. See Leo Bagrow, *History of Cartography*, rev. and enlgd. R. A. Skelton (London: C. A. Watts, 1964), 144.

27. See ibid., 144.

28. *Titus Andronicus*, 3.2.12. For a survey of Shakespeare's references to maps, see Victor Morgan, "The Literary Image of Globes and Maps in Early Modern England," in *English Map-Making, 1550–1650*, ed. Sarah Tyacke (London: British Library, 1983), 46–56.

29. Patricia Parker, *Literary Fat Ladies: Rhetoric, Gender, Property* (London: Methuen, 1987), 138, 154. Montrose argues that this "textualization of the Other" is a gendered "act of symbolic violence, mastery, and self-empowerment," in "The Work of Gender in the Discourse of Discovery," *Representations* 33 (1991): 6.

30. Michel de Certeau, *The Writing of History*, trans. Tom Conley (New York: Columbia University Press, 1988), xxv–xxvi. An analysis of this engraving is offered by Montrose in "The Work of Gender." I am indebted to Montrose's article for bringing this remarkable engraving and de Certeau's reading of it to my attention.

31. It is worth mentioning that two of the most remarkable map makers, Hondius and Mercator, also wrote calligraphy treatises. See Jonathan Goldberg, *Writing Matter: From the Hands of the English Renaissance* (Stanford: Stanford University Press, 1990), 205. Goldberg illustrates, throughout the book, the violence of the scene of writing; he also offers an interesting reading of two remarkable title pages in which feminine sexuality is seen to be the result of "masculine inscription" (137–45).

32. Further references to Lucrece as a city or a fortress abound in the poem. See, for example, lines 438–48, 464–69, and 1170–74.

33. The Artistotelian humoral physiology deployed in this passage is often used as an explanation for women's subordinate position. See Ian MacLean's *The Renaissance Notion of Woman* (Cambridge: Cambridge University Press, 1980), 42–64; also Linda Woodbridge, *Women and the English Renaissance: Literature and the Nature of Womankind, 1540–1620* (Brighton: Harvester, 1984); and Constance Jordan, *Renaissance Feminism: Literary Texts and Political Models* (Ithaca: Cornell University Press, 1990). Shakespeare made use of this metaphor of women as books to be inscribed in *Measure for Measure*:

> Women?—Help heaven! Men their creation mar
> In profiting by them. Nay, call us ten times frail;
> For we are soft as our complexions are,
> And credulous to false print.

> (2.4.126–30)

Further examples occur in *Twelfth Night*, 2.2.28–31; *Midsummer Night's Dream*, 1.1.47–51; and *Othello*, 4.2.72–73.

34. Alice Clark argued that capitalism brought with it the downgrading of domestic work and therefore of women's status; see *Working Life of Women in the Seventeenth Century* (1919; rpt. London: Routledge, 1982). See also Joan

Kelly, "Did Women Have a Renaissance?" in *Becoming Visible: Women in European History*, ed. Renate Bridenthal and Claudia Koonz (Boston: Houghton Mifflin, 1977), 175–99; Lawrence Stone, *The Crisis of Aristocracy, 1558–1641* (Oxford: Clarendon Press, 1965); and Stone, *The Family, Sex, and Marriage in England, 1500–1800* (New York: Harper, 1979). A contrasting view is offered by Judith C. Brown in "A Woman's Place Was in the Home: Women's Work in Renaissance Tuscany," in *Rewriting the Renaissance: The Discourses of Sexual Differences in Early Modern Europe*, ed. Margaret Ferguson, Maureen Quilligan, and Nancy J. Vickers (Chicago: University of Chicago Press, 1986), 206–24. Joan Thirsk reviews both positions in *Women in English Society, 1500–1800*, ed. Mary Prior (London: Methuen, 1985), 1–21.

35. Carolyn D. Williams explores the meanings of rape and relates them to the sparse conviction rates during the early modern age in "'Silence, like a Lucrece' knife': Shakespeare and the Meaning of Rape," *Yearbook of English Studies* 23 (1993) 93–110. She concludes that had Lucrece been an Elizabethan she would have had very little chance of having her case brought to court. The possibility of Tarquin's being convicted of rape could be considered negligible indeed. Her analysis is based on the figures given by Nazife Bashar in "Rape in England between 1550 and 1700," in *The Sexual Dynamics of History: Men's Power, Women's Resistance*, ed. The London Feminist Group (London: Pluto, 1983), 28–42. I thank Williams for letting me see her article before its publication.

36. Roy Battenhouse sees that "she guides the knife downward into her bosom. Emblematically, we have been shown martyrdom in an obscene mode, a religious 'dying' which Shakespeare hints, figuratively, is a kind of masturba-'tory self-rape." Battenhouse, *Shakespearean Tragedy: Its Art and Its Christian Premises* (Bloomington: Indiana University Press, 1969), 28.

37. St. Augustine had presented the dilemma that was to be at the center of this debate as follows: "if she is adulterous, why is she praised? If chaste, why was she put to death?" *The City of God*, trans. Henry Betterson, ed. David Knowles (Harmondsworth: Penguin, 1972), Bk. 1, chap. 19, 29–30.

38. Stephanie Jed analyzes this attitude in Coluccio Salutati's version of the story in *Chaste Thinking: The Rape of Lucretia and the Birth of Humanism* (Bloomington: Indiana University Press, 1989). Philippa Berry's analysis of Lucrece's "voice" renders a different reading of Lucrece's power in Shakespeare's poem. See her "Woman, Language, and History in *The Rape of Lucrece*," *Shakespeare Survey* 44 (1992): 33–39. An alternative perspective on female eloquence appears in Patricia Parker, "Shakespeare and Rhetoric: 'dilation' and 'delation' in *Othello*," in *Shakespeare and the Question of Theory*, ed. Patricia Parker and Geoffrey Hartman (London: Routledge, 1985), 54–74. See also Parker, *Literary Fat Ladies*, esp. 8–35, 81–85, and 97–125; also Lisa Jardine, *Still Harping on Daughters: Women and Drama in the Age of Shakespeare* (Brighton: Harvester, 1983), esp. 37–67 and 103–41; Lynda E. Boose, "Scolding Brides and Bridling Scolds: Taming the Woman's Unruly Member," *Shakespeare Quarterly* 42 (1991): 179–213; and Joplin, "The Voice of the Shuttle Is Ours."

39. Donald Cheney, "Tarquin, Juliet, and Other Romei," *Spenser Studies* 3 (1982): 116.

40. Michael Goldman sees that "In all cases the figure of the crowd is used to suggest some sort of varied population inside the body, a throng of multiple possibilities or competing selves"; see *Shakespeare and the Energies of Drama*

(Princeton: Princeton University Press, 1972), 22. I am, however, inclined to see in this trope the traces of the conquest of the New World which was being emptied out by colonization and epidemics.

41. Using Coppélia Kahn's words, "patriarchy as a family state and a way of defining sex roles was indistinguishable from patriarchy as the basis of all social thinking." See *Man's Estate: Masculine Identity in Shakespeare* (Berkeley: University of California Press), 13.

42. As Platt ("The Republic for Which It Stands," 76) puts it, "the new regime will be a regime of fathers and husbands. . . . In defense of the most private of properties, the chastity of one's wife, the regime is erected."

43. To borrow Joplin's formulation: "female chastity is not sacred out of respect for the integrity of the woman as person; rather, it is sacred out of respect for violence. Because her sexual body is the ground of the culture's system of differences" ("The Voice of the Shuttle Is Ours," 38). Boose ("Scolding Brides," 195) also illustrates that women are "creatures whose bodily margins and penetrable orifices provide culture with a locus for displaced anxieties about the vulnerability of the social community, the body politic." Similarly, Stallybrass and White (*The Poetics and Politics of Transgression*, 144) argue persuasively that "one cannot analyse the psychic domain without examining the processes of transcoding between the body, topography and the social formation." These studies are informed by Mary Douglas's seminal *Purity and Danger: An Analysis of the Concepts of Pollution and Taboo* (1966; rpt. London and New York: Ark, 1984).

44. Donaldson (*The Rapes of Lucretia*, 117) presents Shakespeare's ultimate rashness as a sign of his "royalism." Kuhl, however, argues that "In *Lucrece*, in short, Shakespeare denounces (along with other matters) crumbling outworn political theories—and he does it precisely at the time when these outworn political beliefs were uppermost in the minds of men" ("Shakespeare's *Rape of Lucrece*," 358–59).

"Mon Sans-Culotte Africain": A French Revolutionary Stage *Othello*

JOHN GOLDER

IT is just two hundred years since *Othello* first reached the public stage in France. In some ways it is difficult to understand why it took so long. After all, to neoclassicists of an Aristotelian cast of mind it must have looked very appealing. As Dr. Johnson observed, "Had the scene opened in Cyprus and the preceding incidents been occasionally related, there had been little wanting to a drama of the most exact and scrupulous regularity."[1] Johnson exaggerates, of course, but, despite its great length, *Othello* has a remarkably simple and unified plot. It is a drama of suffocation, in which everything is compressed. Leaving aside the time taken by the voyage to Cyprus, *Othello* pursues its relentless course in some thirty-six hours, a shorter time span than that of any other Shakespearean tragedy. The participants are few, the context is private and domestic, the atmosphere claustrophobic and the theme, sexual jealousy, sickening and degrading. What is more, it is a theme well tested on the French tragic stage, most notably by Racine, in *Phèdre*. It was presumably because of the play's amenability to French tradition, its affinity with the neoclassical aesthetic, that the first two men to translate Shakespeare extensively for a French reading public, La Place (in ten partial and bowdlerized plays between 1745 and 1748) and Le Tourneur (in a complete prose version, unexpurgated, but unexciting, between 1776 and 1783), each chose to open their respective series of translations with *Othello*.

At the same time it is not hard at all to understand why it took so long to reach the French stage, for in many respects it offends seriously against neoclassical convention: a double-dyed villain of central importance, a black-skinned hero, clowns and tipplers, drinking songs and Willow Songs, handkerchiefs and pillows, fits and headaches, and a dreadful finale set in the heroine's bedroom—to say nothing of those ewe-tupping rams, beasts with two backs, and senators in nightshirts, the features of the play that Voltaire, in his tireless campaign to defend the French stage against the English barbarian, held up for public scorn throughout much of the century.[2]

The author who managed finally to reconcile some of these contradictions and bring *Othello* to the French stage was Jean-François Ducis.[3] He began work on the play late in 1782, ten years before it was finally produced. That happened on 26 November 1792, at a crucial moment in French revolutionary history, a matter of weeks after the September massacres and the declaration of the Republic, and less than two months before Louis XVI was guillotined.

Othello was Ducis's sixth, and last, Shakespearean play. Between 1769 and 1791 he had written a *Hamlet*, a *Roméo et Juliette*, a *Roi Léar*, a *Macbeth*, and a *Jean Sans-Terre* [*King John*], all intended for production at the Comédie-Française. The fact that Ducis knew no English caused him bitter disappointment, but access to Shakespeare's language would neither have simplified his task nor made him modify his purpose. That purpose, if I may reword slightly John Dryden's account of his own in writing *All for Love* as he did, was "not to translate Shakespeare's words, or to be confined to his sense, but only to . . . write as he suppose[d] Shakespeare would have done, had he lived [in the late eighteenth century in Paris]."[4] Like Dryden, or more relevantly, like the great French neoclassicists Corneille, Racine, and Voltaire, Ducis was an imitator in the Classical humanist tradition. His plays are not incompetent adaptations based on ignorance or lack of understanding: they are original tragedies, fashioned in part out of the Shakespeare that was revealed to him by La Place and Le Tourneur.

If, as Ducis once said, the memoirs of his life were to be found in his works,[5] then his Shakespeare plays reveal him to have been a peculiarly eighteenth-century figure, pious son, upright bourgeois father, Christian, sentimentalist, citizen and preromantic, a man of deep religious conviction, who held strong beliefs in the theater's traditional educative moral function. Like other *drames* and bourgeois tragedies of prerevolutionary France, his plays are primarily sentimental in tone and domestic in their preoccupations, and offer parents and children, sovereigns and subjects a Rousseauist guide to proper, virtuous conduct, lessons on reciprocal duties, responsibilities and allegiances in both the family and the state. (This explains Ducis's interest in *King John*:

his version concentrates mawkishly on the parent-child relationship of Constance and Arthur. John himself, a secondary role, is offered as a very poor example of the ideal constitutional monarch.)

But I digress. Let me briefly add that in matters of form Ducis was at heart conservative and his impulse was to try to structure regular, quasi-Cornelian tragedies, in which a passion or a dilemma, taken at crisis-point, is made to develop toward an unavoidable outcome in a very short space of time. However, like Voltaire (whose Academy chair, incidentally, Ducis was elected to fill in 1778), he also strove where possible to incorporate some startling English effects—ghosts, witches, storms, for example—some color and movement that might revitalize what had become a rather moribund form by the latter part of the century.

As in aesthetics, then, so in politics, Ducis leaned to the right. In the broad spectrum of revolutionary party politics, Ducis, in his heart a royalist, was only moderately republican and was very probably drawn into the circle of Girondin deputies by Talma, the great tragedian who was just beginning his meteoric rise to stardom, soon to enter into an intimate working collaboration with Ducis and very soon to create the role of Othello.

The outbreak of the Revolution had split the Comédie-Française both ideologically and physically, and in 1791, together with other more politically committed members of the company, Talma had seceded and established himself at a theater that, nailing their colors to the mast, they promptly renamed the Théâtre de la République.[6] Talma's actress wife, Julie Careau, was more drawn than he to the new ideas of the Revolution and her home became a regular meeting place for the moderates of the Girondist Party. To both these gatherings and to his new theater, Talma attracted Ducis, together with his Othello, which the Comédie had been sitting on since 1788. The play was poised to serve a political purpose that Ducis could hardly have anticipated ten years before: Talma's vigorous assertion of revolutionary zeal in the face of charges of counterrevolutionary activities.

On 16 October the Talmas had thrown an elegant after-theater soirée in honor of Dumouriez, the general who had succeeded to the command of the revolutionary army when the deposition of Louis XVI led to the defection of aristocrat General Lafayette. On 22 September, the day the Republic was proclaimed, news reached Paris that Dumouriez had routed the Prussians at Valmy. The Girondins, who most supported the war, were much buoyed by the news. The more radical Jacobins, however, a very influential left-wing pressure group, suspected Dumouriez of secretly sharing his predecessor Lafayette's sympathies for constitutional monarchy, and Jean-Paul Marat, greasy hair tied in a dirty red bandanna handkerchief and, of course, scrofulous, gate-crashed Talma's party in order to confront the general. "This house is a hotbed of counter-revolutionaries," he shouted, but, when the guests braved him, he withdrew. The following morning, however, his broadsheet, the *Journal de la République Française*, carried the headline: "Party given to honor the traitor Dumouriez by the aristocrats at Talma's house with the names of the conspirators who had plotted to assassinate the People's Friend."[7]

Talma was clearly disturbed by Marat's outburst and immediately sought to offer public affirmation of his patriotism by increasing the company's donations to the war effort and the number of revolutionary plays in the repertoire. Within a matter of weeks, following Dugazon's *L'Emigrant ou le père jacobin* and Hyacinthe Dorvo's *Le Patriote du dix août*, *Othello* was rehearsed and mounted.

The play's general contemporary application is anything but obscure. It is set in Venice, a republic that, we quickly learn in the opening scene, owes its stability to a hero who is neither aristocrat nor white, a man who strikes a blow against social and racial prejudice and demands equality on the grounds not of parentage or race, but worth. It dramatizes those liberal principles that were embodied in the Declaration of the Rights of Man and Citizen, a proclamation which in August 1789 was the death warrant of the ancien régime. It is even possible that, in impersonating General Othello, Talma intended to establish at one and the same time his own republican bona fides and that of Dumouriez, who, after all, did resemble Othello in one central respect—he too was a professional soldier, who, without benefit of noble birth, had risen to the rank of maréchal de camp before the Revolution.[8]

But Dumouriez was not colored, of course. Ducis's Moor was, though he was not black: "I thought I could dispense with giving him a black face" Ducis wrote. "I thought that a yellow, copperlike complexion, which is in effect also suitable for an African, would have the advantage of not revolting the public, especially the ladies."[9] The principal objection raised against an *Othello* by one Douin, which failed to reach the stage in 1773, was that "there is something repugnant and unprepossessing about a black hero as the main character [of a play]."[10] This aristocracy of color should not surprise us: in 1785 another at-

tempt to bring *Othello* to the French stage thought to sidestep
the problem by bleaching Othello white! By 1788, however, the
time was much riper, for Brissot de Warville's Society of the
Friends of the Blacks had been founded and the antislavery
movement begun to gain ground.[11] That same year Mme Olympe
de Gouges advised the Comédiens Français to adopt both Negro
costume and color for her *L'Esclavage des nègres*: "never was the
moment more propitious."[12] On 6 November that year Ducis read
his *Othello* to the Comédie.[13] They accepted it unanimously, but
they did not hurry to put it into rehearsal.

Clearly, they recognized the play's potential to offend. Unlike
modern critics, who have laughed at what they regarded as
Ducis's complaisance in the matter of Othello's skin tone,[14] the
actors quickly saw, I believe, that "copper-colored" meant "non-
white," and that in presenting Othello sympathetically the play
was liable to offend against the vested interests of the powerful
colonial lobby. That Ducis was well acquainted with these and
that we may legitimately situate his *Othello* in the context of
contemporary race relations may be safely taken for granted: his
younger brother George was a magistrate and slave owner in the
New World colony of Saint-Domingue. It is surely not fortuitous
that Ducis launched into serious work on the play in 1783, at
the very moment when brother George was back in Paris on a
family visit.[15] What is more, Ducis dedicated the published text
in Year II (probably 1794) to "Citizen Ducis of Saint-Domingue."

In spite of the fact that, in April 1792, the Legislative Assembly
had decreed equal rights for all free whites and mulattoes in the
colonies, Talma continued to feel nervous about *Othello* and
sought to preempt philistine antagonism by having an open letter
placed in the conservative *Journal de Paris*. The author, striking
a suitably Jacobin tone, asserts a connection between neoclassical proprieties and monarchist politics, and proceeds to itemize
those features of Ducis's play that offend against neoclassical
orthodoxy. First among these is the question of skin color:

> I have no doubt that five years ago the men of the court would have
> mocked Hédelmone [Desdemona] who, young and beautiful, loves a
> Moor; but the men of 10 August, whose philanthropy has fought to
> give rights of citizenship to mulattoes, will not employ the aristoc-
> racy of color at the theater and they will find it quite acceptable that
> a white woman loves a man of color somewhat different from her
> own, if that man is young and passionate.

Then follow the Willow Song and the bed:

It will not surprise [the men of 10 August] to see Hédelmone singing a romance in a tragedy, for they know that music expresses those great movements of the soul. . . . [And] they will not be scandalized to see a bed on the stage, for republicans, who have more manners than the subjects of a monarchy, are not, like them, slaves of a false delicacy, which is the hypocritical affectation of decency.[16]

A student of English theater could be forgiven, on the evidence of Talma's fears, for thinking that Ducis had composed a tragedy that was relatively faithful to Shakespeare's.

But they would be wrong. For every Shakespearean feature he accommodates, Ducis omits at least two. True, there is a colored hero, a bedroom finale complete with actual bed and a Willow Song—the French Desdemona goes further than the English and accompanies herself on a guitar for a ballad of seven long stanzas!—but one will look in vain for Shakespeare's colorful array of heralds, sailors, clowns, and courtesans, for drinking scenes, for fits and headaches. The tyrannical rule of decorum proscribes all these and, furthermore, demands that the handkerchief be ennobled into a diamond tiara and the stifling pillow into a conventional dagger.

There is one more, extraordinary, omission: Iago. It is not a case of Ducis being unaware of Iago's significance in Shakespeare's scheme, rather of his being more sensitive to the tyranny of convention:

The execrable character of Iago is depicted . . . with brushstrokes of extraordinary vigour. . . . [However] I am convinced that if the Engish can calmly watch the maneuvers of such a monster on their stage, the French would never for a moment put up with his presence. . . . This is what caused me to reveal the character who replaces him so feebly in my play only at the very end. . . . [I]f the audience had been able, in the course of the play, even to suspect him, through his mask, of being the most villainous of men, since he is the most treacherous of friends, it would have destroyed the entire work.[17]

The feeble replacement is called Pézare, and his name is the only cryptic clue Ducis gives to his perniciousness: in Spanish "pesar" means "to suffer" or "suffering." It has been suggested that in the autumn of 1792 an Othello without Iago might have been a "safer revolutionary play," and that given the volatile state of contemporary politics, the open representation of such treachery as Iago's might well have fueled the general paranoia about conspiracy.[18] But the problem of Iago was of considerably longer date, and, for Ducis, more aesthetic than political. "A simple matter of unfair promotion," wrote one neoclassical theorist in 1776, "is not adequate motive for so many crimes: there may be monsters capable of irrationally committing such atrocities, but luckily they are the exception, not the rule. The dramatist must depict nature, not its aberrations."[19] In other words, the neoclassical theater should confine itself to the universalities, not the particularities, of human conduct: Iagos are improbable, and so unfit for the serious drama. Ducis makes his Pézare plausible by attributing to him a comprehensible motive, extreme jealousy, and one that is, in a sense, sympathetic and sentimental: secretly he shares the hero's passion, for he too loves Hédelmone.[20] However, to cover himself completely, Ducis does not reveal either the motive or the villainy it justifies until the dying moments of the play. Until then Pézare leads a schizophrenic existence. When on stage he is the conventional faithful confidant of classical tradition. Only in the darkness of the wings does he assume something of his former Shakespearean self, and then not until the drama has exhausted its other generative resources.

One might wonder how, without an Iago of Shakespeare's sort, Ducis handles the provocation and development of Othello's jealousy. When the English Moor admits to being "one not easily jealous, but being wrought, / Perplexed in the extreme" (5.2.345–46), he means that, had Iago not hatched his plot, it would never have occurred to him to suspect Desdemona of infidelity. Compare the French Moor, whom Ducis describes in an alexandrine couplet that only appears to resemble Shakespeare's lines:

> A Moor is suspicious [and] terrible in his wrath.
> [And] a Moor, when he loves, is easily jealous.[21]

The point, perhaps not surprisingly, is that Ducis's Moor is as much a product of neoclassical aesthetics as his Iago substitute: blind to the racist implications of what he is doing, he creates a probable, not a possible Moor. His Othello is suspicious by nature, so, when Ducis contrives for him to discover a rival at his mistress's feet, he automatically suspects something. When harmless circumstance can provide, what need a vindictive Ancient?

To this degree Ducis's *Othello* is not about the slow genesis and hideous ravages of jealousy. Nor do the generative resources that propel its plot forward have much to do with either Othello or Pézare. The focal and ongoing complication of this plot, as of so many of Ducis's, concerns a parent and child, here Hédel-mone/Desdemona and her father Odalbert/Brabantio. Indeed, the principal character, as one contemporary journal observed, is Hédelmone.[22] In Ducis, Hédelmone and Othello are not married (though Othello has asked her to marry him secretly) and her intransigent, aristocratic father's strident opposition to the match is what defines the action throughout. The girl is faced with the incompatible demands of passion and family honor, a tragic dilemma of the kind faced by more than one seventeenth-century heroine, most notably Chimène in Corneille's Le Cid. This domestic conflict takes on some political coloring when the Venetian Senate and its doge interpret Odalbert's hostility to-ward Othello as potentially dangerous to national security. A young admirer of Othello's, Lorédan (Cassio) complicates the situation. Fearing for her father's safety, Hédelmone looks to Lor-édan for help. Othello sees them together and becomes jealous. Lorédan brings word that, in order to get back at the Senate, Odalbert may be conspiring with enemies of the Republic. He also indiscreetly blurts out his love for Hédelmone. The Senate deprives Odalbert of his civic rights and impounds his property. At the same time, discovering that Hédelmone and Othello are not married, Odalbert blackmails her into signing a note promis-ing to marry someone of his choosing—who turns out to be Lorédan himself, and the son of the doge! To help him intercede with his father on Odalbert's behalf, Hédelmone gives Lorédan the note and also, in order to raise some money for her dispos-sessed father, a diamond tiara that Othello has given her. In the course of some inscrutably complicated business in the fourth act, mostly in the wings, the note and tiara fall into Pézare's hands. Claiming he found them on Lorédan, Pézare presents them to Othello as ocular proof of Hédelmone's infidelity. Othello responds as one might imagine.

While not wholly approving of the parental intransigence, which is in some measure responsible for the tragic outcome, in the final analysis Othello illustrates a conviction that Ducis shares with the Rousseau of La Nouvelle Héloïse, namely that duty to one's parents may exert higher claims on an individual than those of romantic love and that ultimately that same duty might prove a sounder basis for marriage: a stable marriage is better built on reason than emotion.

This is perhaps the final lesson of the play, and it is implicit in the juxtaposed roles of Othello and Lorédan. Both owe much to Rousseau, having profited from an Emile-type education, far from corrupting civilization, at the bosom of nature. And both, one made famous by birth, the other a child of nature, illustrate another Rousseau principle, that tender feelings are not the natural privilege of the upper classes. Both are *âmes sensibles*, the very playthings of emotion. But whereas Lorédan manages to master his, Othello's emotions erode his natural sound judgment and finally bring about Hédelmone's and his own destruction.

It was in 1794, in a note to Hérault de Séchelles, a member of the Revolutionary Committee of Public Safety, enclosed in a copy of the newly published text, that Ducis referred to his *sans-culotte* Othello.[23] The reference would seem to link Othello with those militant, trousered, professional revolutionaries of the day, who were motivated by crude antiaristocratism and anticlericalism, and who "spent their time at the Section meetings, orating and denouncing in an alcoholic rage."[24] Ducis's own definition of *sans-culotte* is rather more sober: "one without wealth and rank."[25] In this less hysterical sense the label is appropriate both to the play and to its hero. For when *Othello* first reached the French stage, it may indeed have been revolutionary, but it was only moderately republican.

Notes

1. *Dr. Johnson on Shakespeare*, ed. W. K. Wimsatt (Harmondsworth: Penguin, 1967), 167.

2. See, for instance, Voltaire's *Lettres philosophiques* (ca. 1729), his *Appel à toutes les nations de l'Europe* (1761), and his preface to a translation of *Julius Caesar* (1764), in *Voltaire on Shakespeare*, ed. Theodore Besterman, *Studies on Voltaire and the Eighteenth Century*, vol. 54 (1967).

3. On Ducis and Shakespeare, see Sylvie Chevalley, "Ducis, Shakespeare et les Comédiens français," *Revue d'histoire du théâtre* 16 (1964): 327–50, and 17 (1965): 5–37; see also John Golder, *Shakespeare for the Age of Reason* (Oxford: Voltaire Foundation, 1992). On Ducis's and other *Othellos* in France, see Margaret Gilman, *Othello in French* (Paris: Champion, 1925).

4. Dryden, *Essays*, 1.270–71, quoted by L. A. Beaurline and Fredson Bowers, eds., *John Dryden: Four Tragedies* (Chicago: University of Chicago Press, 1967), 190.

5. V. Campenon, "Notice sur la vie et les œuvres de J.-F. Ducis," *Œuvres posthumes de J.-F. Ducis* (Paris: Nepveu, 1826), lxvi.

6. See, in particular, Marvin Carlson, *The Theatre of the French Revolution* (Ithaca: Cornell University Press, 1966), 7–72, and Herbert J. Collins, *Talma: A Biography of an Actor* (London: Faber, 1964), 48–65.

7. See Carlson, *Theatre of the French Revolution* 135–38, and Collins, *Talma*, 81–87.

8. Alfred Cobban, *A History of Modern France*, 3rd ed. (Harmondsworth: Penguin, 1963), 1:191, and Reeve Parker, "Reading Wordsworth's Power: Narra-

tive and Usurpation in *The Borderers*," *Journal of English Literary History* 54 (1987): 302, 323–36.

9. Foreword to *Othello, ou le More de Venise*, tragédie par le citoyen Ducis (Paris: Maradan, an II [1794]). All translations are by the author.

10. "Discours préliminaire," *Le More de Venise*, tragédie anglaise du théâtre de Shakespeare, par M. Douin (Paris: Louis Cellot, 1773).

11. See Daniel P. Resnick, "The Société des Amis des Noirs and the Abolition of Slavery," *French Historical Studies* 7 (fall 1972): 558–69, and, on the general issues, D. B. Davis, *The Problems of Slavery in the Age of Revolution* (Ithaca: Cornell University Press, 1975).

12. *Œuvres de Mme de Gouges*, 3:97, quoted by E. D. Seeber, *Anti-Slavery Opinion in France in the Second Half of the Eighteenth Century* (1937; rpt. New York: Burt Franklin, 1971), 178. See also Ardele Striker, "Spectacle in the Service of Humanity": The Negrophile Play in France from 1789 to 1850," *Black American Literature Forum* 19 (summer 1985): 76–82. Surprisingly, Striker makes no reference to Ducis's *Othello*.

13. Archives of the Comédie-Française, Registre des pièces nouvelles, R. 121/1 (1757–93).

14. C. M. Haines, for instance, in *Shakespeare in France: Criticism: Voltaire to Victor Hugo* (London: Oxford University Press, 1925), 78, says that Ducis had "white-wash[ed] Othello's face." It is worth noting that the dying Louis XV's face was described as "swollen and copper-coloured, like a Moor or a Negro," quoted in English by Vincent Cronin, *Louis and Antoinette* (London: Collins, 1974), 67.

15. Letter from Ducis to Alexandre Deleyre (13 December 1782), in Paul Albert, ed., *Lettres de Jean-François Ducis*, new ed. (Paris: Jousset, 1879), 64.

16. *Journal de Paris*, 10 November 1792: 189. The author of the letter was Carbon de Flins des Olivier, a fellow dramatist and Girondin.

17. Ducis, foreword to *Othello* (Paris: Maradan, an II [1794]).

18. Parker "Reading Wordsworth's Power," 302.

19. E.-C. Fréron, *Année littéraire* 1 (1776): 240.

20. Lytton Strachey's view, quoted in Shakespeare, *Othello*, ed. J. Dover Wilson (Cambridge: Cambridge University Press, 1969), xxix.

21. Manuscript letter from Ducis to Talma, 22 December 1792, Archives of the Comédie-Française.

22. *Journal de théâtres*, 19 pluviôse III [7 February 1795]: 376.

23. Ducis, 10 pluviôse II [29 January 1794], Bibliothèque nationale, n. a. fr., MS 24,005, f.373.

24. Cobban, *A History of Modern France*, 1:227.

25. In a song composed in honor of *la décade* in Year III [1795], quoted by Albert, *Lettres*, lv.

The "Elizabethan Experiment," Part One: Shakespeare's Playhouse of the Future

PHILIP PARSONS

THE New Fortune Playhouse in the Arts Faculty Building at the University of Western Australia was opened in 1964 to make possible practical research into the staging techniques of the Elizabethan public playhouse for which Shakespeare wrote. Experience gained there, first through the inaugural production of *Hamlet,* and later in an experimental production of *Richard III,* prompted a series of productions, chiefly in collaboration with the Sydney Theatre Company, exploring the actor-audience relationship for which Shakespeare wrote, and its potential for modern theater. In this chapter I propose to survey the findings of all these productions and the staging principles that have emerged from them; and to discuss them in the light of the performance tradition inherited by Shakespeare. It is my contention that Shakespeare's theater has too often been seen in the light of notions of progress and evolution from Elizabethan primitiveness to modern sophistication, and too rarely seen in the context of the Elizabethan theater's historical origins in ritual and metaphysics. I shall further argue that the modern stage has confined Shakespeare, and the classic tradition he represents, in a straitjacket that makes practical realization of the full amplitude of his power and vision impossible, and that the Shakespeare we inherit in our theaters is all too often a grotesquely diminished figure.

In the study of theater history there is no such thing as the benefit of hindsight. Hindsight, on the contrary, is a distorting lens. It leads us constantly to see and misinterpret the past in terms of our modern and often unconscious preconceptions. Well within living memory there was a constant, if unacknowledged, search by theater scholars for equivalents, however remote, of the curtained nineteenth-century proscenium arch stage. Curtains were imagined by some earlier scholars, slung between the two stage posts of the Elizabethan playhouse, thus permitting the setup of major scenes behind them while "curtain scenes" were being performed in front. With the notion of a recessed and curtained "inner stage," the search reached its triumphant conclusion. Here was the real Elizabethan stage, a small and no doubt cramped but genuine precursor of the proscenium stage, to which the huge open platform in front of it was merely the "forestage." Crude no doubt it was, but it at least permitted a theatrical imagination formed on current theater concepts to move with some degree of comfort (and, as we now realize, all too often misleadingly) through Shakespeare's texts.

Thanks to Brechtian thinking and practice on the one hand and the Elizabethan-inspired arena staging of Tyrone Guthrie on the other, today's mainstream professional theater is predictably more eclectic, more open to the significance of historical theater research—which has, of course, developed enormously over the last half century. Practical investigation such as my own of theater history may still seem to future scholars absurdly colored by our current notions of theater; but at least it will be grounded in a large and growing body of historical fact.

It was the building of the New Fortune Theatre that first aroused my serious interest in the Elizabethan stage. Its "onlie begetter" was Professor Allan Edwards who presided over an English department that held firmly to the view that drama was written for performance and could not be fully understood without reference to its theater, acting style, and the climate of ideas that brought it into being. The New Fortune is a unique reconstruction of the prime stage and auditorium dimensions of the Fortune Theatre, built at Cripplegate in 1600 by the great Elizabethan actor Edward Alleyn and his entrepreneur father-in-law Richard Henslowe; and already its mere existence had presented me with some new and challenging ideas. At that time the mainstream theater form was proscenium arch pictorial realism and it was only natural that scholarly attention was preoccupied by the stage picture, and especially the players' tiring house, as seen by an audience member positioned in the yard—that is to say, the front stalls in a modern theater. But to walk around the galleries of the New Fortune was to be persuaded forcefully that this was not a modern theater: that the view from the yard, the cheapest part of the house, was of no special significance and that the stage was not pictorial but sculptural. Indeed, for my money the most interesting audience position is about two-thirds of the way back from the stage in the first-floor side galleries, where one is most vividly aware of the three-dimensional stage.

In the second place one is struck by the heroic yet intimate scale of the performance. The Fortune was a square playhouse in which a stage 14 meters broad by 9 meters deep projected from one side of an 18-meter square yard. That is to say, the front of the stage extended to exactly the middle of the yard—a huge, heroic platform, yet giving the illusion of being near enough to touch from any part of the theater. The stage, so the historical evidence suggests, would have been more or less at eye height for the audience standing in the yard. To them the figure of Lear, towering above them, must have seemed formidable indeed; and no less so from the galleries where the actors would have been seen with a sea of faces at their feet. And yet that same towering Lear can ask with domestic intimacy, "Pray you, undo this button."

Also noticeable, and at first puzzling, was what I can only call the dynamic of the theater, which draws even the casual visitor to walk straight downstage to the very edge of the platform and take up a position at its center. To those accustomed to a proscenium arch theater, where the position of dominance is upstage center, this seems an uncomfortable anomaly; but in fact it is from that downstage position at the precise center of the four walls that the actor finds he or she can command the entire auditorium.

The New Fortune was inaugurated with a production of *Hamlet*, directed by the late Jeana Bradley, who had a distinguished record of work in academic theater. It was a sumptuously mounted production, which attracted large audiences to see for themselves how Shakespeare appeared in a theater of his own time. What they found was a stage full of swirling color and movement, somewhat in the Tyrone Guthrie style, against a background of great purple banners, the whole enhanced by moody, atmospheric lighting. The production was a resounding popular success but those looking for some special magic in this unique playhouse could only feel that what they were seeing was not, after all, radically different from the Shakespeare productions to which they were accustomed. It was only with an experimental afternoon performance that the distinctive character and power of a unique actor-audience relationship began to be glimpsed.

According to every conventional expectation this performance should have been no more than a worthy academic exercise. In broad daylight the actors had none of the aids to illusion provided by stage lighting. The Ghost, for example, whose armor, translucent green cloak, and ghastly pallor were so impressive at night, was revealed in the afternoon light to be wearing a fireman's helmet, painted kitchen gloves and trailing yards of green mosquito netting. Astonishingly, where at night he had been impressive, by daylight he was downright alarming.

The Australian Broadcasting Commission was to film the experiment and had promoted it widely. The result was a packed audience, many of whom had probably never set foot in any theater before. But they became totally absorbed in the story, simply taking their cue from the actors. What would have been ludicrous intrusions on the nighttime performance were here simply ignored. Gertrude, scattering her flowers upon Ophelia who had just descended into the grave, was confronted by a cameraman rising from the trap to capture her in close-up. Absorbed in the narrative, the audience simply ignored him. Gertrude, with professional discipline, did the same. There had been some debate among the actors how to cope with the bodies littering the stage at the end—their exits, of course, were regularly covered by a blackout. In this performance they simply got up from the floor to hearty applause.

The whole experience I found deeply impressive. What it revealed most clearly was that this sound conventional production of *Hamlet* was precisely that—conventional. A proscenium production without the proscenium arch. One even had a suspicion that it might have proved more effective behind that arch. But in this theater there was clearly an imaginative power generated by daylight which constituted a different and quite distinctive theatrical experience.

My conviction that the New Fortune's secret lay in the audience creating the play for themselves at the prompting of the actors, instead of passively receiving what the actors had to offer, was confirmed by a similar afternoon's performance in 1965 of the medieval miracle play *Noah's Flood* under the direction of Katharine Brisbane. Although designed for a conventional theater, the style of the production was deliberately one of make-believe, with Noah's ark constructed from painted panels in front of the audience. God was clothed in cotton sheeting with rather an impressive golden mask to set him aside from the other characters. Behind the proscenium the effect was amiable and naive. By daylight in the New Fortune, however, God's appearance was such that small children were alarmed and one vomited. It was the Ghost in *Hamlet* all over again.

From these incidental hints and illuminations the obvious next step was a full-scale Elizabethan production at the New Fortune. It was therefore with real regret that I left the University of Western Australia and the New Fortune in 1965 to join the fledgling School of Drama at the University of New South Wales. The opportunity came, however, in 1968 with an invitation from the Festival of Perth committee to direct *Richard III* with a professional cast drawn from the Perth Playhouse company augmented by the student theater societies. At the university there had been some feeling that, in the absence of a positive policy, the New Fortune was becoming identified less with Elizabethan drama than with contemporary commercial theater. A safe, academic production of *Richard III* would help correct the balance. I determined the production would be thoroughly academic in that no aspect of performance would lack sound historical warrant, though the result was not, perhaps, quite what the university had in mind.

The play was, of course, to be performed at night; but with uniform lighting over stage and auditorium we achieved a simulation of daylight conditions. Taking our cue from the Hope Theatre, where plays and bull- and bearbaiting were on offer to presumably the same audience, we gave the auditorium the appearance of a sporting event by covering the galleries with red and white striped canvas, and throwing in a few banners for good measure. And to further undercut the conventionally reverential approach to Shakespeare generally current twenty-five years ago, we took note that music was a feature of the Elizabethan theater for which one would often arrive early. Audiences approaching the New Fortune could hear popular marching tunes being beaten out by a small combo in the first-floor gallery. The playhouse's spotlit flag flew from its flagpole to complete the impression.

With the assistance of Professor David Bradley of Monash University we achieved a workable reduction of the male cast to sixteen—probably the size of Shakespeare's company at the time the play was written. This involved minor actors playing up to seven roles each; and since all had to be performed without makeup, and often without even an identifying quick costume change, we had brought home to us a basic principle of Elizabethan acting: that it had to be broad and presentational. If the messenger in one scene was to be young and sprightly, the citizen in the next had better be unmistakably elderly. Only by performance could the various roles be made distinct.

As for costume, we took our cue from Peacham's famous *Titus Andronicus* sketch and dressed the company in clothes of the day—black skivvy, trousers, and boots for the men, over which were flung colorful Tudor gowns for period reference and quick character identification.

Our chief problem, however, was to establish movement patterns. I had noticed a suggestive oddity in the Fortune contract, which specified that the stage was to project into the yard by 9 meters, but that it was to be 14 meters long. The term one would have expected, of course, was "broad." Combined with pictorial evidence of the period showing actors performing at the very front of the stage, this seemed a very clear indication of a cricket pitch stage designed for lateral confrontation (the bowler at one end and the batsman at the other).

The result was a quite extraordinary increase in the scale of the performances. When called upon to perform such vituperative confrontations as that, say, between Richard and Margaret, the actors in rehearsal instinctively drew as close as they would on a proscenium stage. The exchange was never more than mildly interesting. But when Richard at one corner hurled his insults to Margaret across forty feet they became, for the audience, creatures larger than life, in intimate and dangerous proximity. This was to be the beginning of an examination of acting style that we are still pursuing in Sydney.

At the time, however, our most exciting discoveries were those concerned with the use of the stage. The upstage area we found was relatively dead. Unless the downstage action happened to expand into it, the actors positioned there simply disappeared from audience interest. Its most useful function, we found, was to hold people unobtrusively who would later be drawn into the downstage action. The messenger who knocks at Hastings's door in the middle of the night first of all knocked naturally enough at the door at the rear of the stage. When Hastings appeared above they realized they could not see each other and the exchange seemed robbed of its urgency. The messenger retreated rapidly downstage. This is entirely in line with Beckerman's contention in his *Shakespeare at the Globe* that, although the action may extend to embrace such comparatively remote areas as the acting space "above," and even the audience itself, the focus of attention always remains the stage; and, I would add, the extreme downstage area.[1]

A stage seen as 14 meters long is not only confrontational but processional; and we soon discovered that all three sides were ideal for purposes ranging from formal pageantry to meetings in the street. Most interestingly of all, they gave us such an effective solution to the appearance of the ghosts before Richard and Richmond in their tents on the night before battle that I strongly suspect it reflects Elizabethan usage. Without lighting effects or symbolic ghostly costuming, we discovered that a simple processional entry to the steady beat of a dead march down one edge of the stage, across the front, then back up the other covered the extent of the ghosts' lines precisely; and further, that the cursing of Richard could very simply be made to end precisely downstage center, while the blessing of Richmond carried them around the corner and to the exit. The procession of arms pointing in accusation and then raised in blessing was all the acting required; the ritual movement did the rest.

Entry down the side of the stage covered a variety of less formal purposes but for urgent entries we found that a simple cross from the entrance to down center was the obvious route. These few basic movements, or some simple variation, seemed to cover all requirements of the text on that vast open stage, except for a few major scenes that brought on the whole cast. Neither we nor, I believe, the audience, felt any need to keep the entire acting area bustling. They were themselves providing the extras.

Shakespeare consistently treats the audience as participating actors. Out of a total cast of sixteen, only three, or at best four, actors are available to witness the hypocritically pious Richard, stationed above, asking Buckingham why he has led here such crowds of citizens. Buckingham is, of course, downstage center, heading, as it were, vast crowds in the pit and galleries; and the savage irony is that they, like a previous crowd whom Buckingham attempted to stir up as partisans for Richard's elevation to the throne, remain mum. As Richard protests that he's reluctantly taking government by popular demand in the face of his own conviction of unworthiness, he points out that we, as citizens, have brought on our own heads all that follows. In the same way, of course, the troops at Agincourt harangued by Henry are in the pit and galleries: "All the world's a stage"—the performance space reaches out to embrace universal proportions. And yet, when Hamlet embraces the audience in his meditation on suicide the stage shrinks to a little patch, just enough to support him alone. The imaginative power generated by that simple actor-audience relationship was borne in upon me as I had never experienced it before.

The capacity of the audience, as we had seen in that afternoon performance of *Hamlet*, to select from the stage what it needed to know in order for the play to proceed, was thoroughly confirmed by *Richard III.* It not only testified to a level of imaginative involvement different in kind and degree from conventional modern theater, but hinted at possibilities for our modern theater culture. These are issues pursued by Wayne Harrison and myself in our recent experimental series of Shakespeare productions.

It was not until 1986 that I was able to resume these investigations of the Elizabethan theater. Thanks to Wayne Harrison, then dramaturg of the Sydney Theatre Company and now its director, I was able to apply a small research grant from the University of New South Wales to an exploratory production of Marlowe's *Doctor Faustus* with a professional all-male cast led by John Howard as Faustus. My thought was to sidestep the vexed question of the tiring-house facade and the hitherto inhibiting lack of an Elizabethan reconstruction in Sydney. That same magical actor-audience relationship must surely have been recreated when the London companies went on tour. It seems highly likely that the fit-up stage on which they performed would have been that in standard use among traveling companies of the period—a platform raised some five or six feet on trestles or perhaps barrels (the same height in fact as that of the London playhouses) backed by a curtained enclosure. By setting up such a stage in the big, daylit rehearsal room of the STC I hoped to achieve a collaborative actor-audience relationship not substantially different from that of the New Fortune.

At the same time I wanted to see what would happen when the actors were faced with a similar hectic production schedule to that routinely experienced by an Elizabethan theater company, who, while performing daily rep—that is, a different play every day—would add a new play to their repertoire on average once a fortnight. Given that our own actors would be able to rehearse full time, it seemed reasonable to give them their scripts on Monday morning for a performance the following Saturday. Direction in the modern sense was clearly impossible. The actors were given the movement patterns that had emerged at the New Fortune and some assistance with the text. Otherwise they were left to direct themselves while desperately learning their lines. Each scene was rehearsed once, with the interesting exception of the clowning scenes, where routines had to be devised.

True to Elizabethan precedent for an outdoor fit-up performance, we provided no seating. The audience promptly arranged themselves in neat rows on the floor. Lesson number one: you can't recreate an Elizabethan audience. There was, however, a small refreshment booth and audiences were invited to move about freely throughout the performance. Enough did so to create an easy fluidity in the auditorium. The result was quite extraordinary. The actors were terrified of facing any audience, let alone this one, with their lines hardly down; and in the first scene there were a couple of "dries." But when the prompter, standing in plain sight, intervened, instead of embarrassment there was cheerful, encouraging applause. The actors quickly realized that instead of confrontation they had eager collaboration. The performance took off like a rocket. As an actors' agent remarked to me, huge waves of energy seemed to flow from the stage, to be returned immediately by the audience. The sense of exhilaration in the room was tangible and at the end we were overwhelmed with requests for further such performances. This was the beginning of Dramaturgical Services Inc., a production company created by Wayne Harrison and myself for the specific purpose of exploring this actor-audience relationship with a series of classical and finally, we hope, modern plays.

I have dwelt at some length on the New Fortune experience and then on *Doctor Faustus* because they have provided the basis for all our subsequent work—*Hamlet* and *1 Henry IV* in 1987, *Othello* in 1988, *1 Henry IV* and *King Lear* in 1991, *Antony and Cleopatra* and *Much Ado* in 1992. Throughout these latter productions our understanding of the actor-audience relationship has developed steadily.

First, we have discovered the importance of a sense of freedom for the audience. The actors announce at the beginning, either directly or through a specially written prologue, that they are about to begin the play and will not stop until the end, but the audience must feel free to come and go throughout the performance (the precedent, of course, is Elizabethan) and to buy refreshments, available in the auditorium. Surprisingly most of the audience always seem happy to sit throughout on the backless benches we provide in lieu of the usual regimented theater seating. Set at liberty in this way, and with no seductive stage illusion to draw them in, the audience must positively choose to go with the story being acted out for them. That is the meaning of "On your imaginary forces work," and audiences love it.

Liberty, the liberated imagination of the listener to the storyteller speaking of wonders—that is the key to Elizabethan dramaturgy. The Elizabethan was not a theater of introspection in the modern manner, where the brilliantly lit actors create a world of their own that draws the audience in. Rather, actors and audience met together in their daylit space in order that a story might be told. And the Elizabethan appetite for narrative was immense. As Harley Granville Barker remarked, the business of the Elizabethan theater was to tell a story, "as fresh and exciting a one as possible; if it can tell two at a time, so much the better."[2] The cultural dominance of the nineteenth-century psychological novel and the rise of Freud have done much to distort Shakespeare's emphasis on the overriding importance of the narrative line.

As a storyteller the actor needs to address his audience, and to do so it is only natural to approach them as closely as possible. That is why the action is concentrated at the front of the stage. It is now widely accepted that the soliloquies of Hamlet are intended to be addressed to the audience, and indeed the actor-audience relationship of the daylit stage makes any other approach absurd: the actor who tries to commune with himself in the manner of modern naturalism simply disappears; the audience feels rightly that whatever he has to say has nothing to do with them.

But direct address to the audience, as we discovered, can be taken much further. Actors in dialogue who face each other are far less effective than if they address each other only initially and thereafter speak directly to the audience, turning only occasionally to the intended recipient. To the audience they appear to have been addressing each other throughout, but the scene registers far more vividly than if they had in fact been doing so. This has become our invariable method. Perhaps the face-to-audience performance of the storyteller, in a context of basic repetitive movement, sounds like visually boring theater. But this is not a pictorial stage. All that matters is the actors, audience, and text. Scenic elements and properties are added only for clear delivery of the narrative. The uniformly positive reviews we have received for our productions indicate we are on the right track. Two further areas of investigation in the DSI productions remain to be noticed.

The all-male casting principle was carried on from *Faustus* to *Hamlet* and *1 Henry IV* in 1987. This had never been possible at the New Fortune, and it now raised the difficulty that, whereas Shakespeare's company had skilled boy apprentices with unbroken voices to play the female roles, we had to cast young men. We were encouraged, however, by the positive audience reaction to the young man who played Lust in *Doctor Faustus* (Helen of

Troy wore a serene female mask) and accordingly Ophelia was played by an attractive but very male young actor, Brian Meagan, while the strapping Hugo Weaving, who had been engaged to play Hotspur, asked for Gertrude also: a remarkably challenging commitment. After some initial giggling, the level of audience acceptance was remarkable. The audience as usual saw what they needed to see and indeed Brian Meagan was among the most affecting Ophelias in my experience. But despite the interest of the experiment, we were at a disadvantage. The fact is that an Elizabethan audience would have taken male performers for granted—and indeed would have been shocked by the appearance of a woman on stage; a modern audience can never completely set aside its expectation that female roles are for women, or if it does, the choice is inevitably self-conscious; and confusion is worse confounded by the intervening traditions of the drag queen and the pantomime dame. In the most real sense male and female casting seems today more faithful to the unselfconscious Elizabethan experience, and mixed casts have performed our subsequent productions with the exception of *King Lear*.

Here we were interested to see whether male performance would bring out certain masculine qualities in Goneril and Regan and, less obviously, in Cordelia. In modern productions her dutiful quietness can appear passive to the point of insipidity. Male casting, we thought, might underline her toughness in refusing to humor her father, and also remind us that this is a woman who can lead an army to his rescue. In both respects we were not disappointed, but surprisingly it was the tenderness of Angelo d'Angelo's Cordelia that most affected the audience. Neither of the actors playing Goneril and Regan felt quite comfortable in a female role, and the hectic rehearsal schedule never allowed them to settle in. Certainly the viciousness of the pair emerged more powerfully than in most productions, but—perhaps for self-defense—the actors were chiefly interested in exploring the hints of comedy in these two businesslike women. Although the experiment is not one I would repeat in a full-scale production, it fulfilled its purpose in providing much useful information for women performing these roles.

The second area of investigation is the most important, and one we continue to explore. A distinctive acting style has begun to develop among those actors who have become familiar with our style. We do not look for through-characterization. We simply ask of each scene, "What does the audience need to know?"

and deliver it accordingly. Our emphasis is, and will always remain, on the text. Shakespeare's plays are the product of an oral
culture where language was a delight; and thanks, I believe, to
our constant reference to the phrasing and pointing of the first
folio (which, of course, has the interest of collecting texts as actually performed by a skilled company with which Shakespeare
was long associated) our productions have developed a distinctive reputation for clarity. But, as Hamlet pointed out, language
should also find expression in appropriate gesture.

Given our deliberately short rehearsal period and the basically
naturalistic training of our actors, we have had little opportunity
so far to work on this visual language. But now the actors are
themselves beginning to find that to unlock emotional truth often
requires broad gestures not unlike those of eighteenth- and
nineteenth-century theater prints. This is, of course, entirely
logical since the acting tradition inherited from Shakespeare's
day flickered out only with the rise of realism in line with the
developing proscenium arch stage. Its last traces can still be seen
in the work of early film actors. The proper exploration of this
external acting tradition and, especially, its roots in the Elizabethan playhouse seems a next necessary step in DSI production
style.

But it is time to call a halt and attempt some overall view.
Is scholarly investigation of the Elizabethan theater simply for
scholars? Or has it something to offer in the way we make theater
today? I believe, with the lively conviction of a theater prac-
titioner, that it has.

The audience is the forgotten factor in our modern theater: it
brings the huge imaginative resources of the human spirit, if
only the theater would use them. By addressing his audience as
inhabiting a universe embracing angels and devils, Shakespeare
gives them huge stature, casts them in their true roles as human
creatures, body, mind, and spirit. Macbeth wrestling with spiritual forces that finally overwhelm his nature is their struggle too.
His world is their world: "Life's but a walking shadow, a poor
player, / That struts and frets his hour upon the stage, / And then
is heard no more."

It is because common day means common reality that daylight
playing—the sharing of this light of common day—is not just
technically important but of profound spiritual significance.
This world of the play is not some carefully prepared slice of
life which we, the audience, are invited to stand off and view, be
moved by, and discuss. It is not the personal vision of some

director in which we are invited to see some comment on life through his or her free interpretation of the text. It is life itself, a reaching out to explore the powers that inhabit the universe of which we are the creatures, and to experience their meaning. It is the theater of revelations. It leads us all deeper into our common life, thanks to the inspired insight of the artist. Tyrone Guthrie affirmed that the function of Macbeth was finally "to reveal something about the nature of mankind, even the nature of God . . . such aspects of the Almighty God as are associated with enlightenment, justice, pity and awe."[3]

Shakespeare's open stage derives originally from the "open stage" of the medieval church. That was the stage for a sacred communal ritual that embraced the participants and the whole universe in its meaning, a unity expressed in the common universe they shared. The medieval secular stage was equally a theater of ritual; and the ritual elements noted in Shakespeare follow on from the folk and religious rituals of the earthy morality and mystery plays and, behind them, from the mass. One need hardly point out, for instance, that Everyman centers on ritual sacrifice.

Ritual is characterized by daylight performance. The priest at mass is not isolated in a spotlit world of his own—he is acting with and for the congregation. Christ, crucified in the medieval marketplace, is acting with and for those who pause to listen: "Is it nothing to you, all ye that pass by?" It is in this sense that Everyman is a ritual sacrifice: he is any member of the congregation, drawn up onto the stage as a redemptive example for us all.

The mystery cycles provide a model for the history plays of Shakespeare. Though the mystery plays span the meaning of the universe from its beginning to its end, the histories build up a comparable moral span, from the introduction of conflict and disharmony into the garden of England to their necessary resolution in blood and renewal. And the tragedies still have the shadow of the mass behind them. They are now far removed from any overt liturgy—the characters are getting more realistic, for example; but they are still daylit: actors and audience are still at one in collaborative celebration, tragic or comic.

Ritual is characterized by simple but significant movement. It is demonstrative, not exploratory. Hence the almost monotonous lateral and processional movement at the front of the Elizabethan stage: the almost hypnotic flow of scene after scene. Hence also the "demonstrational," in the Brechtian sense, nature of the acting, the communication directly with and through the audience.

Ritual of the theater does not suddenly end in the seventeenth century. As long as the illuminated auditorium persists (that is, well into the nineteenth century) there remains something of communal celebration, ritual. Indeed, it withered away only under the onslaught of naturalism and the new spirit of scientific materialism that brought it into being. That is why Shakespeare's playhouse has to be seen, not as a remote precursor of the modern theater, but as the final and greatest flowering of the medieval open stage where the divine and diabolic powers confront Renaissance man in dramatic poetry of enduring and astonishing power.

I suggest that if we really want to hear again the poetry of the great world we must leave our purpose-built theaters to do what they do best and make genuine common spaces into playhouses—halls, warehouses, tents, if need be—the sort of spaces that traveling companies of Shakespeare's day could look for. Whether by day or night, we must become aware again, preferably through clear windows, of the great world we are focusing on our stage. Best of all, let us try to do it by God's good daylight.

Notes

1. Bernard Beckerman, *Shakespeare at the Globe, 1599–1609* (New York: Macmillan, 1962), 87, 92, and passim.

2. Harley Granville Barker, *On Dramatic Method: The Clark Lectures for 1930* (London: Sidgwick and Jackson, 1931), 17.

3. Tyrone Guthrie, *In Various Directions* (London: Michael Joseph, 1965), 37.

The "Elizabethan Experiment," Part Two: Reconstructing Elizabethan Performance Conditions in Sydney, 1986–92: The View from the Audience

PENNY GAY

THE "Elizabethan Experiment" began as the vision of one man, Philip Parsons, with the assistance of his former student, director Wayne Harrison (now the artistic director of the Sydney Theatre Company). The productions of 1 Henry IV and King Lear in 1991, which this chapter is largely based around, composed the fourth short season of the enterprise, which had previously undertaken Dr. Faustus, Hamlet, Othello, and another 1 Henry IV (all texts set for the New South Wales Higher School Certificate). The 1992 season, which I shall also discuss briefly, presented Antony and Cleopatra and had some input into a conventional-stage production of Much Ado about Nothing.[1]

Parsons has described the growth of the experiment, from its germination in Perth in the 1960s at the New Fortune space of the University of Western Australia to its flowering in Sydney in the 1980s. Sydney is the undisputed theatrical capital of Australia (it is also home to the National Institute of Dramatic Art [NIDA] and the Australian Opera); its audiences, arguably, are knowledgeable and keen to try "experiments" such as this (though it is also arguable that Adelaide, host to the biennial Arts Festival, is more ready to welcome avant-garde experiments). Certainly the seasons were well attended by the general public as well as the conscripted school students; performances had the air of a relaxed yet exciting and enjoyable theatrical occasion. Audience and actors, mingling before and after the performances, palpably shared the pleasure.

I Recreating the Stage-Audience Relationship

Practical and economic considerations dictated that the stage for the Elizabethan Experiment was modeled on the fit-up stage of an Elizabethan touring company—"what was there," or what could be easily erected in the various halls, tents, and yards in which the performances took place. The most recent seasons used an old warehouse under the Sydney Theatre Company's Wharf Theatre: a space intersected by huge, rough-hewn wooden pillars, enclosed by a curtained corridor running round the edge of the audience area. Members of the audience were seated on benches, with the option of getting up and walking round, visiting the cake and coffee stall at the back; performances were without an interval, and ran for about three hours. Facing the rows of benches was an open-end stage, 1.5 m. high, 9 m. wide, 3.5 m. deep, with a black-curtained "tiring-house" of three entrances—not a thrust stage, therefore, but modeled rather more on historians' images of the Blackfriars indoor theater (after which it was for the nonce named), though with the addition of the pillars of the outdoor theater's "heavens." Recreations of the Globe must be left to those with considerably more money, and a guarantee of permanent commercial success in the form of tourists—as in Japan, America, or soon beside the Thames—though those who have attended performances at Stratford's Swan Theatre may feel that they have already experienced the actor-audience relationship of the Elizabethan thrust stage as far as it *can* be recreated.

John Senczuk, a designer and theater studies teacher, was brought into the experiment in 1988 in order to regularize this setup and make it as efficient as possible. He comments, "I've now adjusted the height of the stage so that it's eye-height when people are sitting down; historically, the stage was often eye-height for people standing in the street (I'm thinking of the medieval wagons)." The importance of this perspective is explained by his theory of the "horizon line":

> What this Shakespeare stage does is put the performer right on the horizon line for the audience, and you're thus making the performer "superhuman," much larger. You're not seeing any visual image behind you, you're seeing just the performer. The Shakespeare stage brings that horizon line much closer, so that you have superhuman personalities who can expound great moral issues, heroics. We don't use chairs for the audience, but benches, for this reason, it gets people sitting lower, so that they have to look up to see.

Senczuk remarks on the foreignness of modern auditoriums (whether proscenium arch or thrust stage) to the Shakespearean drama: by forcing the audience to look *down* on the performers, "it reduces the significance of the poetic language, and makes the performers look ant-like," which is fine, as he says, for the naturalistic drama, "where you are watching an experiment," but works against the genre of Elizabethan drama, reducing its scale.

This issue is obviously related to the "presentational" style encouraged in the actors by Parsons and Harrison, to which I shall return. I want to comment now on a few other features of the stage and how they were used. The stage was noticeably small and shallow, quite different from what has been inferred of the Globe's huge thrust acting area. There was no audience around the sides, and of course no galleries. On this "wagon model," according to the directors, "all the modern notions of upstage and downstage don't work"; the acting "hot spots" are at the two front corners, not upstage center as in proscenium arch stages. Nevertheless actors had difficulty in breaking the habits of the modern stage, according to Senczuk:

> Most of this drama is direct address, and if a two-scene hogs the center of the stage it becomes too intimate. Separated, the actors have much more scope—it's a much stronger position for them. Also it means that communication between two people becomes much *less* naturalistic, which makes the language more acceptable, and stresses the play's "story-telling."

Finally, Senczuk points to the effects gained by the three curtained entrances at the back of the stage (in fact, two more, on either side of the curtains, were occasionally used): exits and entrances were punctuated by the manual closing of the curtains, fast or slowly, as the occasion suggested. At times one of the curtained areas was used as an "interior," as in *Lear's* hovel (3.6). Furthermore, it was possible to create a sense of an "inner circle" on the stage between the curtains and the two pillars, thus facilitating "overhearing" or "watching" scenes, or alternatively, separate realities copresent on the stage—for example, Emilia and Desdemona on a corner of the stage discussing the loss of the handkerchief, while Cassio stands in the "inner circle" and casually wipes his brow with it. The outer space became a "run-around" or "pageant" area, with actors entering through one of the side back curtains and exiting through the other (Hamlet pursuing the Ghost, for instance), leaving the middle one for ceremonial entrances—Lear's entries in 1.1 and 5.3—and more static, symbolic configurations. Battle scenes obviously made energetic use of the outer circle; and blind Gloucester had a pillar to sit against as he meditated on patience in the midst of the battle. All this seemed "natural," effortless use of the small but uncluttered stage space, and one felt that these must indeed have been the effects gained on the touring company's fit-up stage—effects made much more expansive (and energetic) on the larger Globe stage. There was, however, to a modern eye, something slightly cartoonish about "action" on such a shallow stage, exciting though the proximity to the brilliantly choreographed fights was. The stage also did not allow space for variety in crowded scenes: the actors tended to sort themselves into a straight line along the front, or a shallow symmetrical V—the anti-naturalistic "chorus line" effect.

II   Directors and Actors

The uniform "daylight" lighting throughout the theater had the effect, consciously sought for by Parsons and Harrison, of including the audience in the action. In its simplest terms, this meant that the soliloquies, and some occasional comic turns, were directed unashamedly to the audience. But the most striking departure from modern convention in the acting was in the insistence on a "presentational" rather than "representational" style. The emphasis was on "telling the story" of each scene, and of the play as a whole: technically, this meant a high proportion of any speech was directed out front. Ron Haddrick, who played Lear, describes the technique thus: "You indicate briefly, 'I'm talking to *him*, but *this* [to the audience] is what I'm telling him.'" This had a distinctly alienating effect at first, but actors and audience relaxed as the play progressed, and the strangeness was less noticeable. Haddrick pointed out that it was vital to pinpoint individual members of the audience, even for half a line at a time: a generalized front delivery might as well be spoken into the dark void of the modern theater. The paradigm for the actor was that of the storyteller, always at work to engage his audience, and getting back from them a supportive energy to continue the tale; the audience are silent actors. Thus this "experiment" attempts to revive a perhaps idealized sense of community—an ideal somewhat ambivalently fulfilled when a huge proportion of the audience is schoolchildren, press-ganged into watching a performance of their set text. Though the children did, by and large, enjoy the performances, they were an unrepresentative and, one must assume, at times an unwilling audience. Parsons and Harrison were determined that there should be no playing down to this audience (the "easy laugh"), but sometimes it was the only way to hold their attention. Luciano Martucci, whose Edmund had more than a touch of the swaggering melodrama villain, said, "It is a dangerously thrilling mode of performance: you felt the audience strengthening you—or rejecting you! The challenge was to make them *want* to sit and listen. On a good day, the audience for *Henry IV* responded *passionately*, cheering, booing." On such days the barrier of "high culture" was certainly breached.

The approach to character required of the actors was, as we have seen, that they should simply present the story. Each scene was to be looked at for itself: Parsons's question to the actors was, "What does the audience need to get out of this scene in terms of the story?" Thus the modern actor's technique, in creating a character, of finding a "through-line," a unified motivation for all the character's actions and utterances, was consciously rejected; this was to be, in Harrison's words, "external" not "internal" acting. As Ron Haddrick explained:

> You don't try and do a Stanislavski or a Freud, because Shakespeare didn't know them! So you play that scene for what it is, what the conflict is there. The next scene may contrast, but you play *it* for what it is—it's almost like a jigsaw puzzle. Finally when it's all put together, there you've got the rounded man. But if you decide "Lear is an irascible old man," then you'll miss out on facets of his character.

A nostalgia for the "unified character" still hangs around this; it is significant that the only scene that Haddrick at first had trouble with was in fact the opening scene: what is Lear's real motivation in giving up his kingdom, he wanted to know; what sort of man does this? Parsons told him simply to go for the storytelling aspect: "Once upon a time there was a king, and he had three daughters. . . ." But from the audience's point of view, there is no doubt that for the rest of the play Haddrick was creating "his" King Lear—a plain man used to power. Is it, in fact, possible to retrain actors in such a short time (there were forty hours rehearsal for *Lear*) out of the habit of a professional lifetime, the desire to create a "rounded" character? Haddrick added that he had no doubt that if the season had continued for a longer period (it ran for only ten days), his characterization would have "developed"; the whole play "would have gone further." But this, as Philip Parsons would reply, would be to operate under a different theatrical system than the "repertory" of the Elizabethan companies, with a new play on average once a fortnight.

The young NIDA-trained actor, Luciano Martucci (who played Hotspur and Edmund in the 1991 season), offers a different perspective on the actor's and director's processes in the experiment: the actors, told that they should "direct themselves," were very excited as they began exploring the lines, but found that with the short rehearsal period they were obliged to craft for performance their first choice about a scene (each scene was only rehearsed once): "we had to follow our instinct more than usual." On the other hand, the haste of the whole enterprise meant that the director's power of decision, as the one seeing it from out front, was absolute; there was little time for negotiation, or "trying it another way." Here we must assume that the director's ("academic") ideas and interpretation of the lines' "meaning" took the place of the Elizabethan actor's training and instinct for what was right on the Elizabethan stage: "While directorial interpretation is kept to a minimum, Philip Parsons and Wayne Harrison have deputised for Shakespeare, who presumably had some input into the way in which his stories were told."[2] We might think of this, in critical parlance, as invisible essentialism: a more accurate formulation would be, "What does this twentieth-century Australian audience need to know—what do we, in this context, believe is the meaning of this scene?" There is, after all, no such thing as an unvarnished story; there is a plot, and there are tellers of it; and the tellers, being actors, will embody its meaning for them and for the audience they are communicating with. So, for example, the young but very experienced actor of Gadshill in 1 *Henry IV*, Steven Vidler, made a modern "camp" clown out of the character in 2.1, playing with immense relish the final speech of the scene: "Go to, 'homo' is a common name to all men. Bid the ostler bring my gelding out of the stable. Farewell, you muddy knave." This was certainly not "museum theater," but a living interaction with a contemporary audience and its *twentieth*-century slang.

Wayne Harrison has come to believe that the experiment works best with an active director—not just one who corrects the actors' modern habits, but one who sees a theme or pattern in the play and tries to bring that out in the production, whatever might be its presentational or representational techniques:

I tried to give *Henry IV* an historical context, to increase the audience's understanding of the play [so he began with a potted "vaudeville" *Richard II*]. I tried to run through it some of the ideas of honor and blood. . . . I locked into the political side of the play as well, and tried to play up that historical political through-line that links those four plays.

In the same way, if one were to go by the program notes issued for each play, it might be argued that Parsons wished to see the plays as embodying the "Elizabethan World Picture," and *Lear*, particularly, as illustrating the theme of Christian patience. But for the audience, without the help of symbolic design, the plays remained simply good stories—though they might have gone home and, with the assistance of their program notes, begun reflecting on the plays in terms such as these.

Parsons argues that the Elizabethan theater was an *aural* theater—the word was primary. To Martucci, this emphasis on the plays' aurality meant a certain sacrifice of the actor's visual techniques and the subtleties of naturalism: "You have to demand the audience's attention through being heard and understood." Several of the actors did not in fact have the vocal technique to project as effectively as they might in the acoustically unhelpful ("open-air") space—most of their work had, naturally enough, been on television, where there is nothing to match Shakespeare's complex speeches and rich metaphor, nor any immediate receptors beyond the camera and the boom mike. Thus, the experiment is inherently problematic, although exciting and challenging, for actors trained in the techniques of modern performance.

III   Nonverbal Effects

Undoubtedly the most striking visual effect was the casting, in *King Lear*, of men in the women's roles. What the Elizabethans took for granted (at least, in seeing well-trained boys play these parts), of course, produced considerable unease in an audience used to seeing women's roles played by women. Though the directors cast young, lightly built men (unlike Hugo Weaving's giant Gertrude in 1987), the effect still tended toward pantomime dame; the actors themselves were uncomfortable with the roles, and attempted to compensate for what they perhaps constructed as the audience's contempt with a strongly comic edge to their playing. Parsons claims that he sees, through remembering their original impersonation by males, a "masculine" quality in Goneril and Regan, and even in Cordelia (who eventually leads an army). But would he have seen the same in the young boys with their unbroken voices who first played these roles? What the

Sydney audience saw rather was a not very accomplished drag act, in which "feminine" characteristics such as a housewife's exasperation at untidy guests, or a heartfelt desire to get out of one's good clothes (after the ceremony of 1.1), were delightedly recognized by the audience. Thus Goneril and Regan's descent into evil became the painless mischief of the Bad Fairy, and the heterosexual consciousness that we expect in the play—for example, between Goneril and Edmund, or even between Lear and Cordelia—went by the board. (Harrison had women as the two wives in 1 *Henry IV*; Mistress Quickly remained an effectively comic pantomime dame, as played by John Derum.)[3] In the 1992 *Antony and Cleopatra* the four female roles were taken by women: Sandy Gore's Cleopatra was a serpent of old Nile in the grand style, with a voice to match—her performance drew on music-hall or melodrama modes of acting, comically self-aware rather than "tragic" in the romantic manner, and thus kept that connection with the audience, which is the vital center of the Elizabethan Experiment.

Indeed, there was much that was refreshing about the adoption of Elizabethan performance conditions. At the simplest level, the freedom of the audience to move around meant that for the most part they stayed still, riveted by the story that was being played out so clearly before them, and when they did get up, they did so quietly, keeping their eyes on the stage—not a captive audience in a darkened auditorium, but voluntary *assistants*, with whom the actors maintained eye contact, at a communal event. In this, of course, the uniform "daylight" lighting was immensely coercive. The audience was fascinated by the *presence* of the actors, not necessarily as "stars" "seen through a telescope" (so Martucci described the effect of the modern theater's lighting), but as something more akin to athletes, displaying their abilities "with an almost pugilistic immediacy," as Wayne Harrison says—and with nothing to assist them except for some elementary symbolic costuming. The actors for the 1991 season were dressed in a uniform midblue costume of trousers and shirt, with short modern lace-up boots: Senczuk explains, "the higher up you were in the social hierarchy, the more you embellished yourself" with cloaks and crowns and bits of armor (the actors were instructed to find what they thought suited their character from the STC's wardrobe). In 1992 a rather more conventional control was exerted over costume design, with a curiously liberating effect for the actors: the Egyptians were dressed in colorful "Oriental" drapes, of indeterminate period; the Romans in togas, or, more often, in modern business suits (including the "power-dressed" Octavia). That is, a recognizably modern idea of "symbolic costuming" was operating, rather than the earlier attempt to provide a "neutral" background for archaic symbolic props.

My own favorite "effect" was in the storm scenes in *King Lear*. Sound effects were created by a thunder sheet, a wind machine, and a rain machine: these last two cylinders on a stand, one covered with canvas which scraped against a board as it was turned, the other made of chicken wire and containing polystyrene "pebbles," both creating an immensely satisfying sound of howling wind and driving rain. Actors who were not on stage at the time operated these devices at the side of the stage, a task that required considerable strength and endurance, and which had its own athletic fascination for the audience (a Brechtian effect here!). When the wind and rain machines suddenly stopped we knew that the action had moved back to the interior of Gloucester's castle: nobody missed the electrician's arts.

IV   Conclusions

The simplicity and directness of the "presentational" style meant that the theatrical occasion, while gaining in pace and immediate audience communication, lacked something almost indefinable that we have come to expect of theater—especially of Shakespeare: glamour, perhaps, the mystery of other worlds of experience, certainly. These were people of our world, telling us a story that we vaguely knew already—folktale (*King Lear*), national chronicle (*Henry IV*), a famous love-tragedy (*Antony and Cleopatra*). On the whole, the audience was played to as though it were a "simple" Elizabethan audience, rather than one with four centuries more of human history to deal with, though the costuming of *Antony and Cleopatra* acknowledged the relevance of the play's issues to today as well as yesterday. Obvious "relevance," indicating a directorial intention, had been carefully avoided until the 1992 production, though it is a critical truism to point out that audiences would not remain in the theater if actors did not show the emotional or psychological relevance of their performance to the "now" of the audience.

Ultimately, one is left with the feeling that lighting and scenery, however minimal, and the darkened auditorium, are essential components of the modern experience of "serious" theater as a vaguely spiritual event. I missed the sense of pity and terror that I have occasionally felt at conventional performances of

Lear, the thrilling spectacle of a world of kings and commoners in *Henry IV*. I am of course aware that such expectations are derived from romantic criticism, and that they were not necessarily shared by the audience as a whole—critics' reviews were very complimentary—but I would argue that we cannot undo the cultural attitudes that the past imposes on us. As Parsons and Harrison themselves say, we can't recreate an Elizabethan audience.

The attitudes of the experiment, with its "heroic stage," and the directors' interest in "heroic plays for heroic actors," became particularly problematic when they took on the challenge of Shakespearean comedy, in a proscenium arch production of *Much Ado about Nothing*, with modern lighting and "Elizabethan" costumes. With its strong foregrounding of sex and gender issues, the play is psychologically much more "modern," and encourages a corresponding naturalism in its actors. The Sydney Theatre Company's actors, many of them the same as for the Elizabethan Experiment, were actively discouraged from such psychological naturalism.[4] Senczuk had designed for them an extraordinary imitation, in perspective, of a thrust stage within the wide proscenium of the Drama Theatre, and they were encouraged to move as they had learned to do on the "fit-up" stage, playing largely to the front. The result was that we saw a lot of coarse comedy, desperate mugging into the near darkness of the auditorium—it certainly got the laughs, but at the sacrifice (in my opinion) of anything like charm, wit, or grace, not to mention the tensions of sexuality. Energy, color, and movement the production certainly had, but it fatally lacked the confidence of the actors in the importance of the story. This was not the case with the same season's *Antony and Cleopatra* in the "Blackfriars" theater, in which living theater took precedence over academic ideology. And that appears to be the wisdom that Harrison has learned from the Elizabethan Experiment: "I have to find a way of it [the experiment] helping me come to terms with being a contemporary theater worker instead of someone who's interested in the way it was done in the past. You can use your understanding of the way the text was created and first performed to inform the way you create something for a contemporary audience."

Notes

1. I would like to thank Philip Parsons, Wayne Harrison, John Senczuk, Ron Haddrick, and Luciano Martucci for their time in giving interviews and

providing information. Quotations in the text are from these interviews, unless otherwise attributed.

2. Program notes.

3. This may be a problem peculiar to the Elizabethan Experiment, with its short rehearsal period, and to Australian audiences' perceptions of local actors: Cheek by Jowl's all-male *As You Like It* was very successful both in England and on tour in Australia in early 1992. Harrison says, "I didn't actually think we needed to do it [use all male actors] with *Lear*—we did it with *Hamlet* and with *Henry IV* first time round, and I'd got everything I needed from it. I knew the limitations; I knew how far you could go. . . . It wouldn't have been possible to do *Othello* with an all male cast."

4. Wayne Harrison began by rehearsing it as an "Elizabethan Experiment," and did a run-through on an "Elizabethan" stage after the first ten days, "and then spent the next three weeks just adapting it . . . seeing what happens when you bring it inside [the conventional theater]."

Stabbed through the Arras: The Dramaturgy of Elizabethan Stage Hangings

DAVID CARNEGIE

I

THE impetus for this chapter comes from the creation in New Zealand, by the Wellington Shakespeare Society, of a set of full-size hangings for Sam Wanamaker's Shakespeare Globe reconstruction on London's south bank. The embroidered hangings are now complete, and currently on tour in museums and art galleries in New Zealand prior to a brief international tour. They will then travel to England to be installed in the Globe in time for the official opening. There are four separate panels, approximately 3.5 meters high, envisaged by the international academic committee as covering the three central bays of the five-bay *frons scenæ*. The two large panels, showing Venus and Adonis respectively, each approximately 3 meters wide, will hang either side of the center. The two narrower panels, depicting Atlas and Hercules, about 1.5 meters wide each, will constitute the hangings in front of the central tiring house door.

The distinguished New Zealand theater designer Raymond Boyce designed the hangings. Their size, shape, weight, appearance, and so on were decided in consultation with the academic committee and the project architects.[1] Boyce has pointed out, however, that his experience of professional theater is that over the years curtains and cloths get smaller: bits get cut off and not replaced, or damaged and trimmed, or left behind on tour. The Shakespeare Globe on the south bank, and its associated museum, may well look after these hangings much better than a working theater company such as the Lord Chamberlain's/King's Men would have done. Although the existence now of a "best" set of hangings is both a visual delight and a provocation to practical research, we should be aware that an Elizabethan com-

181

pany or theater might have had other curtains, probably painted cloths, and that there could have been significant difference between one set and another. The stage direction in The Spanish Tragedy, "Enter Hieronimo; he knocks up the curtain" (4.3.0.1), even raises the possibility that characters in the plays had their own curtains.[2]

My research on the use of the hangings, and particularly on the two narrower Atlas and Hercules curtains that are designed to hang over the presumed central opening or discovery space in the tiring-house wall, has been assisted enormously by two things: first, the availability of the actual embroidered hangings themselves (and subsequently a demonstration set made up specially by Raymond Boyce); and second, the willingness of a number of actors, both amateur and professional, to join me at various times in practical workshops instigated by the Shakespeare Globe Centre New Zealand, using the hangings. I have, as a result, been forced to ask questions that had never occurred to me before, and to recognize that our suppositions about Elizabethan stagecraft need to be put to the test far more often and more rigorously than has been possible up to now. This is one of my great hopes for the Shakespeare Globe project.

This chapter, then, is both a demonstration of what I take to be the current state of our knowledge about the theatrical use of hangings in a playhouse such as the first Globe (profiting greatly from the detailed consideration of Shakespeare's playhouse by the late Bernard Beckerman), and also a preliminary further exploration of practical detail about the hangings and their significance for Elizabethan and Jacobean dramaturgy.

Let us consider first two brief extracts from plays performed by the King's Men at the Globe Theatre. These will provide us examples of the main functions on stage of the hangings.

First, Hamlet. Polonius thinks he has discovered the cause of Hamlet's madness: love for Ophelia. His advice to the king is that they should both eavesdrop on a meeting between Hamlet and Ophelia. Polonius tells Claudius:

> At such a time I'll loose my daughter to him.
> Be you and I behind an arras then,
> Mark the encounter.
>
> (2.2.162–64)

In the so-called Bad Quarto of Hamlet, which is, for our purposes here, a very good quarto because it seems to provide evidence of the actors' knowledge of the staging, the lines are slightly different, but they indicate the same stage business:

> The Prince's walk is here in the gallery;
> There let Ofelia walk until he comes;
> Yourself and I will stand close in the study.
>
> (scene 7 [2.2], 104–6)[3]

The "study" where Polonius and Claudius will "stand close" is the space behind the arras.

Let us remind ourselves of the very simple but effective arrangement that the theater hangings allow when this is put into practice: Claudius enters with Polonius, who is leading Ophelia. Polonius places Ophelia, then addresses Claudius:

> Polonius: Ophelia, walk you here.—Gracious, so please you,
> We will bestow ourselves. . . .
> I hear him coming. Withdraw, my lord.
>
> [Polonius and Claudius withdraw behind the arras; enter Hamlet, not seeing Ophelia.][4]
>
> Hamlet: To be, or not to be . . .
>
> (3.1.42–55)

At the end of the "nunnery" scene, Hamlet exits, Ophelia laments the overthrow of Hamlet's noble mind, and Claudius and Polonius emerge from behind the hanging, perhaps cautiously, perhaps even peering around first to make sure Hamlet has gone.

What we see here, and in a form so simple that we need to remind ourselves how expressive and clear the staging can be, is the hangings used as: (1) an exit, (2) an entrance, (3) a place of concealment, and (4) a place for eavesdropping and observation.

To these four uses of the hangings needs to be added a fifth: discovery. In the plays of Shakespeare and his contemporaries the term "discovery" is of course frequently found in stage directions. One of the best known examples occurs at the end of The Tempest (5.1.171.1–2): "Here Prospero discovers Ferdinand and Miranda playing at chess." The sense of discover as "display to view, reveal" is clear. Another example, more typical in that the discovery is of a dead body, is found in act 1 scene 4 of The Revenger's Tragedy (a play performed by the King's Men at the Globe). In this scene, the noble Antonio, one of the very few virtuous characters in the play, displays the body of his dead

wife, who has taken poison after being raped. The stage direction
reads, "*Enter the discontented Lord Antonio, whose wife the
Duchess's youngest son ravished; he discovering the body of her
dead to certain lords*":

> Antonio: Draw nearer, lords, and be sad witnesses
> Of a fair, comely building newly fall'n,
> Being falsely undermined. Violent rape
> Has play'd a glorious act;
>
> [*Antonio opens the hangings to reveal his dead wife
> lying in a religious posture, hands folded on her breast.*]
>
> behold, my lords,
> A sight that strikes man out of me.
>
> (1.4.1–5)[5]

With this example of a discovery, we have identified the five
principal ways in which playwrights made use of the hangings
in the theaters. I want to look in slightly more detail at each of
these uses, and at some very interesting questions they raise. We
should not expect definite answers, because we have too little
information; but if we can ask the right questions, we may get
closer to the nature of the options available to the Elizabethan
actor of Shakespeare.

II   Hangings as Entrance

Although a gap in the hangings could serve the perfectly ordinary function of an entrance or doorway, it is worth looking at a
kind of anticipated entry: "peeping." The popular clown Richard
Tarlton, with his flattened nose and comical appearance, was
apparently able to set an audience rocking with laughter simply
by sticking his head through a gap between the curtain (or tapestry, as it is called here) and the door of the tiring-house:

> Tarlton, when his head was onely seene,
> The Tire-house door and Tapistre between,
> Set all the multitude in such a laughter,
> They could not hold for scarse an houre after.[6]

This implies both a wonderful extempore popular comic performer (one might think in New Zealand of the late Billy T. James,

or internationally perhaps of Rowan Atkinson or John Cleese), and an audience eager to laugh.

> **[Tarlton to put both hands around one end of curtain, then poke head around—react to audience—withdraw (twice?)—poke head through centre gap of curtain—gag to audience if possible (funny faces? disapproval?)—then withdraw behind.][7]**

"Peeping through the curtain" was also a notable trick of at least one later comic actor, Timothy Reade, and may well have been a standard bit of comic business.[8]

It is clear from contemporary illustrations, and from stage directions in plays, that the hangings could sometimes simply serve the function of a doorway; but I don't propose to spend very much time on this aspect because we are so unsure about whether curtains over doorways, or as doorways, were used frequently or rarely. Either way, the use is straightforward.

The comic entrance is worth examining in a little more detail, and we might do this by looking at an example that starts with an exit for concealment. In *The Merry Wives of Windsor*, Falstaff makes the mistake of trying to seduce two citizen wives at once; and worse, Mistress Page and Mistress Ford have no secrets from each other. They therefore plan an appropriate revenge for the fat knight. In 3.3, we see Mistress Ford starting to put it into effect:

> **[Enter Mrs. Ford, pursued by Falstaff.]**

Falstaff: Mistress Ford ... I love thee, none but thee; and thou deserv'st it.

. . . .

Mrs. Ford: Well, heaven knows how I love you, and you shall one day find it.

> **[Enter Robin, a page, in haste.]**

Robin: Mistress Ford, Mistress Ford! here's Mistress Page at the door, sweating, and blowing, and looking wildly, and would needs speak with you presently.

> **[Exit Robin.]**

Falstaff: She shall not see me, I will ensconce me behind the arras.
Mrs. Ford: Pray you do so, she's a very tattling woman.

> **[Falstaff hides, with commotion, behind the arras,**

**centre gap; enter Mrs. Page from the same side Robin
entered; Falstaff looks back out as she enters, and
ducks behind again with a cry of alarm.]**

Mistress Page enters with the news that Mistress Ford's husband
is coming to search the house on suspicion of her concealing a
lover. The two women, overheard of course, as they intend, by
Falstaff, seem unable to decide how to get Falstaff safely out of
the house; in fact, they are greatly enjoying the impression they
hope the words are making on the impertinent Falstaff.

Mrs. Page: In the house you cannot hide him . . . Look, here is a
basket; if he be of any reasonable stature, he may creep
in here, and throw foul linen upon him, as if it were going
to bucking . . .

Mrs. Ford: He's too big to go in there. What shall I do?

**[Falstaff starts a comic commotion behind the hang-
ing (?trying to find the opening); the women observe
with amusement.]**

Falstaff: Let me see't, let me see't, O, [emerging] let me see't! I'll
in, I'll in. Follow your friend's counsel. I'll in.

(3.3.48–138)

And Falstaff does climb into the basket, is covered with the foul-
est dirty clothes they can find, and is carried to Datchet-mead to
be dumped in a muddy ditch.

The points of interest here for us, it seems to me, are several.
First, the way in which an entry from a curtain may be signaled
in advance (as in the curtain calls in the film of *The Dresser*,
where "Sir"—based on the grand old Shakespearean Sir Donald
Wolfitt—plays his exhaustion as he stumbles *behind* the curtain,
muttering to himself, "let them know you're coming," before
finding the gap and revealing himself to the audience). As we
have just seen, part of the comedy of Falstaff's entrance lies in
the potential for delaying it. He can in fact pretend that the arras
is impeding him. There is also potential during his concealment
for the hanging to twitch, but we'll come to that in a moment. A
final point to be made about entries through the hangings is that
if an actor can use them to comic effect, an actor can surely also
use them for serious, even sinister, effect.

III   Hangings as Exit and Concealment

I want next to consider exits and concealment. An exit through
or around the hangings can, of course, be simply the equivalent
of an exit by a stage door. However, as we have just seen in *The
Merry Wives of Windsor*, the exit into concealment has particular
potential for comedy, especially if the actor takes a last look out
(a bit like Tarlton), and either plays to the audience, or is almost
seen by the character entering, or both. With this in mind, let us
take a second look at Polonius and Claudius concealing themselves behind the arras. And although Polonius can be played
for comedy, let us for our purposes regard this as an entirely
serious encounter. Also, we shall include the option of using the
end of the central hangings this time, rather than the central
opening.

> **[Enter Claudius, and Polonius leading Ophe-
> lia; they cross to the opposite side of the
> stage from where Hamlet will enter.]**

Polonius: Ophelia, walk you here.—Gracious, so please you,
        We will bestow ourselves. . . .
        I hear him coming. Withdraw, my lord.

> **[Polonius and Claudius withdraw behind one end of
> the arras, Polonius going last and casting a long look
> back at Ophelia, then at Hamlet as he enters; enter
> Hamlet, not seeing Ophelia.]**

Hamlet: To be, or not to be . . .

Here, I think, Polonius's action in looking back at Ophelia reinforces both the sense of deception inherent in the concealment,
and the very strong link between the place of concealment behind the hanging, and the visible action on stage. The place of
concealment, like an entrance or an exit, exists in relation to the
main stage.

IV   Hangings as Places of Observation or Eavesdropping

The section we have just looked at from *Hamlet* is of course an
example of concealment for the purpose of "observation"[9]—or
perhaps we should say "eavesdropping," since we do not know
whether Claudius and Polonius would have visually reminded

the audience of their presence during the longish scene between Hamlet and Ophelia. Perhaps they would have kept quiet and still, so as not to risk an inappropriate comic effect—or even so that their reappearance would be a slight shock to an audience that had half forgotten they were there.

We do have an example from the Globe of a character announcing his intention to observe. In Jonson's *Volpone*, in act 5 scene 2, Volpone wants to hear and see the reaction of his gulls, after news of his death, to the revelation that he has apparently left all his wealth to his parasite, Mosca, and not, as they expected, to him.

> [Enter Volpone with a stool; speaks to audi-
> ence in glee.]

Volpone: I'le get up,
> Behind the cortine, on a stoole, and harken;
> Sometime, peepe over; see, how they doe looke . . .
> O, 'twill afford me a rare meale of laughter.

> [Exit Volpone with stool through centre gap.]
>   (5.2.83–87)[10]

Notice that he says he'll get up on a stool and "Sometime peep over." This statement has created some difficulty for theater historians trying to ascertain the height of the curtains. What little pictorial evidence we have suggests the hangings should be full height from the stage floor to the balcony; if so, how is Volpone to look over them? The academic committee for the Globe, with Volpone in mind, decided on lower hangings, "covering the whole height of the doors below the arched space which stretches nearly to the entablature," thereby allowing "space for [Volpone's] head between the loops of the hangings and the top of the arched space."[11] This decision was subsequently reversed (I understand to allow for the possibility, suggested by the de Witt hinges, of the tiring-house doors opening outward), with the result that the New Zealand hangings are far higher than Volpone could possibly look over, however high his stool. Workshop experimentation, however, suggests that a standard technique from Italian comedy of the time could serve the purpose with either height of hanging:

> [Enter Mosca as if busy with his inventory;
> to him, Voltore.]

Mosca: Turkie carpets, nine—
Voltore: Taking an inventory? that is well.
Mosca: Two sutes of bedding, tissew—
Voltore: Where's the will? . . .
Mosca: Of cloth of gold, two more—. . .

[Enter to them Corvino.]

Corvino: Ha? is the houre come, Mosca?

[Volpone, up on his stool behind the curtain, puts his head through central gap, speaks in triumph to audience.]

Volpone: Aye, now, they muster.
Corvino: **[seeing Voltore]** What do's the advocate here?

[Volpone laughs as he observes.]

(5.3.1–9)

It seems to me that the slight height given by a stool, plus the conventional comic advantage given by the curtain, allow us to accept with no difficulty at all that Volpone is, as he said he would be, "peeping over." We might also note in passing that Jonson's marginal stage direction does not actually specify that he look over; it says at this point, "*Volpone peepes from behinde a traverse.*" It is not uncommon in Elizabethan stagecraft for a character to announce a very elaborate bit of action, but for the actor to actually do something rather different.[12] In this case, therefore, Volpone's words that he will "peep over" are enough to prepare us for the essential—that he will use the traverse curtain as a hiding place from which to observe his gulls. Are we likely to be concerned if, in the event, he looks through the gap, or even around the end, for instance, rather than over the top?

Let us sum up the use of the hangings considered so far. First, they can serve as an entrance, either in a strictly utilitarian and unremarkable way, or using the malleable qualities of the fabric for comedy or for serious purposes—for instance, Tarlton sticking his head through in preparation for his entrance; Falstaff beating about in a panic, desperate to get out from behind them; perhaps a slightly sinister effect of Claudius reappearing from hiding. Second, they create an exit, again either in utilitarian manner, or with the purpose of the exit pointed by the actor. Third, they provide a place of concealment, as in the case of

Falstaff. And fourth, they are put to use as a place of observation and eavesdropping, whether for comic or sinister purpose. Now I want to turn again to the fifth function of the hangings, the discovery.

V   Hangings for Discovery

A discovery is often a moment when a sight of particular significance, hidden behind the hangings, is suddenly revealed to onlookers (in *The Revenger's Tragedy*, the dead body of Antonio's ravished wife; in *The Tempest*, Ferdinand and Miranda obviously in love over a highly symbolic chess board).

But a discovery can be simply an alternative to a character walking on stage. For instance, in Marlowe's tragedy *Doctor Faustus*, the Chorus finishes his introduction to the audience like this:

> *Chorus:* For, falling to a devilish exercise
> And glutted now with learning's golden gifts,
> He sufeits upon cursed necromancy;
> Nothing so sweet as magic is to him,
> Which he prefers before his chiefest bliss:
> And this the man that in his study sits.
>
> **[Chorus draws curtains open, first one side, then the other, to reveal Faustus sitting at a table.]**
> (Prologue, 23–28)[13]

Certainly the effect here is to emphasize the revelation of the principal, notorious, character. But it also has the useful, if mundane, function of allowing a seated character to, as it were, enter. In fact, the concept was so familiar to the playwrights and actors that stage directions and prompter's notes such as "*Enter . . . at a table, reading*" are commonplace. (It is possible that Othello's stage direction, "*Enter . . . Desdemona in her bed,*" indicates a discovery of this sort; but beds are another complication altogether, not least because they have their own curtains or hangings, so I shall leave them aside from the present discussion.)

A typical example of discovery of a seated character is found in a play for the Globe called *The Devil's Charter* by Barnabe Barnes, acted in 1607, a particularly useful play for our purposes because it has unusually full stage directions. At 1.4, the stage direction reads: "*[Pope] Alexander in his study with bookes, coffers, his triple Crowne upon a cushion before him.*"[14] As is common with discoveries, he is found with significant emblems about him: books of sorcery, like Doctor Faustus; coffers full of the worldly riches for which he has signed the charter of the title with the devil; and the papal crown for which he has bargained his soul. But if he is sitting at his desk, how are the traverse curtains opened? In the case of *Doctor Faustus*, the Chorus could open them; in *The Revenger's Tragedy* and *The Tempest*, Antonio and Prospero could perform the function. But in this case, and often, no characters are on stage. An actor seated behind the hangings is unlikely to be able to open them himself, even if it were desirable. What are the possibilities? Well, two answers seem worth exploring: first, the use of one or more hidden stagehands.

> [Pope] *Alexander in his study with bookes, coffers, his triple Crowne upon a cushion before him.*

> **[Two attendants, hidden by hangings, open the curtains to reveal Alexander, seated, facing the audience.]**

I think I would be more enthusiastic about this option were it not that the reverse process seems rather less impressive.

> **[The two unseen attendants close the curtains.]**

It seems to me that curtains closing "by themselves" draws undue attention, paradoxically, to the hidden stagehands. Moreover, as I have found myself in the course of working with these hangings, the slightest difficulty in drawing them smoothly along the rail is likely to introduce inadvertent comedy. Indeed, in a theater where stage attendants are constantly bringing in tables and banquets, carrying off dead bodies, and so forth, might it not be more likely that stage attendants opened and closed the traverse curtain when necessary in full view of the audience. Let us look at the same discovery again, done that way.

> **[The two attendants enter, and, in full view, open the curtains to reveal Alexander, seated as before; the attendants then close the curtains and exit.]**

This procedure must probably be allowed, in the abstract, as one of the possible Elizabethan conventions for managing the hangings. Dramaturgical considerations, however, lead me to believe that playwrights were sufficiently aware of the potential of the hangings in the hands of an actor that they usually avoided wasting the opportunity with such a neutral operation.

Even as a simple entrance device for a seated actor, the fact of discovery throws a certain focus on the character. Often, this idea of revealing a significant sight is paramount. In *Volpone*, for instance, the play starts with a discovery:

> *Volpone:* Good morning to the day; and next, my gold:
> Open the shrine, that I may see my *saint*.
>
> [Mosca withdraws the curtain and discovers piles of gold, plate, jewels, etc.]
>
> Haile the worlds soule, and mine.
>
> (1.1.1–3)

More common than gold or inanimate objects is the discovery of people, often significantly dead, as in *The Revenger's Tragedy*, or apparently dead, as in the famous final scene of *The Winter's Tale*, when Paulina discovers Hermione as a statue to Leontes, and then the statue turns out to be the living Hermione. What is particularly interesting about this episode for our purposes, I think, is Paulina's control of the traverse curtain. Here is a selection of key moments from 5.3:

> **[Enter Paulina with Leontes and courtiers; Paulina approaches the curtain, turns back to address Leontes.]**
>
> *Paulina:*   prepare
> To see the life as lively mock'd as ever
> Still sleep mock'd death. Behold, and say 'tis well.
>
> **[Paulina opens the curtain, and discovers Hermione standing like a statue.]**
>
> I like your silence, it the more shows off
> Your wonder . . . Indeed my lord,
> If I had thought the sight of my poor image
> Would thus have wrought you (for the stone is mine),
> I'ld not have show'd it.
>
> **[Paulina makes to close the curtain.]**
>
> *Leontes:* Do not draw the curtain . . .
> The fixure of her eye has motion in't,
> As we are mock'd with art.

Paulina: I'll draw the curtain.

[Paulina makes to close the curtain; Leontes counter-mands her.]

Leontes: Let't alone.
                        . . . Let no man mock me,
         For I will kiss her.
Paulina: Good my lord, forbear.
         The ruddiness upon her lip is wet;
         You'll mar it if you kiss it; stain your own
         With oily painting. Shall I draw the curtain?

[Paulina again makes to close the curtain; Leontes again countermands her.]

Leontes: No! not these twenty years.

                                        (5.3.73–84)

The curtain is here a central actor, almost a character in its own right. And it seems to me clear from the intensity of the dialogue, and from Paulina's protective proximity to Hermione, that she controls the curtain herself. Attendants under her direction would be possible, but every dramaturgical advantage lies with giving the physical control to the character and the actor.

However, a difficulty remains that I have not yet confronted. With a split curtain, how does an actor achieve a sudden revelation? Let us return to the example of *The Revenger's Tragedy* and look at several possible solutions.

First, might the body of Antonio's wife be carefully preset to one side of the discovery space, and only that side of the hangings opened? While theoretically possible, I think both the constraints of space and the diminution of spectacular impact make it less than likely.

Second, might the actor open first one side, then the other?

[Enter Antonio and 2 lords.]

Antonio: Draw nearer, lords, and be sad witnesses
         Of a fair, comely building newly fall'n,
         Being falsely undermined.

[He opens one side of the curtains, starting to reveal his dead wife lying in a religious posture, hands folded on breast.]

>   Violent rape
>   Has play'd a glorious act;
>
>   **[He opens the other side of the curtains, completing the
>   discovery of the body of his wife.]**
>
>   behold, my lords,
>   A sight that strikes man out of me.

Although a good actor can slow down the lines in order to suit
a two-stage discovery, I wonder if we find that the action done
thus is sufficient to match the violence of the language that controls this horrific revelation.

A third option would be stage attendants:

> *Antonio:*   . . . behold my lords,
>
>   **[He gestures to 2 attendants, who slowly open the
>   curtains.]**
>
>   A sight that strikes man out of me.

A fourth possibility would be a pulley system, similar to that in
domestic use for curtains in many homes today. If it were hidden,
the effect would, of course, be identical to having hidden stagehands. If it were visible, however, the dramatic character would
be evidently in control. (I have already suggested how important
I think this is in the case of Paulina in *The Winter's Tale.*) I do
not have a pulley set on the hangings I have been working with,
but the situation can be imagined by having Antonio mime pulling on a cord, while hidden stagehands imitate the operation of
the pulley opening the curtains.

>   **[Antonio miming pulley cord; hidden attend-
>   ants opening curtains.]**
>
> *Antonio:*   . . . behold, my lords,
>   A sight that strikes man out of me.

For myself, I find all these less than satisfactory.

Another solution would be to use a single curtain, with no
central split in it at all. This is in many ways the most attractive
option, and solves all the problems of control by one actor. The
principal objection is that the few illustrations of hangings for

English stages all show a central split (see, for example, the Roxana, Messalina, and Wits illustrations).[15]

However, it occurs to me that we might have our cakes and ale, and eat them, even using a pair of hangings with a central gap, if we assume that at least one end is free to slide. In that case, our scene would look like this:

Antonio: . . . behold, my lords,

[Antonio draws the entire curtain open from one end.]

A sight that strikes man out of me.

This does seem to answer most of our needs. Some slight problems remain, however: closing the curtain again has to be done in two stages. Furthermore, as anyone who has worked in theater will know, curtains that are not secured at the ends invariably come adrift just when you most need them for concealment of what is behind. However, unless a wide, symmetrical opening ever had to be created by pulling both hangings back from the middle, the two center rings could be overlapped so that the central opening always fell closed; full discoveries could then always be made by treating the hangings as a single traverse curtain.

I should like to consider two last examples of the dramaturgical use of the hangings by playwrights writing for the Globe. The first is from *The Devil's Charter*, a play from which we considered the discovery of the evil pope Alexander. Alexander is discovered again, later in the play. The stage direction at the start of 5.6 reads:

Alexander unbraced betwixt two Cardinalls in his study looking upon a booke, whilst a groome draweth the Curtaine.

[Enter Groom and open curtain from one end, discovering Alexander between 2 Cardinals.]

Notice the "groome." It is not clear whether he is a dramatic character, Alexander's groom, or a stagehand, one of the theater's grooms. But either way, the stage direction specifies that he opens the traverse curtain. A moment later Alexander walks out onto the stage, still with his book, and a further stage direction (3294–96) says: "*They place him in a chayre upon the stage; a groome setteth a Table before him.*" Presumably the groom also, for reasons we shall come to in a moment, closes the curtain. Alexander dismisses the two cardinals, and meditates on his inevitable end:

Alex: Oh wretched *Alexander*, slave of sinne
       And of damnation; . . .
       Out, out alas, my paines, my guttes, my liver;
       And yet I feare it not: though in security
       Once more I will, with powrefull exorcismes,
       Invoke those Angells of eternall darkenesse
       To shew me now the manner of my death.

   ["Alexander draweth the Curtaine of his studie where hee discovereth the divill sitting in his pontificals, Alexander crosseth himselfe starting at the sight."]

(3314–38)

What does Alexander see, and react to with such fear? The Devil, discovered, wearing Alexander's pontifical robes. Furthermore, the sense that Alexander is seeing not only his own death, as he wished, but also what he will be after death, is enormously strengthened by two elements. First, that Alexander himself, not the groom, makes the discovery; and second, that the Devil is sitting precisely in the chair in which Alexander was himself discovered when the scene started—but, of course, without the holy cardinals to offer advice.

The final example I want to offer of the use of a curtain, hanging, tapestry, traverse, or arras is also perhaps the most famous. I'm referring to *Hamlet*, of course, when Polonius conceals himself in order to be a witness to what Hamlet says to Gertrude:

   [Enter Polonius with Gertrude, giving her urgent advice.]

Polonius: 'A will come straight. Look you lay home to him.
           Tell him his pranks have been too broad to bear with,
           And that your Grace hath screen'd and stood between
           Much heat and him. **[gesture to arras]** I'll silence me even here;
           Pray you be round [with him].
Queen: I'll [warr'nt] you, fear me not. Withdraw,
           I hear him coming.

   [Polonius hides behind the arras, at central gap, taking a last long look as he goes. Enter Hamlet.]

Hamlet: Now, mother, what's the matter?

Queen:	Hamlet, thou hast thy father much offended.
Hamlet:	Mother, you have my father much offended.
Queen:	Come, come, you answer with an idle tongue.
Hamlet:	Go, go, you question with a wicked tongue.
Queen:	Why, how now, Hamlet?
Hamlet:	What's the matter now?
Queen:	Have you forgot me?
Hamlet:	No, by the rood, not so:

You are the Queen, your husband's brother's wife,
And would it were not so, you are my mother.

| Queen: | Nay, then I'll set those to you that can speak. |
| Hamlet: | Come, come, and sit you down, you shall not boudge; |

You go not till I set you up a glass
Where you may see the [inmost] part of you.

Queen:	What wilt thou do? Thou wilt not murther me?
	Help ho!
Polonius:	[**Behind**] What ho! Help!

[Polonius creates a commotion behind the arras, which Hamlet sees and reacts to.]

| Hamlet: | How now? A rat? |

[Thrusts his rapier through (?the gap in) the arras.]

Dead, for a ducat, dead!
Polonius: [**Behind**] O, I am slain.

[Polonius falls, still behind arras.]

| Queen: | O me, what hast thou done? |
| Hamlet: | Nay, I know not, is it the King? |

[Hamlet draws arras from one end, slowly, to discover   Polonius.]

| Queen: | O, what a rash and bloody deed is this! |

[Actors hold position looking at dead Polonius.]

(3.4.1–27)

This well-known scene incorporates almost every element we have looked at in the stage use of hangings. First, Polonius uses the hangings to exit. He exits to concealment. It is for the purpose of observation and eavesdropping, which may well be signaled as he leaves by a significant last look. Notice the words, "A rat."

It was proverbial Elizabethan lore that rats draw attention to themselves, and therefore conspire in their own deaths. This fits well with Gertrude's later description of how Hamlet, in his lawless fit,

> Behind the arras hearing something stir,
> Whips out his rapier, cries 'A rat, a rat!'
> And in this brainish apprehension kills
> The unseen good old man.
>
> (4.1.9–12)

When we looked at Falstaff, we noticed the potential for comic commotion behind the hangings; now we see the equivalent in tragedy.

The death itself also uses the hangings. That dreadful schoolboy joke, "Polonius was stabbed through the arras," is, unfortunately, true. There is certainly all too much potential for a melodramatic death clutching the arras, even, as has been done, bringing the hangings down on top of him. To do this, however, misses revealing the full dramatic significance of the final discovery. Editors of *Hamlet* usually supply a stage direction such as, "*Hamlet lifts up the arras, and sees Polonius.*" But given what we know of the use of the hangings for discovering significant sights, very often of unfortunate deaths, I would suggest that part of the power of this scene lies in the way Shakespeare leads up to the inevitable and utterly appropriate use of the arras for discovery. The full opening of the arras then formally associates this discovery with the wider implications of the general theatrical convention. The discovery is not only of the "unseen, good old man," the innocent Polonius; it is the discovery of a death that now casts Hamlet as victim as well as avenger. His justice in pursuit of Claudius will henceforth be shadowed by Laertes' pursuit of him—another son avenging a father. Like Alexander in *The Devil's Charter*, Hamlet has looked into the discovery space at his own death.

It is evident that the technical and the dramaturgical are inseparable, and that one of the virtues of the reconstruction of the Globe that is going ahead on London's south bank is that it will present us with both the need and the opportunity to explore these questions in detail. The simple existence of the Globe hangings created by the Wellington Shakespeare Society has led me to consider questions that never presented themselves so precisely before, and for that I am grateful. It is essential that the actor playing Antonio, or Prospero, or Paulina, or Falstaff be enabled to make the best possible use of a central piece of theatrical equipment. It is our job, therefore, to investigate every element of the Shakespearean playhouse as rigorously and creatively as possible.

Notes

1. Raymond Boyce, "The Shape of the Globe," and "The Interior of the Globe," *Renaissance Drama Newsletter*, supplement 8 (autumn 1987): 84–89.

2. Thomas Kyd, *The Spanish Tragedy*, ed. Philip Edwards, The Revels Plays (London: Methuen, 1959).

3. Shakespeare, *Hamlet: The First Quarto, 1603*, ed. Albert B. Weiner (Great Neck, N.Y.: Barron's Educational, 1962).

4. My stage directions, here and throughout the paper, are intended as directorial rather than editorial decisions.

5. Cyril Tourneur [or Thomas Middleton], *The Revenger's Tragedy*, ed. R. A. Foakes, The Revels Plays (London: Methuen, 1966).

6. Quoted in Andrew Gurr, *The Shakespearean Stage, 1574–1642* (Cambridge: Cambridge University Press, 1970), 65.

7. Stage directions in bold, here and throughout, indicate the staging at the conference where this paper was delivered with the set of demonstration hangings, and with actors portraying the scenes described.

8. Gerald Eades Bentley, *The Jacobean and Caroline Stage* (Oxford: Oxford University Press, 1941), 2:541.

9. Bernard Beckerman, *Shakespeare at the Globe, 1599–1609* (New York: Collier, 1962), 192–95.

10. Ben Jonson, *Volpone*, in *Ben Jonson*, ed. C. H. Herford and Percy Simpson, vol. 5 (Oxford: Oxford University Press, 1937).

11. "The Shape of the Globe," 88.

12. See, e.g., Alan C. Dessen, *Elizabethan Stage Conventions and Modern Interpreters* (Cambridge: Cambridge University Press, 1984), 58–59.

13. Christopher Marlowe, *Doctor Faustus*, ed. John D. Jump, The Revels Plays (London: Methuen, 1962).

14. Barnabe Barnes, *The Devil's Charter*, ed. Jim C. Pogue (New York: Garland, 1980).

15. See R. A. Foakes, *Illustrations of the English Stage, 1580–1642* (London: Scolar, 1985), 72–73. See also John H. Astington, "The Origins of the *Roxana* and *Messalina* Illustrations," *Shakespeare Survey* 43 (1991): 149–69.

Shakespeare and Performance Practices in Sweden

JACQUELINE MARTIN

I Early Shakespeare Productions

THE first performances of Shakespeare in Sweden were *Romeo and Juliet* (1776) in Norrköping, by the German Seurerling and his troupe, later by the resident French theater troupe under Monvel's direction, and *Hamlet* (1787) in Gothenburg by a Swedish troupe.[1] When *Hamlet* was performed in Stockholm in 1819 it was the result of many years' struggle between the old French classical school, which had dominated theater life in Sweden under Gustav III, and the new German romantic one. In spite of the fact that it was translated into prose rather than blank verse, and that many scenes were cut, such as the gravediggers' scene, Hamlet's journey to England, and Fortinbras with his invading Norwegian army, *Hamlet* was regarded as a great success for many years. However, there was no further Shakespeare production until *Othello*, in 1827; the translation was blank verse, the actors declaimed in a semicircle downstage front, Desdemona was stabbed rather than suffocated and a great deal was cut—all attempts to find a balance between the classical and romantic ideals, but finally satisfying neither.[2]

During the 1850s and 1860s a marked wave of interest in Shakespeare arose in Sweden, which resulted in a number of famous productions at the Royal Theater (Kungliga Teatern) and at a private theater in Stockholm (Mindre Teatern). Contributing strongly to this revival were C. A. Hagberg's excellent translations, upon which the majority of nineteenth-century productions were based,[3] and a more historical way of playing Shakespeare that had emerged in England and Germany.

Initially the emphasis was on the tragedies, such as *Hamlet* with new premieres (1853 and 1864), *Othello* and *The Merchant of Venice* (1857) with the colored actor Ira Aldridge in the title roles, and *Coriolanus* and *Timon of Athens* (1866). The interpretations of Othello and Shylock were related to problems in the Swedish society of the 1850s—a subject of growing interest to the new reading public. But even the comedies, *A Midsummer Night's Dream* (1860), *The Comedy of Errors* (1861), and *Twelfth Night* (1864), were included in the repertoire at the Royal Theater. On the other hand, the choice of plays in the repertoire at Mindre Teatern complied with the trends of the times, where romantic motives were the order of the day in plays such as *All's Well That Ends Well* (1854–55), *Romeo and Juliet* (1858–59), and *The Taming of the Shrew* (1860–61), and were intended to satisfy the middle-class theater-going public.[4]

In terms of performance practices, the new modern realistic style in vogue at the Gymnase in Paris was becoming more evident, particularly in the acting of Edvard Swartz, whose Hamlet and Richard II (1863) were more reflective and less declamatory in style than his predecessors had demonstrated. Elsie Hvasser's Puck was an outstanding exception to acting practices of the day, while later her Lady Macbeth (1886) demonstrated a psychological-realistic, though physically quite statuesque, style. Otherwise German influences were followed in terms of staging, taking inspiration from the efforts of Ludwig Tieck and his experiments with formal Shakespearean stages and the possibility of playing the text uncut while preserving the scene order. Music was used to great effect in most of the productions, either adding to their exotic and grand atmosphere, or assisting entrances and exits and supporting a fast-moving action. Overtures and entr'acte music were also an integral part of the theatrical experience.[5] The enormous changes in lighting techniques that accompanied the development from gas to electricity allowed scope for fantastic scenic effects. Similarly costume designs were more harmonious and more historically founded.

II   Outstanding Twentieth-Century Directors

The production of Shakespeare in Sweden in the twentieth century has been steered in the main by three directors, Olof Molander, Alf Sjöberg, and Ingmar Bergman, all of whom have shared a fascination for the visual possibilities of the theatrical space. In his Shakespeare productions from the 1920s, 1930s, and 1940s, Olof Molander was always concerned with metaphysical questions such as man's relationship with God. His fas-

cination for psychology resulted in penetrating dramatic
analyses and led to brilliant interpretations of Shakespeare from
the directorial point of view as well as the acting. Actors he
worked with acclaimed his exceptional capacity for bringing out
all the nuances of the text and he was bitterly critical if they did
not measure up to his expectations for the spoken word. Molander believed that the art of acting was synonymous with really
understanding the text and was always extremely well prepared
in advance of the rehearsals. However, the visual aspects of
performance also interested him enormously, even though to him
they were merely an accompaniment to the lines of the text.[6]

In his interest in scenographic possibilities, Alf Sjöberg continued in Molander's footsteps at the Royal Dramatic Theater in
Stockholm, as was demonstrated by his twenty-nine Shakespeare
productions, spanning over fifty years. In his early productions,
Much Ado about Nothing (1940), Twelfth Night (1946), and Romeo and Juliet (1953), Sjöberg's fascination with the theatrical
space often threatened the literary dimensions of the text.[7]

For Sjöberg, Shakespeare represented both a poetic theater and
a theater fighting for a political breakthrough. As he became more
politically aware, Sjöberg's Shakespeare productions demonstrated special interpretations, such as The Merchant of Venice
(1944) which was a protest play directed against the treatment
of the Jews by the Nazis, and Richard III (1947) which was intended as a warning "for clowns who can emerge and completely
cast spells over the people—not least with their brilliant rhetoric."[8] Similar motivation can be seen in his portrayal of the ty-
rants in Hamlet (1955) and King John (1961) where he expressed
fascination for how "one person can emerge from the masses and
throw the whole world back into the feudalism of the Middle
Ages."[9] In his production of Troilus and Cressida (1967), Sjöberg
attempted to show the meaninglessness of war "in a broken mirror of a world without meaning and sense, a fragment of the
classical vision we thought we could see in school."[10] He tried
to show the strong parallels between the play and the world
situation, in particular "America's feudal attitude to the rest of
the world—with its messiah role as a knight setting out to save
the world with God, the bible and napalm in its hands."[11] In
order to create more relevance, the Prologue had been rewritten
to include the following: "Aristocrats came from the Middle
Ages, they have nothing to do with the modern world, so you
will see a war game which is very much on your level."

Ingmar Bergman has also staged visual Shakespearean master-

Troilus and Cressida, Royal Dramatic Theater (Dramaten), Stockholm, 1967.
Directed by Alf Sjöberg. Photograph by Beata Bergström.

pieces following strong directorial lines, such as his *Macbeth*
productions (1940, 1944, 1948), while in later years his fascination has extended to experiments in time and place, with a particular interest in the portrayal of the protagonists in *King Lear*
(1984) and *Hamlet* (1987). Bergman's first production of *Macbeth*
with a group of students coincided with the German invasion of
Denmark (1940) and attracted widespread interest. His second
one (1944) also used the theme of Nazi totalitarianism in a simple setting, where the visual effects were projected against a bold
but effective background of red and black. A tendency toward
textual modification was particularly in evidence in this *Macbeth*, in which the heath was depicted as a battlefield where the
bereaved wives of the fallen had gathered and where the most
talkative of the witches had been translated into a fortune-
teller![12] His third *Macbeth* (1948) was an elaborate split-level
setting of Wagnerian proportions, where silhouettes of hanged
men hung from a gigantic oak on one side "like overripe fruit"
and the witches, transformed into seductive creatures, writhed
alluringly through its branches.

King Lear, **Royal Dramatic Theater (Dramaten), Stockholm, 1984. Directed by Ingmar Bergman. Photograph by Hans Hasselgren.**

Bergman set his production of *Twelfth Night* at the Royal Dramatic Theater (1975) in an Elizabethan innyard, with a musicians gallery across the back for musicians to accompany the action. A special feature of this production was that the actors were in full view of the audience awaiting their entrances, a technique that had impressed Bergman at the Comédie Française and which he was to incorporate in further Shakespeare productions, believing that it kept the actors concentrated and involved in the play. The production was received very positively by the critics, who applauded the simplicity of Gunilla Palmstierna-Weiss's scenography, claiming that it drew attention to the text.

Many of these features were seen in Bergman's production of *King Lear* (1984) at the same theater and with the same scenographer. Maximum empty space was utilized in the stage setting and a red carpet covered the entire stage floor and walls. This setting remained throughout the performance—abstract in character—with no particular reference to time nor place, until the last scene, when the red walls collapsed revealing the naked black walls of the theater, underlining a theme of "all the world's a stage." Extras were choreographed back and forth in special groups and configurations, thereby shifting the action and proxemic significations. Time shifts were emphasized in costumes, which ranged from the Renaissance court to *Star Wars* futurism. Entrances and exits were seldom made, as the characters remained seated on the stage floor throughout. In this proscenium arch theater, the stage frame itself was outlined in black, emphasizing the distance between the stage and audience. On the whole it was a visual experience: 34 percent of the text was cut, while many of the lines were given to other characters or shared and many scenes were rearranged. Although it was received enthusiastically by most, one discerning critic had difficulty in reconciling the theme of *King Lear* with a choreography that he derisively referred to as pure *Swan Lake*.[13]

In his production of *Hamlet* (1986) at the same theater, Bergman showed many similarities of approach and even used the same translator in order to arrive at an "understandable and believable" text, although this resulted in one-third of the text being trimmed away. Again the setting was an empty abstract space in which the actors, who remained on stage observing the events, were used choreographically to create certain effects, such as a row of judges all wearing long courtroom wigs, or a group of umbrella-twirling mourners at Ophelia's funeral. Timelessness was emphasized in use of costumes, with Hamlet in black polo-necked jumper and grey trousers hiding behind black sunglasses, Claudius and Gertrude in reconstructed Renaissance red, Polonius and Horatio in sober grey modern business suits, Rosencrantz and Guildernstern in sporty golfing attire, and Ophelia in what looked like a simple blue nightdress.

A mood of distanced theatricality was established in the opening scene with the use of three curtains, the last black one being opened to the strains of the popular *Merry Widow* waltz. In this way the directorial line was established and thereby the motive for Gertrude's behavior—later born out in drunken, bawdy scenes with Claudius. Again a Beckettian effect was used in the last scene to herald the unexpected arrival of Fortinbras and his army who exploded through an imitation back wall. On the whole, the theme of the play was shifted to the war between the sexes, where the overthrown Ophelia was the central witness, wandering distractedly around the periphery of a marked-out circle—even after her death. Hamlet had become impotent, physically and emotionally, trusting only Horatio, whom he kissed passionately, while Rosencrantz and Guildernstern sniggered. Although Bergman was praised for his visually fantastic

Hamlet, Royal Dramatic Theater (Dramaten), Stockholm, 1986. Directed by Ingmar Bergman. Hamlet played by Peter Stormare, Claudius by Börje Ahlstedt, Gertrude by Gunnel Lindblom. Photograph by Bengt Wanselius.

dramatization, reactions from both public and press were mixed, many remarking that Bergman had gone his own way through Shakespeare's drama with his trendy modernizing and sexual overtones.

A more political production was Ralf Långbacka's *Timon of Athens* at the Gothenburg City Theater (1969), set in the 1920s in an old car graveyard, and the leading characters played as criminals. In this Marxist interpretation Timon's change throughout the play was seen not as a human being's development through accident, but as a social development, enforced by the relationship between people and money.[14] Långbacka's *Troilus and Cressida* at the same theater (1981) followed the same Marxist interpretation, where he endeavored to show how war deforms and cripples both the losers and the winners and that hero-worship and love are dependent upon situations in one's environment and in society.[15] This was realized in performance by a sandbank setting representing the Greek camp, and in the background a devastated Troy, while the costumes, mostly uniforms from ancient Greece to the present, underlined the "timelessness" theme. In both these productions much of the text was cut or rearranged, or additions were inserted, in order to support the directorial vision. His current approach to *Macbeth* at the Stockholm City Theater (1992), although more faithful to the text, follows the same lines in its concern with investigating the kind of society that can produce such monsters as Macbeth and Lady Macbeth, and Långbacka draws many parallels with the present world situation.

III   The Elizabethan Project

In terms of acting practices, the Stockholm City Theater's Elizabethan Project was initiated in an attempt to discover an acting style based on new translations of Shakespeare's texts. During its short life span (1983–86) the Elizabethan Project presented four new translations of Shakespeare to Swedish audiences, most of which were received with great enthusiasm: *Romeo and Juliet* (February 1983), *The Taming of the Shrew* (September 1984), *As You Like It* (November 1984), and *Pericles* (February 1986). Its intentions were pedagogical: a small ensemble of selected actors was gradually to acquire a new acting style and more direct contact with the audience by using verse and rhythm as the support for their characterizations. It hoped to combat the naturalistic acting style which was becoming more and more prevalent, and to say something about contemporary life. It was intended that after a number of productions the results of this project would transfer to other theaters.[16]

The intention was not to reconstruct an Elizabethan theater with any historical accuracy, although it had served as an inspiration, but rather to construct a modern one, built with modern techniques in wood and steel. The main aim was to use a stage design that could strengthen stage-audience contact; to produce, in the words of its designer, Gunnar Steneby, "a theater with a maximum living contact—an open stage, surrounded on three sides by the public, who can sit very close. A theater that really places the actors in the center and can function with a minimum of properties and scenography."[17] The atmosphere they were trying to create was that of a barren riding school, and its width (25 meters) would demand a larger than life playing style, although the distance from the front of the stage to the back row was only 8.5 metres, which would allow the actor maximum possibilities to direct his acting out to the public.[18]

In *Romeo and Juliet* attempts at modernization were apparent, particularly in male costuming, as references to the Renaissance were combined with contemporary 1980s fashion trends such as leg warmers, tight trousers, and broad-shouldered black jackets. In keeping with the principles of the Elizabethan formal stage there was no extraneous decor, and although the action was directed mainly to the forestage, it often extended down into the audience. The balcony was also used. In spite of the closeness of the audience and the occasional eye contact made, the acting was not particularly different or noteworthy, although the actors repeatedly turned toward the audience. The marked differentiation between the generations, clearly indicated in costuming and acting style, was obviously in line with the director's intentions. This was a young person's play, where the overriding theme was "misunderstood youth taking out its aggressions on each other and its parents"—a topical issue in Sweden at that time, where street gangs and violence had become more prevalent.

The new translation and its modernizations were received very warmly and obviously assisted the interpretation. Many contemporary expressions were received with great delight by the audience—particularly the young—thereby strengthening the ties between the Renaissance and the present. On the whole, however, public reaction was not very enthusiastic, partly because many people in the audience were disturbed by being able to see each other throughout the performance, partly because of the hard wooden seats, and partly because many were disappointed by the acting.[19] With expectations so high for the success of this project, and the acclaim that the new translation of *Romeo and Juliet* had received, it met with unanimously negative reviews in the press. Many criticized the poor quality of the direction, many (such as Fagerström in *Aftonbladet*) drew attention to the fact that none of the actors was capable of reading verse, and Björksten (*Svenska Dagbladet*) complained that he could not hear what the actors said—a dilemma that has been dealt with elsewhere.[20]

In subsequent productions, a new director and translator were used in *The Taming of the Shrew*, and a director from the Royal Shakespeare Company, John Caird, was brought in to direct *As You Like It*. This latter experiment was a most rewarding one for the actors, many of whom admitted that they learned about speaking verse for the first time. At the same time, the Elizabethan Project ideals had become somewhat diffuse: Caird, assisted by a team of colleagues from the RSC, introduced a strong scenographical solution for the transfer to the forest of Arden and literally broke up the existing world, ripping up the wooden planks that formed the stage setting to the accompaniment of specially composed illusionistic music. The ensuing production in the main theater, *Pericles*, took these visual indulgences to an even further extreme, by which time the direct acting style had all but been forgotten, together with many of the other aims of the project. Another major reason for the project's lack of success, according to Johnsson, was its failure to keep a permanent ensemble of actors: out of a total of fifty-one actors, not one was present in all the productions.[21] Many different directors were involved too, with conflicting ideas about the actor's working process as well as what the Elizabethan Project had as its aim.

IV   The Group Theater Approach

During the 1990s deconstructionist theory has come to play a significant role in the interpretation of Shakespeare in Sweden. This was particularly obvious in the case of two special theater groups, whose aesthetics have found ready expression in the deconstructionist point of view. In its staging, Folkteatern's *Amledo* (1990) drew our attention to the fact that this was both Shakespeare's *Hamlet* and not it at all. It deconstructed history in its attempts to unite pop culture with the Renaissance, mixing traditions from the Peking Opera with Swedish folk traditions in its use of music, dance, costumes, and song. Obvious influ-

As You Like It, Stockholm City Theater's Elizabethan Project, 1984. Directed by John Caird. Rosalind played by Stina Ekblad. Photograph by André Lafolie.

The Tempest, Unga Klara, Stockholm, 1990. Directed by Etienne Glaser. Ariel played by Malin Ek. Photograph by Lesley Leslie-Spinks.

ences came from Mnouchkine's Noh-inspired Shakespeare cycle and more recently from Brook's choice of location for staging *The Mahabharata*.[22] The scenography was minimalistic—just two crossed logs in the center of the platform and one balanced precariously at the side of the stage—making simultaneous references to the Swedish countryside in the immediate vicinity as well as to the Middle Ages. The acting was highly stylized and the mise-en-scène a ritualistic, tightly structured formation choreographed visually and audially. The central character, Amledo, was played by a rock artist of Italian Swedish origins and his interpretation cast new light on contemporary conceptions of Hamlet as an outsider.

In the same vein, Unga Klara's *The Tempest* (1990) was a fragmented and physical production set in a world of no definite time nor place, where to the continuous accompaniment of "exotic" music the "old structure" of the comedy was exploited and undermined by surfaces that were not so much concerned with yielding textual depths as with reflecting other surfaces—in other words, with deconstructing the surface-depth opposition.

V Conclusion

As can be seen, certain trends have come to characterize the performance practices of Shakespeare in Sweden: an expansive exploration of scenographical solutions; a theatricalization of the mise-en-scène by incorporating music, song, and dance; an unflinching reworking and modernizing of the text in support of special interpretations; a physical rather than a verbal theater; experimentation with time and place; and an attempt to make Shakespeare relevant for contemporary audiences.

Notes

1. See Nils Molin, *Shakespeare och Sverige intill 1800-talets mitt. En översikt av hans inflytande* (Göteborg: Elanders, 1931), 10f.

2. See Ann Fridén, "Att vara eller inte vara, Shakespeare på Kunglig scen i 1800-talets Stockholm," *Den Svenska Nationalscenen* (Lund: Wiken, 1988), 102–23.

3. During the 1840s Carl August Hagberg (1810–64) had translated all of Shakespeare's plays into Swedish with the exception of *Pericles*. He rejected the German translators, Tieck and Schlegel, as advocates of romanticism in Shakespeare. His translations followed the verse meter faithfully, and at the time they were written were good examples of his moralistic and antiromantic ideology. This ideology and rather outdated vocabulary produced translations that have been criticized for their lack of poetry and ignorance of philological research, although praised for their dramatic content. For further details see T. Olsson, "Carl August Hagberg," *Kgl. Dramatiska Teatern program* 79–80: 12–15.

4. See Kerstin Derkert, "Repertoaren på Mindre Teatern, 1854–63," dissertation, Stockholm, 1979.

5. See Dag Kronlund, "'Musiken, låten ljuda, mina vänner!' Musiken i talpjäserna på Kungliga teatern vid 1800-talets mitt," dissertation, Stockholm, 1989.

6. See Jacqueline Martin, "Eloquence Is Action: A Study in Form and Text's Influence on the Vocal Delivery Style of Shakespeare in Sweden, 1934–1985," dissertation, Stockholm, 1987, 83–87.

7. See S. Ek, "Alf Sjöberg—regissören och humanisten. En studie i hans regikonst under 30-talet," *Dramatik på svensk scener 1910–75*, Umeå University, 1 (1977): 3f.

8. Alf Sjöberg, "*Richard III*," *Kgl. Dramatiska Teaterns Program* (Stockholm: Dramaten, 1947).

9. Interview with Alf Sjöberg, cited in *Perspektiv på teater. Document och studier*, collected by U. Gran and U. B. Lagerroth (Uddevalla, 1971), 110f.

10. Sjöberg, "*Troilus och Cressida*," *Kgl. Dramatiska Teatern Program* (Stockholm: Dramaten, 1967).

11. Sjöberg, Interview in *Dialog* 2 (Stockholm: Bonniers, 1968).

12. See Jacqueline Martin, *Voice in Modern Theatre* (London: Routledge, 1991), 82–95.

13. Leif Zern, "Ingen förstår Shakespeare," *Dagens Nyheter*, 13 January 1985.

14. Ralf Långbacka, cited in K. Aspelin, *Timon från Aten. Ett drama, en uppsättning, ett möte med publiken* (Köten: Boc-serien, Bo Caverfors Bokförlag, 1971), 133.

15. R. Långbacka, *Dagens Nyheter*, 30 January 1981.

16. In the words of the project leader, Göran O. Ericksson, "One wanted to cultivate a theater that was dependent upon the relationship between the actors and the public and thereby reduce the amount of technical apparatus." Interview with Göran O. Ericksson, cited in Jakob S. Johnsson, "Projektet som kom bort," unpublished essay, Theater Studies Department, University of Stockholm, 1984.

17. Gunnar Steneby, "Brädor som föreställer världen," *Romeo och Julia*, program, Stockholm Stadsteatern, 1983.

18. Cf. the work of Philip Parsons in Sydney, described in articles by Parsons and Gay in this collection.

19. See Willmar Sauter, Curt Isaksson and Lisbeth Jansson, *Teaterögon: Publiken möter föreställningen: upplevelse-utbud-vanor* (Borås: Liber, 1986), 231–57.

20. Cf. Martin, "Eloquence is Action."

21. Johnsson, "Projektet som kom bort."

22. See Martin, *Voice in Modern Theatre*, 75f.

The *Chronicle of Macbeth:* Suzuki Tadashi's Transformation of Shakespeare's *Macbeth*

Ian Carruthers

I am not aware that William Shakespeare ever traveled to the Orient except in disembodied form; however, only a few years before he wrote *Macbeth* (ca. 1606)—in fact, in the year that *Hamlet* was playing in London—another William became the first Englishman to reach Japan, in 1600.

The first years of William Adams's sojourn in Japan were at least as important for Japanese theatergoers as they were for Shakespeare's audiences, for the early 1600s saw the birth of Kabuki.[1] This new craze was started by a priestess called Okuni who abandoned a quiet life in the great Izumo Shrine to perform outrageous dances to popular love songs on the streets of Kyoto. A true performance artist in the mould of Mary Frith, "The Roaring Girl" of Dekker and Middleton's 1611 play, Okuni strutted her stuff in samurai garb with two swords at her side and a cross around her neck. She was, of course, no more a Christian than Madonna is today, but she was sporting her difference, and Christianity also happened to be new and strange.[2] Whether Will Adams ever saw Okuni perform, we know from the diaries of Captain John Saris and his factor Richard Cocks that they and Adams had many times seen "caboques, or women players" and had even "made a maskerado" with some of them.[3]

In 1600 William Adams also became the first European to show a Japanese head of state a map of the world and to warn him of the expansionist trade wars of the Spanish, Portuguese, Dutch, and English.[4] His master, Tokugawa Ieyasu, was quick to turn European technology to his own advantage, using the firearms on Adams's ship to help him establish hegemony over Japan at the battle of Sekigahara (1600). In the next fifteen years Ieyasu went further, employing Adams and his Japanese son to build and sail oceangoing ships down the coasts of China, Siam, and the Philippines to compete with European traders.[5] But in this trade war he seems to have been a hundred years too late—or, more accurately, some three hundred years too early.

Sailing fast forward into the present, 1991 saw the first "Festival of Japan" in Britain. This featured everything from Sumo wrestling and horseback archery in Hyde Park to a Kabuki version of *Hamlet*, in which both Hamlet and Ophelia were played by the same quick-change artist. This year we are treated to Suzuki's experimental *Macbeth* in the Antipodes. It has been framed by two historical moments. Starting just after the Hawke government's recognition that Australia's future lies less in Europe than on the Asian Pacific Rim, and finishing in Hobart on ANZAC Day as Mr. Keating kissed the Kokoda Trail, Suzuki's *Macbeth* has been positioned as either a cultural invasion or a new transfer of technology—though no one has chosen to notice that such an invasion or technological transfer once went the other way during the Meiji and Victorian periods.

The *Chronicle of Macbeth* production by the Melbourne theater company Playbox, with its modest cast of twelve, is Suzuki's third and most faithful version of Shakespeare's play.[6] His first was a very free rendition, staged in 1975 as *Yoru to tokei* (Night and the clock). This involved a nightly game of role-playing among asylum patients, all vainly attempting to become Macbeth. It used two pop songs, selected passages from *Chushingura* (the Kabuki classic about the revenge of the forty-seven Ronin), and Tsubouchi Shoyo's turn-of-the-century Kabuki-style translation of *Macbeth*. The performance emphasized Japan's shadowy past and her contemporary situation rather than the world of Shakespeare's tragedy. According to Goto Yukihiro's account, an aged man, confined to the asylum since 1941, gloomily uttered dialogue exchanged between Ross and Macduff: "Alas, poor country! Almost afraid to know itself!" (4.3). He then dismembered a grotesque-looking doll and scattered its intestines over the floor while passionately singing a mid-seventies pop song about lost love, "O Night in Ginza."[7]

The treatment was typical of Suzuki's early use of surrealist techniques to break down ingrained, habitual audience response. In Goto's words "Dream-like hallucinatory images, dialogue out of context, and acts of provocation are all used to induce the spectator's subconscious response to the dark mood of the performance" (Goto, 130). A video of Shiraishi Kayoko per-

Suzuki Tadashi rehearsing *Macbeth*. Photograph by Rei Zunde.

forming Chekhov's *Cherry Orchard* shows how effective these techniques can be.[8] Suzuki taught the actress to find her physical sensations first "because it is her body that gives expressive form to the words" (Goto, 180). For him "a true sense of theater language is not the drama of the playwright but the actor's physicalization" (178). In an early essay called "Body, Space, Language," Suzuki wrote:

> The history of the actor in Japan is one of devising artificial and painful ways to use the body. For actors know full well, to deceive the spirit, first one must deceive the flesh. One must enter into an aggressive relationship with the physiology of one's own body. Forcibly restricting the breath, then opening up and letting it go free for example, going into convulsions, groaning, relentlessly piling up phrase upon phrase in speech are ways for the actor to apply artificial pressure to physical being. The aim is to use the rhythmic tension which results in order to set the spectator's or the auditor's own body into shared resonance. The spectator, caught up in this physiological rhythm, becomes a participant. In the end . . . the spectator is released, refreshed from the experience; catharsis sets in. (Goto, 174–75)

Suzuki's second version of the play was presented at Mito, Japan, in 1991 as part of a trilogy based on *The Bacchae*, *Macbeth*, and Chekhov's *Ivanov*; that production had a cast of twenty-four. (Suzuki intended to produce yet a fourth version at the Toga Festival this year with just three actors: Macbeth and Lady Macbeth played in English, and a member of the Suzuki Company of Toga [SCOT] playing all the other roles in Japanese.) The fact that Suzuki could have put *Macbeth* together with *The Bacchae* and *Ivanov* to form a trilogy says a lot about his confidence and powers of imagination. As he says in an interview,

> I am often asked why I use foreign texts. Well, if I use Shakespeare or Euripides, for example, I don't feel I'm using a foreign text, rather the heritage of the human race. If Europeans consider this to be a peculiarly European drama, I think that shows excessive self-consciousness on their part. If the English think that Shakespeare is part of their exclusive heritage, then Shakespeare is of no interest. It's precisely the ability to impress other nations that makes Shakespeare so excellent.[9]

The radical way in which Suzuki reshaped these plays to give them contemporary and personal significance is indicated in the title for the trilogy: "The Farewell Cult." He says it was inspired by the Jonesville Massacre, in which members of an American New Age Cult committed mass suicide on the orders of their religious leader.

For Suzuki, the common theme linking these three otherwise very different plays is fanaticism. *Dionysus* (which was Suzuki's reworking of his 1989 version of the *Bacchae*) was to represent the rise to prominence of the Farewell Cult. *Macbeth* (in the Mito version) showed the cult overreaching itself, and *Ivanov* described its decline. Since this trilogy was run over three separate nights (like Brook's *Mahabharata*) each play was given a prologue and epilogue that recontextualized it in relation to Suzuki's theme. Ironically enough, Suzuki wrote these in the spirit of Beckett's *Endgame*.[10] Lest we jump to the conclusion of one incensed observer that "Suzuki should make his own plays and stop attacking Western classics,"[11] we should ask ourselves why we accept Peter Brook's *Mahabharata* as "innovative" and balk at Suzuki's new synthesis.

Before going on to discuss the Playbox *Macbeth*, however, I should provide some background information. The Suzuki-Playbox project was the brain-child of Playbox's artistic director, Carrillo Gantner, who first put to Suzuki the idea of directing Australian actors in an all-male production of Mishima Yukio's *Madame de Sade*. This initial proposal would have involved cross-dressing, but it came to nothing when the American publishers, acting on behalf of Mishima's widow, refused to grant performance rights. Suzuki next offered to direct a stripped-down version of his Mito *Macbeth* production, and this was accepted. Negotiations then took place between Carrillo Gantner and Suzuki over the casting of key roles: Gantner insisting on major roles for Playbox-associated actors, plus inclusion of more female performers, and Suzuki holding out for Elizabethan-style all-male casting, or an offshore Lady Macbeth. Eventually a compromise was reached in which a cast of ten Australian male actors, most of them associated with Playbox, were joined by Katia Molino (Australia) and Ellen Lauren (America).

The latter has proved to be a particularly wise choice, for none of the Australians in the cast has trained with Suzuki for more than a few months, let alone acted in one of his plays, whereas Ellen Lauren (who plays Lady Macbeth) has worked with Suzuki over a period of ten years and came to this production fresh from playing Agave in the Mito *Dionysus*.[12] Ellen Lauren's performance skills provide a useful mark for the Australian actors to aim at, and have the added advantage of giving audiences a means by which to measure their energy, skill, and commitment.

The video of Kayoko Shiraishi playing Madame Ranyevskaia in *The Cherry Orchard* allows audiences to compare Lauren's skills with those of Shiraishi, the greatest exponent of Suzuki acting. I say this not to be negative. After watching what Suzuki calls "the daily battle of rehearsals" over four weeks, I have the greatest respect for all, even those who had not yet reached their full potential. However, I believe that one of the most important things we can learn from Asian theater training is that long-term commitment to communal theater training gives the greatest return in performance quality. As Suzuki has told the cast, theater, like sport, is about the refining of intense energy: the process does not produce "gold" overnight. Investment costs are high and the real benefits are long-term. It's not for nothing that the show's chief sponsor is Shell!

Two important questions that audiences may have are these: how new is this production of *Macbeth*? And how Australian is it? The latter is certainly a question that concerns Peter Curtin, the actor who plays Macbeth in the production. However, Suzuki has said (in interviews with myself and Norman Price of Melbourne University) that he is trying to get at "the essence of *Macbeth*," what is still of universal and contemporary significance in it.[13] We can hardly expect local color (Scottish-Australian accents or scenery) but we are, of course, meant to relate the play to our own dark experiences.

In concentrating on Macbeth's inner vision (which I'll return to in the context of Suzuki's opposition to naturalism and realism), the Playbox version is remarkably faithful to Shakespeare's text. The latter was performed in an adapted Japanese translation, whereas the Playbox text is a cut version of the original. The *Chronicle* set is new, and the costumes for the Australian production, though brought from Japan, have been redesigned here.[14] Some scenes are completely transformed. For instance, one of the most remarkable at Mito was the Banquet scene (3.4), which brought the whole company on stage for a gorgeous, lavish, and very funny meal.[15] The Playbox version is more astringent, more like something out of Ionesco's *The Chairs*. The dinner guests are only "present" in the imaginations of the Macbeths, and the last image we are left with at the end of the play is of twelve incandescent chairs awaiting the arrival of new occupants.

"Come, come, come, come, give me your hand. What's done cannot be undone. To bed, to bed!"—Photograph by Rei Zunde. (Lady Macbeth, Ellen Lauren)

The Playbox text also strips away what Suzuki believes is inessential to his theme. It focuses much more narrowly on the psychological world of the Macbeths and reveals as vividly as possible the inner landscapes of their fears and desires—"making the invisible visible" as Suzuki calls it. In so doing, Suzuki wants us to look closely at "the disease that Shakespeare calls Macbeth." For Suzuki, "he is not a thane of ancient Scotland but rather a man who speaks the words of Macbeth in his own life, as himself."[16] The names dropped by Suzuki into the "bad sleep well" of his actors' imaginations—to make them think about the way the "Macbeth virus" can spread—ranged from Hitler and Stalin to Saddam Hussein and George Bush.

Familiar to many of us is the idea of institutions as places of covert power-brokering and fanatical cultisms—whether they be states, churches, tertiary institutions, prisons, or nursing homes. A surrealist collage of fragmented images is deliberately used to widen the associative net. As Suzuki explained to the cast on day two of rehearsals:

1. The play is the evocation of the memories, the consciousness of the person we're going to call "Macbeth."
2. He is a person who, in some sort of way within this organization (the Farewell Cult), they've "killed."
3. What we are to realize is the visual workings on stage of that person's spirit.
4. Real present time ends when "Macbeth" first gets up from his chair and begins again only when he returns to it at the end of the play.
5. The person who facilitates the realization in point three, whether as psychologist or shaman, is the Reverend Father (Carrillo Gantner's character).
6. The theater is the space in which the Reverend Father performs the psychodrama as "kill-or-cure."

To the actor playing Macbeth (Peter Curtin), Suzuki explained, "At the very beginning of the play, on your first entrance, your personality is already fractured, broken. You are not well. It is the end of your life. You sit at the front of the stage to show that everything taking place behind you is in your head."[17] After fifteen days of rehearsal, when the ending of the play was finally reached, Suzuki went on to explain to Curtin how, as the music comes in on "The Queen, my Lord, is dead," he must go through a psychic collapse and revert to being a senile old man as he mutters "Blow wind, come wrack":

> You get to the point where your only "salvation" lies in someone killing you. The image should be that of an old man in a nursing home having dinner, just waiting for the angel of death. If Hitler had been put in a nursing home, what fantasies would have filled it![18]

Suzuki's psychologizing, existential approach to *Macbeth* is clearly mining toward something at the core of the play which he sees as having contemporary resonance. But his approach is one that he has refined since his student days at Waseda University in the sixties, when the influences of Freud, Jung, Sartre, and Surrealism were paramount. For example, his first international success, *On the Dramatic Passions II* (1970), was set in

> a confinement room where a solitary madwoman recalled fragments of numerous plays from the past, performing them one by one. Through the fiction of the drama, the passions which she was never able to satisfy in real life exploded with dreadful force. (SCOT, 59)

Over the years, the same set of Suzuki concerns have reemerged in similar formal configurations.[19] *The Trojan Women* (1974) stages an internal situation in which "an old woman who has been driven from her gutted home by the fire-bombing of Tokyo in 1944, lives through the legends of Troy in her fantasy" (SCOT, 60). *The Bacchae* too is "restructured into a fantasy embodying the hopes and aspirations of an old man (Cadmus) oppressed by a totalitarian and despotic ruler" (27). *Clytemnestra* (1983), a reconstruction of no less than six ancient Greek plays, is "intended to present an internal view of contemporary man . . . isolated . . . in a spiritually chaotic state" (37). *The Tale of Lear* (1988), which Suzuki sees as "an exploration of modern man's tendency towards psychological decay," is set in a nursing home where a nurse reads *Lear* to a senile old man (47). And, again "making the invisible visible," *The Chekhov* (1989) is "a portrayal of the expansion of desires and fantasies within [a young girl's] daily life until the illusory world becomes all consuming" (44).

In concentrating on Macbeth's inner vision, the Playbox version is remarkably faithful to Shakespeare's text, as the following table shows (for minor deletions and insertions, see the Appendix).

Table of scenes from *The Chronicle* and from *Macbeth*:

Suzuki   Shakespeare

Scene I
Reverend Father and chorus of believers:
History / If only it could be thrown away /
We could rest / Could sleep / But until then /
No, I understand / A thousand and one and
many many times that / That's all there is /
Of my life / Farewell to history /
Farewell to memory / But once it's finished /
That's no good either / Cannot rest now /
Will not rest now / Right away, another one /
But this one / Is different from always /
Finish this one / Then there can be rest /
A lifetime that is already long /
No matter what people say / A certain
amount of misfortune / That is enough /
After a hundred years / After an eternity /
It's impossible to understand, but / Die /
Break / Farewell to history / Farewell to memory.

Reverend Mother: Today we shall do
                    Macbeth. Begin reading.

Chorus of Believers: 5.5.19–28
                                          Tomorrow, and tomorrow, and to-
                                          morrow / Creeps in this petty
                                          pace from day to day, / To the last
                                          syllable of recorded time; / And
                                          all our yesterdays have lighted
                                          fools / The way to dusty death.
                                          Out, out, brief candle! / Life's but
                                          a walking shadow, a poor
                                          player, / That struts and frets his
                                          hour upon the stage, / And then
                                          is heard no more. It is a tale /
                                          Told by an idiot, full of sound
                                          and fury, / Signifying nothing.

Scene 2   1.7, "If it were done when 'tis
                                          done."

Scene 3   2.1.33–49, "Is this a dagger. . .?"
                                          62–64, "I go and it is
                                          done . . ."

Scene 4	4.1.35–36, "Double double, toil and trouble."
Scene 5	2.2.13–end, "I have done the deed."
Scene 6 Scene 7	3.1.47–end,"To be thus is nothing . . ." "Aye, i' the catalogue . . ."
Scene 8	3.2.8–end, "We have scorched the snake . . ."
Scene 9	3.4, "You know your own degrees, sit down . . ."
Scene 10	4.1.35–36,"Double double, toil and trouble." 48–end (minus last 20 lines).
Scene 11	5.1, "Out damned spot."
Scene 12	5.3, Seyton scene. 5.5, "The Queen, my Lord, is dead."

Scene 13
Reverend Father and chorus of believers:
History / If only it could be thrown away /
.... (*as above*) ....
Farewell to history / Farewell to memory.

Reverend Mother: This concludes today's labours.
              Thank you. You may go home.

Chorus of Believers including "Macbeth": 4.1.35–36,Double, double
                                        toil and trouble:
                                        Fire burn, and
                                        cauldron bubble.
                                        (*repeat*)

The Beckettian framing device works on a number of levels. It recontextualizes *Macbeth* as an absurdist tragicomedy ("Signifying nothing") and Shakespeare as "our contemporary." It also helps characterize the radical reductivism of the Farewell Cult through the semantically dislocated but rigidly repetitious and circular ritual of chanted invocation and choral response. These qualities allow for audience analysis of this "disease called Macbeth" since, as one psychologist has remarked on seeing the play,

> The relation between Suzuki's frame-story and the stripped-down version of Shakespeare's *Macbeth* is effective because it underlines the dreadful compulsion to repetition if we refuse fully to "know" our history.[20]

Moreover, the litany gains another level of meaning through the actors' performance of it, night after night. The gruelling physicality of their labors turns them into battle-scarred veterans who "Cannot rest now" and for whom there is always "Right away, another one" (another performance) which "is different from always." For them, if not for their audiences, this may be accompanied by a painfully direct awareness of heroic futility in which, like existentialist philosophers or absurdist clowns, they must construct their own raison d'être in a world divested of any ultimate truth. What Suzuki calls "the daily struggle" of performance offers only temporary respite, and its tempering of the actor for future occasions of skillful display has to be its own reward. Like Vladimir and Estragon obliged to wait out what Suzuki's prologue calls "A lifetime that is already long," they are caught between the wish to say "That is enough" and the contradictory tug of pride which says "Finish this one / Then there can be rest." For the performer there is always "Tomorrow, and tomorrow, and tomorrow." And for this reason, I think, Suzuki has lifted out Macbeth's great "Life's but a walking shadow" speech to insert at the very beginning of *The Chronicle*. The circularity, the doubleness that Suzuki sees at the core of *Macbeth* is formalized and foregrounded in *The Chronicle* by the repetition of the "Farewell to History" at beginning and end of his play, and by the cyclical repetitions of "Tomorrow, and tomorrow, and tomorrow" and "Double, double, toil and trouble."

This last assertion can be checked swiftly against the Suzuki-Shakespeare table, the "Tomorrow" speech being used in the "Farewell Cult" prologue (where it functions like a *shidai*)[21] and also in its proper sequence at the end of the play (5.5). The Witches' "Double, double" refrain is not only used in its proper place (4.1) but also between 2.1 and 2.3 (during the murder of

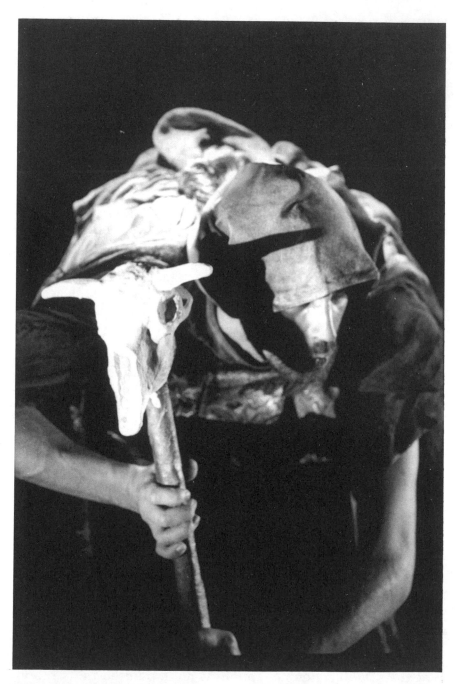

"I'll charm the air to give a sound
While you perform your antic round"—Photograph by Rei Zunde (Witch 2,
Olivier Sidore)

Duncan). It is at this stage, as Macbeth exits to do the deed, that the witches crash across the stage with their goat's-head staves, stoking the fires and stirring the cauldron of Macbeth's desires. The Chorus's criss-crossing of the stage (from side to side or from upstage to downstage and back) may be seen as choreographing the external and internal planes on which the action of the play develops; it certainly echoes the large inverted cross that hangs threateningly over the upstage center exit, behind the royal rostrum with its running blood-red carpet. And the severe frontality of the acting serves to highlight the entrances and exits down it as eruptions from and irruptions into the subconscious.

Shakespeare scenes omitted include all of act 1, scenes 1–6 (everything up to and including Duncan's arrival at the castle of Macbeth). Act 2, scenes 3 and 4, are also missing (these include the Porter scene, the discovery of the murder, and the escape of Malcolm and Donaldbain). Three scenes are cut from act 3: the murder of Banquo (scene 3), Hecate (5), and Lennox's conversation with a Lord (6). Gone from act 4 are scenes 2 (the murder of Lady Macduff) and 3 (Malcolm's testing of Macduff). Finally, in act 5, the scenes involving the English army are omitted (2, 4, and 6), and those involving Macbeth's death at the hands of Macduff (7–9).

As can be seen, Suzuki's stripping down of Shakespeare's play is done largely in the interests of intensification. He starts *in medias res* and allows no secondary themes to distract us from his single focus on the Macbeths.

Having said that Suzuki is surprisingly faithful to Shakespeare's *text*, I also need to add as a paradoxical rider that he quite consciously de-forms Shakespeare's *play*. I quote from our interview on 3 October 1991: "One isn't so much seeing Shakespeare presented as seeing my deformation of Shakespeare, the Suzuki style" (7). However, by recontextualizing a stripped-down version of the play, he is giving it unexpected new life. In the same interview Suzuki says,

> Ultimately it's an adaptation not on the level of words but on the level of the acting, the physical situation. On the visual level, what is presented is very different from what one might imagine by just reading the text. But the words are the same. (7)

As the title *The Chronicle of Macbeth* makes clear, the play is as much Suzuki's as Shakespeare's, and yet Suzuki would claim "it's . . . of the essence" of Shakespeare (7). Ironically, Shakespeare here becomes the source, the vehicle for Suzuki's contemporary synthesis, much as Holinshed's *Chronicles of Scotland* was raw material for Shakespeare (and much as Shakespeare's plays were adapted as vehicles for virtuoso eighteenth-century actors).

The chief advantage of a classic play is that it is widely known and appreciated. "With Shakespeare," Suzuki told me, "the audience are able to see what's done to that story (in my adaptation). They can enjoy that; it's a deeper experience to compare their own perceptions of that story with the presented version on stage." However, he goes on,

> For me the theme of a man hallucinating in an insane asylum comes first. The words chosen from the Shakespeare text are only those which relate to the situation, which feed that image. The words used are taken from Shakespeare but they're put into a new context. (6)

The classical Japanese term for this process is *honkadori* (the echoing of words, or sometimes only the situation or conception of a well-known earlier poem or story in such a way that recognizable elements are incorporated into a new meaning).[22] For me, it is most brilliantly used by Suzuki toward the end of *The Chronicle of Macbeth*. In their new contexts such familiar lines as "I have supped full with horrors," "Curses not loud but deep, mouth-honour," and the innocuous line "Bring me my armour" leap to new life, bristling with provocative but intelligent energy. We see an old man "armed" for supper with bib and fork by a sympathetic cafeteria staff member—while the nursing staff (doctor and nurse) simper and fawn in front of "the old tyrant," and titter and leer behind his back.

Honkadori is a technique that has been refined within Japanese literary and dramatic tradition over the last thousand years, and it is important to recognize that Suzuki does not jump to international prominence *ex nihilo*, either in terms of his dramaturgical skill or in terms of the actor-training method that complements it. Suzuki's strengths, and the strengths of the cultural-theatrical traditions behind him, are brought into controlled collision with Shakespeare (our cultural flag-bearer) in order to create a new international work of collage art. In order to appreciate this new work more fully, we need to know something of what it borrows and recycles from Japanese tradition as well as what it borrows from our own.

If the words of Suzuki's play are 95 percent Shakespeare's,

the structure is more like that of a Japanese ghost play—more accurately, a *mugen* or phantasmal Noh play. Let me briefly describe the structure of such a ghost play to clarify the point. A traveling Buddhist priest (played by the *waki* or "side person") stops at a spot made famous in history to pray for the soul of the famous person who once lived there. While praying, he meets a local villager (played by the *shite* or principal actor, literally "the doer of the action"). This person-of-the-place seems to know so much that the priest's suspicions are aroused. The local person then vanishes, only to reappear in his or her true form as the spirit of that famous person. So obsessed is the ghost by its unsatisfied desire for something in the land of the living (a false lover, a lost child, or even the failure to get a poem published in an imperial anthology of poetry) that it cannot achieve karmic release. Knowing this, the *waki* questions the *shite* to help the suffering spirit recognize its problem. Telling its story to the priest and acting it out in a final dance can have therapeutic effect for the *shite*'s character. In some Noh plays the spirit does achieve enlightenment and release; however, in others it remains stubbornly and tragically attached, furious and suffering to the bitter end.[23]

Noh is thus a form of psychomachia and, since the *waki* priest functions as a kind of analyst and the *shite* character acts out an obsession in order to achieve release, it also has affinities with psychoanalysis and psychodrama.[24] Suzuki consciously takes advantage of this ambiguity of reference to work in both traditional and contemporary, national and foreign modes.

It is also important to note that, although Noh action starts in real time, it quickly slides into the fantasy world of the *shite*. For the disembodied spirit, reality exists only in his or her imagination. This may help us to appreciate Suzuki's approach to *Macbeth*. In Suzuki's words: "What we're trying to achieve is a visualization of the unconscious of the person who plays Macbeth. Everything that takes place behind him on stage should be seen as taking place in his mind."[25] For this reason the acting is largely frontal, as it is in Kabuki theater.

In *The Chronicle* the only real time occurs in the "Farewell Cult" scenes at the beginning and end of the play. What remains of the bare bones of Shakespeare is resuscitated by religious fanatics, murderers, the senile, a doctor, a maid, and a cook at a play reading. At the end of a prologue that begins with a farewell to history and memory, one of the cult leaders announces "Today we shall do Macbeth." The story is then read and acted out. We

"Thou art too like the spirit of Banquo; down!
Thy crown does sear mine eyeballs. . . .
. . . Now I see 'tis true,
For the blood-bolter'd Banquo smiles upon me,
And points at them for his." Phograph by Rei Zunde.

can now see, I think, that, in stripping away Shakespeare's multiple plotting, Suzuki is making *Macbeth* conform structurally to the demands of a Noh play, which is why we have such a tight focus on the psychological state of a single person or couple.

Other important structural elements that Suzuki recycles from Noh theater are the *shidai*, to which I have already referred, and the *michiyuki* (travel song). In the Noh the effect of travel is conventionally presented by the actor taking a few steps while chanting a poetic description of famous beauty spots seen along the way. To a Japanese, however, Suzuki's *michiyuki* is more likely to recall Chikamatsu's in the puppet play *Sonezaki Shinju* [The love suicides at Sonezaki]. In this, a grimly ironic effect is created by the juxtaposition of visual and narrative elements; we see two desperate young lovers moving slowly toward their place of suicide while the *joruri* chanter describes the beauty of the night and the happiness of revelers along the riverbank. Suzuki's *michiyuki* is less poetically ironic than brutally dramatic, each jarring crash of the witches' staves on the ground suggesting both the blood pounding through Macbeth's adrenalin-filled veins as he wills himself toward the sleeping Duncan—and, offstage, Duncan's waking to a bloody, frantic death. Suzuki spent much time coaching Peter Curtin to create a reentry from Duncan's chamber that would vividly convey the precise manner in which Macbeth had killed. Scene 4 is a coup de theatre that many audience members comment on, largely because of these compelling sounds and images.[26]

Suzuki's is a theater of tensions and oppositions that trains the performer in just such intense emission and repression of physical power. In his book *The Way of Acting*, Suzuki describes the basic exercise of stamping, which he uses to help the actor develop energy and control. The stronger the stamping, the more the energy generated—but the harder it becomes to maintain control. The actor must try to prevent the stamping from producing "shake" or "wobble" in the upper body (which then looks weak). This can be done by learning to "block" or control this energy in the area between the hips (the actor's center of gravity), which must remain firm in all stage situations if the body is to be truly expressive. The stamping exercise is just one of many in which obstacles to stability are set up in order to stimulate the actor to develop the powers to overcome them.

Of course it takes time. Speaking in an interview on 3 October 1991, nearly four months before the start of rehearsals, Suzuki made the point very clear:

> Working with Australian actors whose primary influence has been Naturalism, it makes no sense to ask them to do something of which they're completely incapable, and so the process has to be one of slowly weaning them away from what they have been doing towards the image I have, but also to try to tap into what they have that's good, to find the best mixture of what's asked of them and what they already have. *In five years time one could imagine being able to create something of a very clearly defined style with such a new group.* But the body can't change quickly, nor can the understanding of the actor. Until they've actually done *Macbeth* they won't have a clear sense of what it is they're trying to do. So it's necessary to go through this process.[27]

If we bear these observations in mind as we watch the show, we are less likely to mistake the beam in our own eye for the mote in Suzuki's.

The Chronicle of Macbeth challenges us to notice our own cultural blind spots, increase our aesthetic tolerance, and extend our theatrical understanding.[28] Suzuki does not merely repeat

"Wake Duncan with thy knocking! I would thou could'st!"
Photograph by Rei Zunde.

the techniques of traditional Japanese theater any more than he simply follows Shakespeare, for he is a master of *honkadori*. What he gives us for the nineties is an "Empire of Signs" inflection of "Shakespeare Our Contemporary," and, if we have trouble recognizing the author, it is probably because our understanding of "Our" is too narrowly possessive. Shakespeare is also Suzuki's contemporary.

We may not be used to seeing the Bard taken seriously as musical dance drama in an absurdist mode. However, if Peter Brook's *Mahabharata* can command our admiration, so should Suzuki's adaptations of Shakespeare. It is no coincidence that at the 1992 Mitsui Festival in Tokyo (of which Suzuki is the artistic director), the Playbox *Macbeth* will be given its final performances alongside Ratan Thiyam's contemporary Indian adaptation of *The Mahabharata*.[29] The empire strikes back. Suzuki's experiment in "doubleness" may offer us a timely lesson in the dangers of not coming to terms with our cultural imperialist past: it may return to haunt us. The last image he leaves us with is one of fanatics stirring the cauldron of history with a book.

Notes

1. "[T]he first mention of *kabuki odori* in written records occurs in 1603. By that time, however, it already seems to have acquired a certain celebrity." Gunji Masakatsu, *Kabuki* (Tokyo: Kodansha International, 1985), 19.

2. Gunji, *Kabuki*, 20; also Donald Shively, "The Social Environment of Tokugawa Kabuki," in J. Brandon, W. Malm, and D. Shively, *Studies in Kabuki* (Honolulu: University of Hawaii Press, 1978), 63.

3. The first reference occurs in the entry for 29 January 1618 in Edward Thompson, ed., *The Diary of Richard Cocks*, vol. 2, Hakluyt Society, First Series no. 67 (1833; rpt. New York: Burt Franklin, 1964), 11; for the second see the entry for 1 September 1612 in Ernest Satow, ed., *The Voyage of Captain John Saris to Japan, 1613*, Hakluyt Society, Second Series no. 5 (1900; rpt. Nendeln/ Liechtenstein: Kraus Reprint, 1967), 147. In the diaries of Saris and Cocks I have counted 53 occasions on which they saw plays or entertained guests at dinner with Kabuki interludes; besides 47 explicit references to "caboques" (Kabukis), it is clear that they also saw Chinese opera, Shishi mai, Bon odori, Kagura, Noh, and Kyogen. "No day passed without playes, I meane comodies or tragedies," Cocks writes (17 October 1616); "And we had the cabokis after supper ashore, who plaid and dansed till after midnight . . . being 8 women and 6 or 7 men" (26 December 1616); "the caboques took Tome prisoner for 15 *tais* he owed them for lechery" (4 January 1617). No wonder the Council for the East India Company at Batavia fulminated to Cocks, "We expect to have a reformacion in the lavish expenses for the shipps companie" (Cocks, 2:343).

4. Thomas Randall, *Memorials of the Empire of Japon*, Hakluyt Society, First Series no. 8 (1850; rpt. New York: Burt Franklin, 1963), 39.

5. For the battle see P. G. Rogers, *The First Englishman in Japan* (London:

Harvill, 1956), 13–14; for Adams's trading, see Rogers, 83–99 passim; and for details of Adams's voyages in 1614, 1615, 1617, 1618, and 1619, see various entries in Cocks's diary for those years.

6. Since delegates were to attend the Adelaide Festival preview of Suzuki's *The Chronicle of Macbeth* on the last day of the conference, this paper offered a number of the contexts within which Suzuki's adaptation might be better appreciated. To this end, I and Deborah Leiser, who has completed Suzuki Masterclass training in Japan, also held a workshop during the conference; our purpose was to give delegates a taste of Suzuki's distinctive actor-training method and a sense of its relation to traditional Japanese theatre training.

7. Goto Yukihiro, "Suzuki Tadashi: Innovator of Contemporary Japanese Theatre" (Ph.D diss., University of Hawaii, 1988), p. 153. Referred to hereafter as Goto.

8. *Japan: Live Performance*, Channel 4 (Melbourne, 1989), counter nos. 15.00–16.30 and 17.00–19.00.

9. Suzuki, interview, *Japan: Live Performance*, counter nos. 16.40–17.00.

10. When Richard Moore asked Suzuki in rehearsal if he had based the "Farewell Cult" prologue on Francis Fukuyama's *The End of History*, his response was "No, no, no! Beckett. *Endgame.*"

11. Questionnaire distributed to audiences attending *The Chronicle*, put out by Ian Carruthers and Patricia Mitchell, respondent number 9.

12. Suzuki's American assistant-director and translator, Leon Inglesrud, also comes from the cast of the Mito *Macbeth*, and was company translator for Suzuki's American *Lear* adaptation, so the American presence is a vitally necessary link.

13. Suzuki, unpublished interview with Ian Carruthers and Norman Price at the Playbox Malthouse, 3 October 1991, 7.

14. Suzuki has created the costumes himself, with the help of Aizawa Akiko, from secondhand silk kimono pieces bought at temple fairs and resewn in Melbourne. For the Mito *Macbeth*, according to Leon Inglesrud, the actors created their own individual costumes. In the interview cited earlier, Suzuki made it clear that the production was not prepackaged: "I'm not clear yet what I want to do with this production. So, as things unfold in February during rehearsals, we'll have to see" (4). "The whole thing is more strongly focused as his hallucination" (3).

15. See photographs in *SCOT: Suzuki Company of Toga*, Japan Performing Arts Center, Kamimomose, Toga-Mura (n.p., n.d.), 98–99. Hereafter referred to as SCOT.

16. "Suzuki on Macbeth," Program, *The Chronicle of Macbeth*, Adelaide Festival of Arts (1992), 4.

17. Author's Rehearsal Notes, Day 2 (Friday, 24 January 1992), 7.

18. Notes, Day 15 (Saturday, 8 February), 18.

19. Richard Moore has referred to this phenomenon as "the Suzuki formula" but to my ear this sounds pejorative. I would prefer to use the term "formula-frame" in the sense that it is used by Parry and Lord in Albert B. Lord, *The Singer of Tales* (Cambridge: Harvard University Press, 1971). It is worth remembering that Japan too has had an illustrious tradition of oral formulaic epic poetry, its best-known example being *The Tale of the Heike*. See Kenneth Butler, "The Textual Evolution of *Heike Monogatari*," *Harvard Journal of Asiatic Studies* 26 (1966): 5–51.

20. Questionnaire, respondent no. 15.

21. *Shidai*: the short poetic opening passage in a Noh play that provides the central image around which subsequent action crystallizes.

22. Earl Miner et al., eds., *The Princeton Companion to Classical Japanese Literature* (Princeton: Princeton University Press, 1985), 277.

23. See Suzuki's *The Way of Acting: The Theatre Writings of Tadashi Suzuki*, trans. J. Thomas Rimer (New York: Theatre Communications Group, 1986), 30, for his own synopsis of phantasmal Noh.

24. Jan Kott, "Noh, or About Signs," in *The Theater of Essence and Other Essays*, ed. Martin Esslin (Evanston, Ill.: Northwestern University Press, 1984), 115; also Sirkku Hiltunen, "Initial Therapeutic Applications of Noh Theater in Drama Therapy," *Journal of Transpersonal Psychology* 20. 1 (1988): 71–80.

25. Rehearsal Notes, Day 2 (Friday, 24 January), 7.

26. Questionnaire. Papers based on this material were presented by Patricia Mitchell at two conferences in 1992: the Melbourne Performance Research Group conference "Reading the Suzuki/Playbox *Macbeth* Project," Melbourne University (October); and the Australian Drama Studies Association conference "Local Knowledges," Wollongong University (November).

27. Suzuki, interview, 3 October, 1–2 (my italics).

28. While the difficulties for inexperienced Australian actors of trying to do justice to Asian theater traditions is to be appreciated, this is not the place to comment on audience perception, actor training, and cross-cultural theater experimentation. For more thorough treatment of these issues, see Mitchell (n. 26); and my "Traditions in Transformation: The Suzuki/Playbox *Chronicle of Macbeth*," *Meanjin* 3 (spring, 1992): 615–31, and "Noh as Transformation: the Transformation of Noh," *Proceedings of the Asian Pacific Confederation of Arts Educators Conference* (Melbourne: Centre for Continuing Education, Monash University, 1994).

29. Tony Chapman, dir., "The Mitsui Festival," *Dateline*, SBS television, 19 June 1992.

Appendix
Table of Suzuki's Minor Deletions from and Additions to Shakespeare's *Macbeth*

Line numbers refer to Kenneth Muir's edition of *Macbeth*, The Arden Shakespeare (1951; rpt. London: Methuen, 1987).

3.1.72 deletion: *Re-enter Servant, with two Murderers.*
(Macbeth) "Now, go to the door, and stay there till we call."
New stage direction reads An *illusion of Macbeth appears and speaks Macbeth's lines.*
3.2.36 deletion: (Macbeth) "O! full of scorpions is my mind."
   46–50 deletion: (Macbeth) "Come, seeling night . . . Which keeps me pale."
3.4.2 deletion: (Lords) "Thanks to your Majesty."
   5–8 deletion: (Macbeth and Lady Macbeth) "Our hostess keeps her state . . . they are welcome."
   38 *addition*: (Macbeth and Lady Macbeth) "Cheers!"
   38 deletion: (Lennox) "May it please your Highness sit?"

51–57 deletion: (Rosse and Lady Macbeth) "Gentlemen, rise . . .
Feed and regard him not."

61–65 deletion: (Lady Macbeth) "This is the air-drawn dagger . . .
Authoris'd by her grandam."

72–73 deletion: (Lady Macbeth) "What! quite unmann'd in folly?"
(Macbeth) "If I stand here, I saw him."

74–82 deletion: (Macbeth) "Blood has been shed ere now . . . This
is more strange than such a murther is."

91 deletion: (Lords) "Our duties, and the pledge."

98–105 deletion: (Macbeth) "What man dare, I dare . . . The baby
of a girl."

115–20 deletion: (Rosse) "What sights, my lord? . . . A kind good-
night to all!"

122–25 deletion: (Macbeth) "Stones have been known to move . . .
The secret'st man of blood."

127–31 deletion: (Macbeth and Lady Macbeth) "How say'st thou
. . . but in his house I keep a servant fee'd."

4.1.69 deletion: (Witch 1) "He knows thy thought."

113–22 deletion: (Macbeth) "and thy hair, Thou other gold-bound
brow . . . Horrible sight!"

135–56 deletion: (Lenox and Macbeth) "What's your Grace's will?
. . . Come, bring me where they are."

5.1.40 deletion: (Lady Macbeth) "The thane of Fife had a wife: where
is she now?"

72–6 deletion: (Doctor and Gentleman) "Look after her . . . Good
night, good Doctor."

5.3.1 *addition: Seyton plays Macbeth a sentimental pop song about
being consoled by flowers.*
(In production this indication of a radical shift into the present,
from castle to infirmary, was instead signified by Seyton's meal-
trolley and mock-French chef outfit; here Suzuki saw the relationship between "Seyton" and "Macbeth" as like that between Sancho
Panza and Don Quixote.)

30 deletion: (Seyton) "What's your gracious pleasure?"

55–56 deletion: (Macbeth) "Pull't off, I say . . . Would scour these
English hence?"

61–62 deletion: (Doctor) "Were I from Dunsinane away and clear,
Profit again should hardly draw me here."

5.5.29–51 deletion: (Macbeth and Messenger) "Thou com'st to use
thy tongue . . . Ring the alarum bell!"

52 deletion: (Macbeth) "At least we'll die with armour on our back."

"This Last *Tempest*": Shakespeare, Postmodernity, and *Prospero's Books*

PAUL WASHINGTON

"WHAT happened to culture may well be one of the more important clues for tracking the postmodern," writes Fredric Jameson,[1] a suggestion that will bear some paraphrasing: for example, that recent uses of the "postmodern" contain clues as to what is happening to culture now. My subject is not, however, culture but rather "Shakespeare" and in particular the fact that postmodernity and Shakespeare are terms that have not frequently been put together, a nonrelationship that, potentially, has some interesting implications for Shakespeare criticism at a time when the value and cultural power of Shakespeare are widely under scrutiny. The past decade has seen the rise of cultural materialism and new historicisms in Renaissance studies, and it has occasionally accepted the consequent politicization of the subject with a less than pressing interest in theoretical elaboration of the conditions of possibility of these readings, or in the specific meanings of their implied terms. Postmodernism is one such term, so I want to discuss a text—Peter Greenaway's *Prospero's Books*—and some recent descriptions and formations of Shakespeare studies, to lend force to an argument about the usefulness of postmodernism as a critical term for continuing rereadings of Shakespeare, both where they already happen and where they may yet: in Australia, for example.

British director Peter Greenaway's film *Prospero's Books* is the latest retelling of the now (self-evidently, it often seems) postcolonial paradigm text, *The Tempest*, the play that in many ways has taken over from the "great tragedies," *Lear* and *Hamlet*, the role of providing critics with a text on which to state their positions on Shakespeare and on which to stake other claims with less obvious bearings on criticism. As Gary Taylor remarks in his recent flirtatious history of Shakespeare, *Reinventing Shake-*

speare, "We have made love to *The Tempest* so many times that the act of textual intercourse itself has begun to bore us."[2] Taylor devotes a chapter to sketching the pedagogical and geographical vastness of Shakespeare studies in a single year, from the activities of the RSC in London to a meeting of the International Shakespeare Congress in West Berlin, so that the appearance of *Prospero's Books* might easily pass as unremarkable, as merely another salute to Shakespeare.

Graham Holderness observes that, on the whole, "Shakespeare films exist on that important but peripheral fringe of cinematic production, where the values of high art can be held to justify or compensate for the lack of commercial success . . . and they can scarcely be regarded as central to the mainstream practice and development of the cinema."[3] Holderness made this remark in 1985, and while it remains broadly true, the release of *Prospero's Books* was preceded by a decidely mainstream film of *Henry V* and the Zefirelli and Gibson "star-studded" production of *Hamlet*, giving us three cinema-size Shakespeares in two years that enjoyed varying degrees of commercial success, and carried the values of high art a little further than the "peripheral fringe" of cinematic production and consumption. Almost certainly, these films reached a smaller overall audience—students, secondary and tertiary, and "average viewers"—than has, say, the BBC Shakespeare series (intended, according to Russell Miller, to "be faithful to the Bard rather than the Box . . . [and even to] be a thoroughly proper, perhaps scholarly version of the Compleat Works"),[4] but they still represent a remarkable "upsurge in Shakespeare's mass-cultural visibility," as Linda Charnes says. Charnes, writing from America, attributes this

to Shakespeare's position as iconic guarantor of liberal humanism, at a time when as a society we desperately need to find ways to justify our moral authority as we throw our weight around. Like so many other products in American consumer culture, Shakespeare is used to reinforce our sense of "distinction": like the best cars, the best furnishings, or the best wine—Shakespeare, the best that's been thought, said, and felt.[5]

It is harder, then, to situate in criticism and culture a film like *Prospero's Books* than it is to account for projects like the BBC Shakespeare, which, committed to the notion of the authentic Shakespeare, are precisely what have motivated the development of *political* and *alternative Shakespeares*.[6] It is difficult to situate

Prospero's Books because it is difficult to establish under what conditions, and how, "radical productions of Shakespeare, or productions advertised as radical, do occur."[7] According to Gary Taylor we now "find in Shakespeare only what we bring to him or what others have left behind; he gives us back our own values."[8] Skepticism is something a critic must bring to new readings of old texts, particularly when those old texts are invested with the preeminent cultural power of the name of "Shakespeare"; and such skepticism is advisedly brought to *Prospero's Books*, which closes its telling of *The Tempest* precisely by saving from the wreckage of Prospero's insubstantial pageant's fading nothing more nor less than the name of Shakespeare in the form of a book, *the* Book, the First Folio. I want to dwell on this scene because of its—to use a tired word—undecidability: its moment of ideological closure is not one of ideological resolution, as it serves merely to stage the centrality of the Book to the power of Shakespeare/Prospero. What matters is that it *does* stage this moment, and explicitly, as failing to arrest the production of potentially postcolonial meanings that precipitate this scene in the first place and that interrupt the relations of power and authority structured by the colonizer's use of his books. Greenaway's telling of *The Tempest* is highly equivocal: it simultaneously uses the technological advantages and capacities of film, as opposed to those of writing, to develop the postcolonial reading, and yet disregards this reading as the film culminates—back at the precise moment when the possibility of Shakespeare as an instrument of empire began—with the singularity of the Book. The film unsettles the paradigm that shapes it, either as colonial or as postcolonial text.

This late sequence in *Prospero's Books* runs like this: as the John Gielgud/Shakespeare/Prospero character is drowning his books in the sea, presumably "deeper than did ever plummet sound," two things happen.

Only two books are left—a thick volume called *Thirty-Six Plays* . . . and—bound identically—but much slimmer—Prospero's unfinished *The Tempest.* Turning both books slowly in his hands—we can see that on the spine of *Thirty-Six Plays* is the name William Shakespeare—opening the book we catch—as the pages turn—the many familiar names of Shakespearean plays—the text is written entirely by hand—Prospero's hand.

Prospero makes a decision and throws them both into the sea.

Then:

> The books land together on the water and Caliban surfaces—spurting
> and spouting water from a long underwater swim—he snatches both
> books and disappears again under the surface. The water is calm
> . . . as though it had never been a witness to the destruction of so
> many books.[9]

The recent uses that have been made of, and the readings that
have been produced from, The Tempest have served to carry over
one of the most canonical texts of Western culture into a central
place in discussion of postcolonialism, in departments of literature at least. This is a possible meaning of this "insertion," when
Prospero magically fills the nineteen pages left blank at the beginning of the book of Thirty-Six Plays with the book he has
just written, The Tempest. The play is thus put into play as an
intervention and as a supplement at the same time that it com-
pletes the Book, filling the blank part of the text with the colonizer's narration. Prospero discards the Book, and Caliban
retrieves it: what might he have written in that blank part of the
text? This is the postcolonial question, but one that Prospero's
Books only poses in what is almost its final scene, making the
question itself supplementary to the plot, the part of it that remains unwritten. Whatever else it does, and it may be all that it
does, the film problematizes and unsettles the new orthodox
readings of The Tempest—at least if we take it at face value—
foreclosing on histories that are unwritten, and leaving the question of whether productions of Shakespeare can ever be contestatory or "radical" as troublesome as ever. But in completing the
Book with the colonizer's narration Prospero's Books does make
trouble for postcolonial readings of The Tempest.

I want to say more about this moment in which the film stages
an ideological closure on postcolonial meanings, for it seems to
me that the undecidability of this scene poses a difficulty for
contestatory readings of Shakespeare texts (of which the postcolonial Tempest is only one form), a difficulty from which only
historicizing strategies of reading promise any release. Such a
commentary on Prospero's Books seems all the more plausible
for the fact that in some ways comparable discussions followed
the release of Branagh's Henry V, as what has been termed
Thatcher's Shakespeare became polarized into the subject of
radical critique (Political Shakespeare, The Shakespeare Myth,
etc.) and an exercise in scholarly translation—of the authentic

Shakespeare of the First Folio into the stagey authentic Shakespeare of the BBC. The film on the whole struggled to assert
itself independently of the powerful persona of Branagh himself,
whose industrious rise to fame and fortune from a Belfast up-
bringing has led to his being described as an "icon of Thatcherite
initiative."[10] Despite this his film has provided at least one reading that has found it to be the source of some interesting reflections on cultural and nationalistic anxieties in Thatcher's
England, focusing on the suggestively named Shakespeare Cliff
near Dover, so that it can also be seen as offering something
both to the culture critic and to anxiously patriotic Thatcherites,
speaking, as it will tend to, to those ideal subjects who "per-
sonify the sacred values of religion, hard work, health, and self-
reliance."[11] It seems that while contestatory productions of
Shakespeare may be possible, it is not possible to divest a production of Shakespeare of the cultural power, authority, and
somehow essential authenticity of "Shakespeare."

How, then, can it be helpful to talk about postmodernity and/
or postmodernism to find a way beyond these, as it were, each-
way readings? For the specific case of *Prospero's Books* it is worth
giving some attention to the disclosures Greenaway makes in the
published filmscript, disclosures that explicitly frame discussion
of the film as a technological achievement, a subordination of
the Book to the new possibilities created by the representational
apparatus of the nineties' film. Thus, we are enabled to read
through the filmic narration into the technological conditions of
its possibility, to understand it precisely as "other" to the singularity of the Book, and to read it against what Jameson calls that
"peculiar postmodern feeling about our own multiple subjectivi-
ties and points of view."[12] Among the prefatory sections of the
filmscript is one entitled "The Paintbox Images" in which
Greenaway gives a description of the "digital, electronic Graphic
Paintbox" with which Prospero's magical volumes are produced.
The volumes, those provided for him by Gonzalo on the night
he fled Milan, are the means by which he has controlled the
subtleties of the isle and they structure the film's presentation
of the events that Prospero simultaneously performs, narrates,
and records in the play he will call *The Tempest*. It appears
important to Greenaway to tell us something of how these
Graphic Paintbox volumes work.

The machine links the vocabulary of electronic picture-making with
the tradition of the artist's pen, palette and brush . . . its possibilities

could radically affect cinema, television, photography, painting and printing (and maybe much else), allowing them to reach degrees of sophistication not before considered . . . For the paintbox can change the shape, form, contrast, colour, tone, texture, ratio and scale of any given material, then store the resulting infinite solutions for reappraisal . . . [to] be reproduced as film, as audio-tape and as still photograph. If uniqueness is considered desirable, it is possible to make a unique image. . . . However, its potential, as always, depends on the audacity, imagination and pictorial sophistication of the user. (28)

The Graphic Paintbox's potential is to sublimate electronically the user's pictorial sophistication, combining and arranging the traditional elements of an artist's representational apparatus like so many parts of an elaborate equation to present the finished product, indifferent to material limits or requirements, for any medium that could be desired—a machine of positively Baudrillardian dimensions producing hyperreality where simulation "is no longer that of a territory, a referential being or a substance . . . [but] the generation by models of a real without origin or reality."[13] Greenaway foregrounds the simulacra machine as the very condition of possibility of his movie, and by inference, of Prospero's magic too. Suddenly, the production of the Shakespeare Book, the First Folio, appears not only to effect an ideological closure on postcolonial meanings, but to do so with a power without "origin or reality," to do so with the cultural power of a name without origin or history, the "always already" of "Shakespeare," the name that can expand to fill any amount of blank text to displace postcolonial readings as easily as any other. If the purpose of Greenaway's use of the Graphic Paintbox is to capture, to frame, the cultural power of Shakespeare, or at least the logic by which it works, then in a sense this Tempest is tracking what, under the sign of postmodernism, has happened to culture/Shakespeare. And the cost of doing this, of demonstrating the power of that name, is to abandon the assumption that The Tempest can be read as anything more than an incitement to postcolonial, or any contestatory, reading and never as immanently postcolonial itself.

This logic is carried over into the film's representation of Caliban, which in part fixes on the moment when Miranda teaches him a language, her own:

> I pitied thee,
> Took pains to make thee speak, taught thee each hour
> One thing or other. When thou didst not, savage,

Know thine own meaning, but wouldst gabble like
A thing most brutish, I endow'd thy purposes
With words that made them known.

(1.2.353–58)

Much has been made of the fact that Caliban uses the new language to curse, conceivably turning the colonizer's instrument of oppression against him, or her in this case. But, as Jonathan Dollimore writes in his recent book *Sexual Dissidence*, perhaps

> the most important thing about this passage is that of which it (or Miranda) is completely unaware: the possibility that Caliban already had a language. A different language, the language of the colonial subject, is perceived only as brutish gabbling. This blindness is a crucial factor in the imposition of the dominant language.[14]

Over and above the fact of the imposition of the colonial language is the possibility that the new language—presumably the duke of Milan was teaching Caliban English—was not in fact a language in which Caliban's purposes could be made known.

There are many examples of untranslatability, and cultural difference is an otherness that may not translate, the site of not only difference but of "différends," the term Jean-François Lyotard uses to describe a situation in which a speaking subject suffers a wrong for which no language or idiom exists that could express that situation.[15] While John Gielgud/Prospero/Shakespeare speaks all the speeches of the film until the time of abjuring his rough magic, speaking over and through all other characters including Caliban when he speaks in the colonial tongue, Caliban alone has another means of expression, that is not exactly a language but nonetheless marks the otherness of his place in Prospero's imported world order. Caliban, played by Michael Clark, has been given the language or rather, the figure, of dance through which to express himself, gliding or hurling in balletic movements through the film, signaling his agitations and sinuating his insinuations as he works through the plot that Prospero will forget, not surprisingly since it falls outside of representation. As deconstruction, through Derrida, and more explicitly through Lyotard has taught us, there is a figural Other to all discourse, an Outside that can never be brought fully into representation nor, as Lyotard has stridently insisted, be reduced to textuality. The otherness of Caliban is, oddly enough, saved from obliteration precisely by being so very other, silenced by the colonizer without recourse to any possible justice but retained as a silent trace of a culture that was already there and different.

The figure or figurality of dance associated with Caliban might stand for what has been pressed out of representation in this text by the colonizer, Prospero, but if so, then it signals also the need to make new openings in history, to reopen discursive spaces that have been closed or to create wholly new ones. Here in Australia, for example, where Shakespeare has been accepted unproblematically as just as much "our" playwright as England's for the past century, there remains to be written the kind of cultural history that would study those processes of naturalization of "Shakespeare" that complement other aspects of imperial history—the invention of nationalisms, the identification with distant metropolitan centers, the pressures brought to bear on Australian culture by such complex signifiers of value as "Shakespeare." In general terms the work of opening such spaces in history, literary or otherwise, has been modeled by Lyotard as an exemplary postmodern act. The postmodern, he writes,

> would be that which, in the modern, puts forward the unpresentable in presentation itself; that which denies itself the solace of good forms, the consensus of a taste which would make it possible to share collectively the nostalgia for the unattainable; that which searches for new presentations, not in order to enjoy them but in order to impart a stronger sense of the unpresentable. A postmodern artist or writer is in the position of a philosopher: the text he writes, the work he produces are not in principle governed by pre-established rules, and they cannot be judged according to a determining judgment, by applying familiar categories to the text or to the work. Those rules and categories are what the work of art itself is looking for. The artist and the writer, then, are working without rules in order to formulate the rules of what *will have been done.*
>   . . . it must be clear that it is our business not to supply reality but to invent allusions to the conceivable which cannot be presented.[16]

While postmodernity has become visible at a particular historical juncture it is also for Lyotard a moment in all discourse that disrupts the rule of meaning and the order of representation, and, signaling the presence of the unpresentable, of something ever more about to be, appears or irrupts in the discourse of modernity and the struggle for control of the representational space of political discourse, as a crisis. Indeed, whether we accept Lyotard's description of postmodernity in terms of the breakage of metanarratives, or rather look to Jameson's description of postmodernism as the cultural logic of late capitalism, the postmodern is always the name of a crisis and thus of an invitation to criticism. In this at least, Baudrillard's simulacra machine and Greenaway's gadget, the Graphic Paintbox, Lyotard's postmodernity and Jameson's are all in rough accord—that "postmodern" has something to do with crisis. Indeed, according to Gayatri Spivak, it is the function of postmodernism to manage the crisis of postmodernity.[17]

We can make use of this critical moment and of the crises of postmodernity to open the spaces in which it would be possible to begin to write our own histories and to establish what have been the rules of the critical and cultural processes by which we have met, inscribed, and reproduced the cultural power of Shakespeare, and participated in the institutional practices in which that power is realized. And I want to argue that this possibility is particularly important in Australia—which exemplifies all the cultural complexity and difficulty of a settler culture— where the desire to be able to analyze Shakespeare-in-Australia in something like our own terms, as it displaces and yet engages *The Tempest*'s postcolonial allegory once again (this time into our relationship to the imported rhetoric of critical practices invented in the northern hemisphere to answer to northern hemisphere situations), is also the desire to allude through historicizing readings and practices to, as Lyotard says, the "conceivable which cannot be presented."

My argument works toward showing how the Greenaway film *Prospero's Books* begins to break up the colonial and postcolonial paradigms within which its foster text *The Tempest* has long been reproduced and received, by ambiguously emplotting the iconic Book, the First Folio, and by using the thematics of postmodernity to display the infinite variety of the name of Shakespeare whose power must be critiqued not in abstract terms but rather with attention to the specific meanings and values it produces in heterogeneous discursive forms and locations. What the film frames as undecidable in such readings is in fact an effect of an overvaluation of textual power and textual practice to the exclusion of detailed consideration of institutional practices:[18] *The Tempest* can never tell more than its own colonialist narratives, and mere readings of the text, no matter how refined or scholarly, can tell us nothing of what becomes of the play when it is put to work in the classroom or the lecture theater, on the stage or on the BBC. I want to conclude then by rehearsing in this context an argument that has already been made about the relationship of postmodernism and postmodernity to the new historicism, in the belief that it is under the rubrics of new historicism and cultural materialism that we find the most powerful strategies for producing new readings of how Shakespeare matters today.[19]

If we align the newness of the new historicism with the project of modernity, which is also (at the risk of a profound simplification) about newness, and do so with some attention to the history of historicism, then it becomes easy to see how the postmodern, testifying to the unpresentable in the modern, is a continual challenge to historicist reading. Very briefly, the new historicism clearly defines itself against an old historicism, which itself in its time made promises for the study of history. Its time was the nineteenth century and its place was the Germany of Leopold von Ranke, whose work went under the name *Historismus*. Brook Thomas, in his account of Ranke's work, writes: "Although *Historismus* claimed to break with moral philosophy, it smuggled in its own moral vision through the narratives that it used to structure its stories of the past. These narratives yoked together the modern sense of linear temporality with the celebrated logocentrism of Western thought to produce teleological narratives of progressive emergence" (189). Such a narrative is the one that attaches to Enlightenment rationalism, which foresaw the universal rational subject coming to find itself more and more at home in the world, the vision that culminates in modernity and which coincides in its historical trajectory with the trajectory of *Historismus*, and both of them with the progression of Western imperialism. Paradoxically, as Thomas writes,

> the very success of Western imperialism invited a questioning of the assumptions of *Historismus*, since as the West dominated other cultures it was forced to adjust its narratives about the unfolding of world history to include them. To be sure, these non-European cultures were absorbed into a Eurocentric narrative that denied them proper representation. Nonetheless, the presence of these repressed "others" allowed the possibility of a decentering of the Eurocentric version of history. (189)

The crucial feature of the new historicism is that while there "may be nothing new about [its] claim to make history new . . . its difference from past historicisms is its effort to take shape in a postmodern age in which poststructuralism has called into question the assumptions of the modern upon which historicism depends" (199). The new historicism understands the present uses and inscriptions of Shakespeare as the present ending of a complex process of negotiation between discourses and across cultural and historical differences, in which the new historicism and postmodernity work against each other in such a way that the act of enclosing the irreducibly different narratives of other discourses and other cultures in a historicizing project is signaled as a crisis that we can call a crisis of postmodernity, in which is presented the unpresentable of which we can nonetheless conceive. Among those things of which we can conceive is some sustained criticism of how Shakespeare has been so naturalized in Australia as to have been a compulsory subject in our schools and our universities too; and the question of how it is that a Melbourne cinema can find five audiences a day for a difficult adaptation of a play written in Jacobean England as easily as, say, the Oxford Shakespeare manages to market here an editorial policy. We can ask these questions neither as Prospero nor as Caliban but only from a position in between, as complicit in the literary, institutional, and, in a very recent sense, Shakespearean practices to which we are also subjected.

Notes

1. Fredric Jameson, *Postmodernism or the Cultural Logic of Late Capitalism* (London: Verso, 1992), x.

2. Gary Taylor, *Reinventing Shakespeare* (London: Vintage, 1991), 349.

3. Graham Holderness, "Radical Potentiality and Institutional Closure: Shakespeare in Film and Television," in *Political Shakespeare: New Essays in Cultural Materialism*, ed. Jonathan Dollimore and Alan Sinfield (Manchester: Manchester University Press, 1985), 182.

4. Russell Miller, "Shakespeare on the Big Screen, the Small Box, and in Between," *Yearbook of English Studies* 20 (1990), 73.

5. Linda Charnes, "What's Love Got to Do with It? Reading the Liberal Humanist Romance in Shakespeare's *Antony and Cleopatra*," *Textual Practice* 6.1 (1992): 1, 13.

6. John Drakakis, *Alternative Shakespeares* (London: Methuen, 1985).

7. Isobel Armstrong, "Thatcher's Shakespeare," *Textual Practice* 3.1 (1989): 1.

8. Taylor, *Reinventing Shakespeare*, 411.

9. Peter Greenaway, *Prospero's Books*, film script (London: Chatto and Windus, 1991), 162. Hereafter referred to as Greenaway.

10. Graham Holderness, "'What ish my nation?': Shakespeare and National Identities," *Textual Practice* 5.1 (1989).

11. Norman K. Denzin, *Images of Postmodern Society* (London: Sage, 1991), 150.

12. Jameson, *Postmodernism*, 151.

13. Jean Baudrillard, *Simulations* (New York: Semiotexte, 1983), 2, 3.

14. Jonathan Dollimore, *Sexual Dissidence* (Oxford: Clarendon Press, 1991), 110.

15. Jean-François Lyotard, *The Differend*, trans. Georges van den Abeele (Manchester: Manchester University Press, 1988).

16. Jean-François Lyotard, *The Postmodern Condition*, trans. Geoff Bennington and Brian Massumi (Minneapolis: University of Minnesota Press, 1984), 81.

17. Nikos Papastergiadis, "Identity and Alterity: An Interview with Gayatri Chakravorty Spivak," *Politics of Writing, Arena* 97 (1991): 66.

18. Alan Sinfield's recent book *Faultlines: Cultural Materialism and the Politics of Dissident Reading* (Berkeley: University of California Press, 1992) is "designed to epitomize a way of apprehending the strategic organizations of texts," and is motivated in part by the way in which "the very excellence achieved by North American academics may effect a kind of blinkering; sophistication, cleverness, abstruseness, difficulty, and professionalism screen out the wider culture" (8, 9).

19. Brook Thomas, "The New Historicism and Other Old-Fashioned Topics," in *The New Historicism*, ed. H. Aram Vesser, (New York: Routledge, 1989). I am drawing heavily on Thomas's argument here.

Notes on Contributors

MICHAEL BILLINGTON has been Drama Critic for the *Guardian* since 1971. He broadcasts on radio and television, runs a theater course for London-based students of the University of Pennsylvania and is the author of several books. His most recent publication is *One Night Stands*, a collection of theater reviews, and he is currently working on a critical study of Pinter.

ANN BLAKE is Senior Lecturer in English at La Trobe University, Melbourne. She has published on Shakespeare and Jacobean drama, particularly on Shakespearean comedy and the boy actors, and on Christina Stead and women crime writers. She is currently working on two books, *Christina Stead's England* and *Shakespeare's Children*.

MERCEDES MAROTO CAMINO is Assistant Lecturer in English and Romance Languages at The University of Auckland, New Zealand. She has published articles on gender and colonialism in the early modern period, including studies of Shakespeare, Spenser, and Maria de Zayas. She is currently working on early modern women's utopian "cartography."

DAVID CARNEGIE is Professor of Theatre and Film at The Victoria University of Wellington in New Zealand. He has published in the areas of Elizabethan drama and staging and New Zealand theater history and drama, and has worked as a dramaturg in professional theater. He is coeditor of the Cambridge edition of the works of John Webster and is editing *Twelfth Night* for the Bell Shakespeare.

IAN CARRUTHERS is Lecturer in Theatre and Drama at La Trobe University, Melbourne. In 1993–94 he held a Japan Foundation Fellowship to further his work in Japan. He has published widely on Suzuki's Shakespeare and other cross-cultural adaptations, is editing a casebook on Allan Marett's Australian Noh play, *Eliza*, and is writing a book on Suzuki as director.

249

TREVOR CODE is Associate Dean in the Faculty of Humanities, Deakin University, Geelong.

ROBIN EADEN is joint editor of *The Annotated Such Is Life* by Joseph Furphy (Melbourne: Oxford University Press, 1991). Her research interests include Australian literature, seventeenth-century literature, and garden history. She works as a freelance editor.

PENNY GAY is Senior Lecturer in English at the University of Sydney, where she also teaches in Performance Studies. She is the editor of *The Merchant of Venice* for the Bell Shakespeare and author of a feminist stage history of the comedies, *As She Likes It: Shakespeare's Unruly Women* (Routledge).

JOHN GOLDER is Senior Lecturer in the School of Theatre and Film Studies, University of New South Wales. He is President of the Australian and New Zealand Shakespeare Association and a General Editor of the new Bell Shakespeare series of critical editions (Science Press, Sydney). *Shakespeare for the Age of Reason* was published by the Voltaire Foundation (Oxford, 1992).

WERNER HABICHT is Professor of English Literature at the University of Würzburg. He has been President of the Deutsche Shakespeare-Gesellschafte West (1976–88), was founding editor of *English and American Studies in German* (1969–82), and is currently editor of *Jahrbuch der Deutschen Shakespeare-Gesellschaft West* and coeditor of a bilingual study edition of the plays of Shakespeare.

HEATHER KERR is Lecturer in English, University of Adelaide, and General Editor of *Southern Review*. Her publications are in the areas of early modern drama and legal history. She is collaborating on a volume of feminist essays on medieval and early modern writing and coediting a collection of Australian women's fictocriticism.

JACQUELINE MARTIN is Associate Professor of Theatre Studies at the University of Stockholm. She is the author of *Voice in Modern Theatre* (London: Routledge, 1991) and "Understanding Theatre" (forthcoming) and she is Editor in Chief of *Nordic Theatre Studies*. She has directed a number of plays and operas and coordinates masterclasses for the European League of Institutes of the Arts.

MADGE MITTON is Lecturer in English, University of Adelaide. Her research interests are Victorian literature, especially the work of Trollope and Wilkie Collins, British drama, and crime fiction by women writers.

MICHAEL MORLEY is Professor of Drama at Flinders University of South Australia. His publications include *A Student's Guide to Brecht* and articles on modern drama and Brecht and his musical collaborators. He is President of the International Brecht Society and a member of the Advisory Council to the Kurt Weill Foundation.

PHILIP PARSONS (1926–93) was Senior Lecturer in the School of Theatre Studies, University of New South Wales (1965–87). He pioneered the Australian study of Elizabethan theater practice and in 1986 began experiments with the Sydney Theatre Company into daylight performance of Elizabethan drama. In 1971 he founded Currency Press with Katharine Brisbane. He was awarded membership of the Order of Australia in 1993. Following his death, an annual memorial lecture on the performing arts was instituted by the New South Wales Ministry of the Arts. The encyclopaedic *A Companion to Theatre in Australia* was published by Currency Press and Cambridge University Press in 1994.

MARTIN PROCHAZKA is Assistant Professor of English and Comparative Literature at Charles University, Prague, where he teaches English Renaissance literature, English and European romanticism, and literary theory. His book *Romanticism and Personality* is forthcoming and he is writing an introduction to poststructuralist theory and cultural history for Czech readers.

JYOTSNA SINGH is Assistant Professor of English and Cultural Studies at Southern Methodist University, Dallas. She has published essays in *Renaissance Drama* and *Theatre Journal* and is coauthor, with Dympna Callaghan and Lorraine Helms, of *Weyward Sisters: Shakespeare and Feminist Politics* (Oxford: Blackwell, 1994). She is currently writing a book entitled *Colonial Narratives/Cultural Dialogues*.

PAUL WASHINGTON is Lecturer in English and Cultural Studies at Charles Sturt University, New South Wales. His current research is focused on settler cultural production of Shakespeare.

Index

Page numbers in italics refer to illustrations. Shakespeare's plays are indexed individually by title.